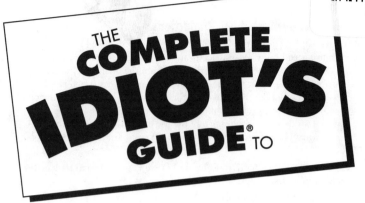

THE COMPLETE IDIOT'S GUIDE® TO

Taoism

by Brandon Toropov and Chad Hansen

ALPHA

A Pearson Education Company

International Standard Book Number: 0-02-864262-7
Library of Congress Catalog Card Number: 2002101638

04   03   02   8   7   6   5   4   3   2   1

Interpretation of the printing code: The rightmost number of the first series of numbers is the year of the book's printing; the rightmost number of the second series of numbers is the number of the book's printing. For example, a printing code of 02-1 shows that the first printing occurred in 2002.

Printed in the United States of America

Note: This publication contains the opinions and ideas of its authors. It is intended to provide helpful and informative material on the subject matter covered. It is sold with the understanding that the authors and publisher are not engaged in rendering professional services in the book. If the reader requires personal assistance or advice, a competent professional should be consulted.

The authors and publisher specifically disclaim any responsibility for any liability, loss, or risk, personal or otherwise, which is incurred as a consequence, directly or indirectly, of the use and application of any of the contents of this book.

Publisher: *Marie Butler-Knight*
Product Manager: *Phil Kitchel*
Managing Editor: *Jennifer Chisholm*
Senior Acquisitions Editor: *Renee Wilmeth*
Development Editor: *Joan D. Paterson*
Senior Production Editor: *Christy Wagner*
Copy Editor: *Michael Brumitt*
Illustrator: *Chris Eliopoulos*
Cover/Book Designer: *Trina Wurst*
Indexer: *Angie Bess*
Layout/Proofreading: *Svetlana Dominguez, Ayanna Lacey, Stacey Richwine-DeRome*

Contents at a Glance

Contents

Appendixes

Foreword

Taoism has both an ancient pedigree and a vibrant modern life. Its origins are the subject of endless scholarly debate, and its current expression is as near as the words you are reading and the breath you are taking right now.

Centuries ago, the paradoxes and penetrating insights of Taoism's core texts had a profound influence on the emerging Zen Buddhist tradition. Taoism has had, in China and elsewhere in the East, an incalculable impact on religious life, on medicine, on the arts, on intellectual life, and on politics, among many other disciplines. In recent years, Taoism has served in the West as both an important spiritual and philosophical influence and as a catchall prefix of uncertain but apparently profound meaning. People speak casually of the Tao of the Internet, the Tao of television, the Tao of sales training, and so on.

What's all the fuss about? What *is* Taoism?

Does that (deceptively) simple-sounding question intrigue you? Good. Read on.

If you are looking for a guide that will help you learn more about this ancient and massively influential tradition and deepen your insights into its many expressions around the world, then you've found it here. *The Complete Idiot's Guide to Taoism* is a useful handbook that offers a good starting point for beginners interested in exploring the basic features and guiding principles of Taoism. It is a significant and valuable aid to the basic understanding of one of the world's great philosophical and religious traditions.

And you don't have to be an idiot to use it!

Zen Master Bon Yeon (Jane Dobisz)
Cambridge, Massachusetts

Introduction

Our aim with this book is to make it easier for people to learn about a tradition whose very name has for centuries defied adequate explanation.

As its title implies, a volume like this is best understood as a beginning, rather than the final word on anything. In keeping with the spirit of *The Complete Idiot's Guide* series, though, we'd like to offer at the very beginning of this book a single idea that may help you as you make your journey through this book (and perhaps, through life). Here it is:

Individuals in search of the truth can benefit most, not by grasping or striving, but by means of a patient, accepting focus on natural patterns and influences that are worthy of being emulated.

Think of *The Complete Idiot's Guide to Taoism* as a flashlight; judge its effectiveness by what it helps you to see more clearly as you make your own way along the path.

What You'll Learn in This Book

This book is divided into five sections that will help you learn more about one of the world's great philosophical and religious traditions.

Part 1, "What Is the Tao?" gives you answers to some of the fundamental questions about Taoism.

Part 2, "Landmarks on the Path," gives you information about the history and development of Taoism in the East.

Part 3, "The Music of the Tao," shows you some of the things Taoism teaches about nature, skill, and life and death.

Part 4, "Tao Jones: The West Discovers Taoism," examines Taoist overlaps with the West's popular culture, science, and environmental movements—and shows how Taoism is influencing the ongoing search for meaning and spiritual fulfillment in the West.

Part 5, "Here and Now," gives you resources, reviews, and writings to support further exploration and practice.

At the end of the book, you'll find appendixes with even more information about books and organizations with a Taoist focus.

Extras

You will probably want to take advantage of the little nuggets of information distributed throughout the text. They will help you gain an immediate understanding of some aspect of the topic under discussion. Here's how you can recognize them:

Taoist Tip-Off

These boxes will alert you to common misconceptions and potential problem areas.

Tao Then, Tao Now

These boxes offer illuminating examples or insights into points of contact between ancient Taoist practice and contemporary thought.

Spoken and Unspoken

Here you'll find concise summaries of key terms that may not be familiar to you.

On the Path

Background facts or supporting information that can accelerate and streamline the exploration process are found in these boxes. We think you'll be fascinated by what you find here.

Acknowledgments

We thank Renee Wilmeth, Joan Paterson, Christy Wagner, and the entire team at Alpha.

Grateful thanks also go out to Gene Brissie, Bert Holtje, Judith Burros, David Toropov, Jane Dobisz, Glenn KnicKrehm, and Mary Toropov. Without their help, support, and encouragement, this book would not have been possible. The staff at the Peabody, Massachusetts, Starbucks outlet also provided a peaceful weekend haven for work on this project that was essential to its completion. Their patience, good humor, and fine taste in music were and are much appreciated.

Trademarks

All terms mentioned in this book that are known to be or are suspected of being trademarks or service marks have been appropriately capitalized. Alpha Books and Pearson Education, Inc., cannot attest to the accuracy of this information. Use of a term in this book should not be regarded as affecting the validity of any trademark or service mark.

Part 1

What Is the Tao?

In this part, you learn about the fundamentals of Taoism. You'll find answers to some basic questions about the Tao, learn about key concepts within the tradition, and get an introduction to the *Daode Jing* and the *Zhuangzi*, two of the most influential books ever written.

Don't Try to Define It

In This Chapter

- ◆ Why a book about Taoism?
- ◆ What is the Tao?
- ◆ What is Taoism?

Why would anyone write a book about Taoism? That's a good question—one that came to us instinctively when we started thinking about how to write this book. (Foreshadowing alert: Listening for one's own instincts can be extremely important when it comes to writing books … or doing anything else!)

In this chapter, you'll learn our answers to some of the most important questions about Taoism, one of the world's oldest philosophical and religious traditions.

From one point of view, a book about Taoism is unnecessary, and writing one is a violation of Taoism's spirit. Still, the great Taoists themselves wrote and, furthermore, wrote in a style that contributes hugely to the appeal of Taoism. Much of Taoist thinking revolves around its ambivalent view of language. We want to explain enough that you can understand why such paradoxes arise in Taoism.

Warning: A Little Mysticism Can Be a Dangerous Thing

But be careful: Just about everyone who has studied formally or informally within this tradition has had an experience something like the following:

◆ **Step one.** Read a Taoist scripture or experience some Taoist-influenced teaching. Such a teaching might take the form of a Zen story, a reinterpretation of something you've heard for years in a church or synagogue, or even, believe it or not, a line from one of the *Star Wars* films:

> "Luke! Let go of your conscious feelings!"
>
> "Reach out with your feelings!"
>
> "Never his mind on where he was; what he was doing!"

◆ **Step two.** Take time by yourself to process this teaching quietly. You might meditate, you might take a walk in the woods, or you might do the dishes and glance out the window at a cardinal perched on a branch outside.

◆ **Step three.** Experience, silently and with little effort, what might appear to be some kind of spiritual insight related to the teaching experienced in step one. ("I *got* it!")

◆ **Step four.** Mess up the silence by trying, noisily, to explain your insight to somebody else. ("Hey! Lookie here, everybody! I *got* it! I *got* it!")

◆ **Step five.** Wonder what happened to the suddenly inert "insight" you experienced in step three. ("I guess I don't get it after all.")

So relax. We won't be trying to convey our mystical experiences to you.

Shut Up Already!

There is probably no more effective way to undermine others' trust that you understand Taoism than to start claiming that you understand. Any time we try to learn an idea system from a great distance in time and culture, our best answers will be filled with guesses. But Taoism, one can argue, is a special case, because it is so very fond of paradox and doubtful of words. An ambivalent attitude about language (the great Taoist masters were masters of ancient Chinese literary expression!) and a belief that language can never replace practice are common themes in Taoist philosophy.

A thought: Instead of reading a book like this, you could be out working in your garden … or drawing a picture of a river … or taking a walk … or doing anything completely enough to lose yourself in it (or do we mean find yourself in it?).

Why You Should Read the Book Anyway

Still, we believe that if we arm our readers with cautionary warnings like the previous ones, there is a place for our book. Here are three reasons why we believe this.

First, the entry point is absolutely valid. This is a book about Taoism for beginners. It's intended as a starting point, which works for us. The title, *The Complete Idiot's Guide to Taoism*, means we can assume readers want to learn something about it. And while we're on the subject of idiots, please note: One precept of Taoism is to prefer "idiots" to "sages." We offer what follows on these pages in the spirit of sharing what we have learned from this ancient tradition, but we acknowledge here and now that we all have a lot to learn about Taoism.

Second, Taoism is one of those traditions people talk about (at least in the West) a great deal without taking the trouble to explore it at any length. The word *Tao* itself has, for better or for worse, become a kind of shorthand for "tough-to-figure-out metaphysical stuff." Religious readers substitute "Tao" for "God" and complete the familiar picture with a creation story, faith, soul, redemption, and heaven without making any attempt to connect faith in God to any recognizable element of Taoist thought. What a shame!

> **Tao Then, Tao Now**
>
> "Those who know to act do not speak; those who speak do not know to act."
>
> —*Daode Jing*, chapter 56
>
> (In this book, unless otherwise noted, we cite Chad Hansen's provisional translation of the *Daode Jing*. You can find it at www.hku.hk/philodep/ch.)

This book is intended to help beginners connect some of the dots. If you're interested in learning what is interesting and valuable in Taoism as it relates to physics, ecology, popular entertainment, or any of a host of other subjects, you've come to the right place.

Third, we think that reading this book might just help people become ...

◆ More fully present at any given point in the day.

◆ More nonjudgmentally open to the experiences they encounter.

◆ More observant of the skills and instincts that arise spontaneously in daily living.

Writing this book has certainly had that effect on us. So go ahead: Read the book. Just remember that what's most important is not any sequence of words that may appear in this or any other text, but the ability to engage directly and powerfully in one's own life. And know that it's okay to go outside and take a walk, too.

On the Path _____

An old wandering monk was drawn to an obscure village by a powerful feeling of vital energy. He entered the tiny hut that was the source of this energy, expecting to encounter an advanced master. What he saw and heard was a humble peasant meditating and chanting incorrectly! The monk interrupted the farmer, taught him the correct version of the chant, and then set off upon his wandering way. Months later, he passed the same hut but did not feel any of the energy that had drawn him before. Stepping inside, he saw the obedient peasant farmer chanting "correctly"—but without inspiration. Moral: If it works, don't fix it!

What Is the Tao?

Tao is a word that's easy to translate from the Chinese but not so easy to define. We'll tackle the easy part first. Tao may be translated as "way" or "guide." The most common English translation is "Way" with a capital W.

Spoken and Unspoken _____

Tao can be understood as the way things reliably operate in the sense of (1) the *guidance itself* or (2) its *actual operation*. In this book, **Tao** (with a capital T) refers to the sum of all guidance in the universe *or* to its result—the entire course of history (past and future) from the big bang to the big collapse. (Taoist texts call this the "Great Tao.") We use a lowercase *tao* to refer to some part of that guidance such as a moral code, a set of instructions, an intuition, or a teacher's example.

That capital letter points us toward the difficult job of explaining the Great Tao. This concept is the basic source of Taoist incoherence. Most accounts take all uses of tao to involve these contradictions. A famous saying from Taoist scripture has been read, by most readers, to say that all language distorts the Tao. Literally, it reads:

> tao can tao not constant tao
>
> name can name not constant name

A middle-of-the-road translation by J. H. McDonald (from his 1996 translation available at www.wam.umd.edu/~stwright/rel/tao/TaoTeChing.html), reads as follows:

> The tao that can be described is not the eternal Tao.
>
> The name that can be spoken is not the eternal Name.

The paradox "all language distorts the Tao" is itself a piece of language! Whatever says or implies that distorts the Tao. So … does the first sentence contradict itself? Was the author speaking tongue in cheek?

Language trips us up again. Consider the following:

1. Ancient Chinese has no "the."

2. The word *tao* occurs *three* times in the passage, not twice.

Translators usually read the middle tao as "speech." They put the contradiction inside the first by saying "the Tao" and read their familiar Christian mysticism ("God can't be defined") into this sentence.

So maybe this sentence is not about the Great Tao. Let's try this translation on for size:

> To guide what can be guided is not constant guiding.

> To name what can be named is not constant naming.

However we read this famous passage, it seems to point to some problem about words and using words to guide us. We'll explore this problem more in later chapters.

Because this is a book, though, and because people reading books like to have some idea of what they're reading about, we would like to go beyond the simple synonyms Way or guide. The problem is that the English way is about as hard to define as the Chinese tao. How about some examples?

A concrete example: A tao is a road, a path, or a series of signposts that get you from one point to another.

Taoist Tip-Off

Ancient Greeks were fixed on defining words. Ancient Chinese seldom spoke of definitions.

On the Path

In her article "The Search for Tao" (quoted at users.ntplx.net/~bbarrett/intro~tao.html), author Madelyn Hamilton defined Taoism as follows:

> "In a nutshell, Taoism is the consolidation of a number of concepts and practices that make up the 'path,' or 'Way,' of living. The consolidation of ideas and concepts include basic principles or theories regarding the body, diet, breathing and physical exercise, uses of herbs, philosophical inquiry, and, of course, meditation. All of which the Taoist feels brings a human being into closer alignment with the 'natural order' of life and living."

A provisional definition: When you ask "How do (or should) I (blank)?" the answer will be a tao.

In the end, though, it's probably best to consider the word *Tao* as something like a cross between ethics and the laws of nature.

On the Path

For familiarity's sake, we have retained the old-style westernization of the Chinese terms Tao and Taoist in this book, since these are the forms most familiar to those who have heard of this school of thought. (If we used the word Dao in the title of our book, some bookstores and readers might believe it to be something other than Tao.) However, we have used the official spelling of other terms. This may confuse you because the two most famous Taoists are Laozi and Zhuangzi (once known in the West as Lao Tzu and Chuang-Tzu). This new spelling is now used by native Chinese and Chinese students around the world. After all, more people speak Chinese than English!

Why Define the Simple?

The problem with defining the English word *way* (like the Chinese word *tao*) is that it is too simple. Any word we would use in the definition, you probably learned later in life than the word *way* and learned it by using the word *way*. Tao is like that in Chinese. In English, we can do little more than offer a near-synonym that is just as primitive.

Here are some familiar English synonyms for way. Each could be a possible translation for tao.

- ◆ Course
- ◆ Method
- ◆ Manner
- ◆ Mode
- ◆ Means
- ◆ Practice

And so on. Such ways are intrinsically practical and answer a wide range of "What-to-do?" questions. But a way presupposes we already know where we want to go … and to know a tao is both to know *where to go* and *how to get there*.

Other problems exist. Chinese language lacks plurals and not simply the forms, but the whole grammar of pluralization. (By this we mean agreement in number, the plural forms of verbs, and all the rest of that bother from high school English.) To get a sense of what this would mean in English, imagine speaking with only nouns like poultry, wood, venison, mutton, beef, instead of chicken, trees, deer, lambs, cows. In Chinese, nouns refer in this *collective* way. They have many ways of counting the things they refer to in this collective way—words rather like "piece of," "blade of," "ream of," and "slice of" in English. The nouns themselves do not say what counts as a single item of that type.

Tao is no exception. That is why we gave you two definitions of the whole of Tao (the Great Tao) and its parts (the rules or laws for this thing or group of things). When we see "tao" in a Taoist text, it may refer to any-size part, from the most particular (the way I typed this t) to the entire history of time.

This brings us back to the lowercase t tao: the tao that refers to some *part* of that guidance, such as a moral code, a set of instructions, an intuition, or a teacher's example. The word *tao* is used throughout classical texts of Chinese thought, first by Confucius, then by the philosophers who argued with him about ethics and politics. They all disputed about tao. In this sense, taos are spoken, heard, forgotten, transmitted, learned, studied, understood and misunderstood, distorted, mastered, and performed with pleasure.

In the end, the picture that emerges is that of an idea that doesn't quite yield to the valiant effort of countless translators to make it conform to the English language. A tao is something you can follow, though, we can tell you that much. When you follow it, that is practice, conduct, behavior, action, and living.

What Is Taoism?

Here's one answer: a fiction. As one scholar quipped, "Zhuangzi never knew he was a Taoist."

There was no classical Chinese association or group calling themselves Taoists. The name was coined in the Han dynasty (206 B.C.–A.D. 220—a rough Chinese equivalent of the Roman Empire). A Han historian (Sima Qian, writing around 98 B.C.), faced with the task of classifying the philosophers of the classical period who didn't belong to schools, came up with two categories: Taoist (Tao-school) and Legalist (Fa-school). His names pointed to a central term in their writings of the two groups he "created." Laozi and Zhuangzi became Taoists long after they were dead … essentially because they talked about tao a lot!

Many of the ruling class in the Han dynasty were attracted to Huang-Lao—a superstitious cult of ruler lore. It worshipped the Yellow (Huang) Emperor and Laozi. The cult mixed naive popular cosmology with the philosophy of Laozi and Zhuangzi. Thus Taoist religion grew out of Taoist philosophy.

> **Tao Then, Tao Now** _____
>
> The classical tradition of China, like that of Greece, was lost with the onset of a philosophical Dark Age initiated by the Qin dynasty (221 B.C.). Sima Qian (ca. 145 B.C.–ca. A.D. 90) wrote "I have gathered up and brought together the old traditions of the world which were scattered and lost." China had two "enlightenments"—one with the transmission of Buddhism at the end of the Han dynasty (A.D. 220) and the other with the rise of the Song dynasty (A.D. 960) Neo-Confucianism.

Here's another answer to the question "What is Taoism?" The Huang-Lao groupings existed from the time of Laozi and transmitted the authentic expression of Laozi's *religious* ideas. Sima Qian was talking about this religion when he coined the term. Zhuangzi learned Taoism from this cult, though he honored only Laozi. Thus Taoist philosophy grew out of an original Taoist religion.

Both views have their proponents. Tune in here in 75 years or so—maybe the matter will be settled. As you will learn in Chapter 9, "Fifteen Epochs," the timeframes in question in either approach are impressively vast.

Religious Taoism, as you will learn in Chapter 3, "All About Laozi," can look considerably more diverse than the philosophical school from which it draws its name. It denotes a wide range of Han Chinese practices, the Han yin-yang cosmology, alchemy, and rituals that may seem to expand well beyond the core ideas of Taoism as expressed within the philosophical school. Yet religious Taoism regards as sacred the same texts that brought that school into existence.

A Philosophy or a Religion?

Taoism can be approached from either direction, or from both. It's up to you. Many (perhaps most) Westerners seem to celebrate Taoism's religious insights, yet have minimal interest in the intricate specifics of traditional Chinese religion. They would prefer to focus fairly narrowly on the guidance offered in the two core texts of Taoism, the *Daode Jing* (attributed to the Taoist sage Laozi) and the *Zhuangzi* (attributed to the Taoist sage Zhuangzi).

This book focuses primarily on the teachings of Laozi and Zhuangzi, because these appear to be the objects of greatest interest to the Western readers. In addition, *The Complete Idiot's Guide to Taoism* offers some insights on and descriptions of Taoist religious practice.

In short, if you acquaint yourself with some of the key teachings from the *Daode Jing* and the *Zhuangzi* and examine their modern implications, you'll probably be in a good position to take the journey in any direction you choose after you finish this book.

Do Taoists Believe in God?

To the extent that the word *God* refers to a creator of nature, or a supernatural person with a "plan" for humans in particular, or a supernatural ruler and judge, the best answer is probably "no."

To the extent that the word *God* refers to some unknown meaning or purpose of nature, or the guide that operates in natural and human action, then the best answer is probably "yes."

If one's conception of God does not preclude God from being everywhere, all at once, then religious Taoism is likely to complement that conception. In a sense, Taoist religiosity expresses itself in awe of nature itself, rather than in awe of an imagined creator or author of nature.

Is There a Single, Big Idea to Taoism?

We'll examine a number of big ideas in later chapters of this book, but as a starting point, awe of nature will do. The natural beauty and complexity that inspires Western religion to postulate God also inspires Taoists. Nature has an awesome richness and complexity of process that seems to guide everything in a splendid balance. Grass doesn't need lectures to grow properly; rivers don't have to be bullied into finding the sea. Humans, a Taoist would hold, are an integral part of this nature, not a separate agent to exploit or act on it.

The Taoist ideal of human behavior, then, is one in which forceful striving, grasping, artificiality, social posturing, and short-sighted manipulation of one's environment have passed away. In the place of these things, there is a relaxed acceptance of our nature and our unity with it. This inspires a view of human action as an elegant expression of natural spontaneity.

Here's a familiar description of this particular "big idea" that we think you'll appreciate:

> "True people for [Zhuangzi] are those who have merged their thoughts and actions with the ever-changing transformations of the universe. Once at one with the Tao, such people act from their innermost being; they no longer deliberate or think about their actions. Free from all choice, they reflect the situation with perfect clarity and duly respond in the only possible and perfectly appropriate way."
>
> —Livia Kohn, *Early Chinese Mysticism* (Princeton University Press, 1991)

How Many Taoists Are There?

Here's one answer: about six billion! How can anyone who exists not be a part of nature? In another sense, there is only one Taoist—the natural universe as a whole. How many people identify themselves as Taoists? That's harder to say. In China, a conservative estimate of the total number of self-conscious religious Taoists runs at 40 million. In the West, there are far fewer who call themselves Taoists, but there are many who regard Taoism as informing their spiritual or philosophical outlook in important ways. Zen Buddhism is a product of Taoism (a Taoist insight applied to Buddhism), so one might include all Zen Buddhist adherents as "technical" Taoists.

In the end, the total number of Taoists doesn't measure a Taoist's goal nearly as well as does the influence Taoism has had on arts, on ideas, and on the way people in a remarkably diverse array of cultures live their lives.

What's Next?

Keep reading—and you'll find out about the *Daode Jing*, one of the most translated books in human history.

The Least You Need to Know

- ◆ Ancient Chinese didn't speak of definitions, but Taoists have a vague concern about the relation of language and tao.
- ◆ Our provisional definitions of tao are "the totality of natural process" and "the human parts of that process, including instructions, examples, morality, rituals, and so on."
- ◆ The key link: Humans are an integral part of nature, and human tao is natural tao.
- ◆ Philosophical Taoism and religious Taoism are distinctive strands within the Taoist tradition.
- ◆ Taoists do not speak of God, but of nature. The tradition's religiosity stems from the awe of nature that motivates others to worship a creator of nature.
- ◆ Taoists do not think of humans as separate from nature; they view their own actions as continuous with natural spontaneity.
- ◆ Taoists do not count members, but the cultural, artistic, religious, and philosophical influence of Taoism pervades the Far East as well as the modern West (partly through Taoism's influence on Zen).

Laozi and Zhuangzi

In This Chapter

- ◆ Introducing Laozi
- ◆ May we present Zhuangzi
- ◆ Some thoughts on the origins of Taoism

In this chapter, you get an introduction to the two most important figures in Taoism—Laozi and Zhuangzi. The "mysterious sage" Laozi is the traditionally recognized author of the *Daode Jing* (*Tao Te Ching*), the most beloved and widely translated Chinese philosophical text.

The figure of Laozi has always been shrouded in ambiguity. This ambiguity has a strange way of deepening, rather than dispersing, as more is discovered about the texts. Many scholars dismiss Laozi as mythological or use his name as shorthand for "the author(s) of the *Daode Jing.*"

The Traditional View

Tradition regarded Laozi as Confucius's (sixth century B.C.) teacher and the "founder" of Taoism; a "doubt tradition" movement in modern China gave influential arguments for dating the text to a period a few centuries later. The discovery of a first-century B.C. version of the text suggested that the text was in flux over a long period of time.

Taoist Tip-Off _____

Little is known of Laozi (also known as Lao-Tzu), the presumed author of the _Daode Jing_. Speculation regarding his lifespan, if he had one, ranges from 600 to 200 B.C. We take the skeptical approach of assuming the text to have Laozi as its creator and leave for others the debate over whether Laozi ever existed and the precise historical development of the text. When we say "Laozi said that (whatever)" we mean only "the _Daode Jing_ says that (whatever)." We sometimes call the _Daode Jing_ the _Laozi_. This reminds us that the other "masters" of Chinese thought whose names are also the titles of books probably didn't write those, either. (Although unlike Laozi, we tend to believe the others actually existed.)

Confucius (551–479 B.C.), also known as Kongfuzi, fostered an influential school of thought in China that emphasized social obligation, etiquette, and ritual. The Confucian school has been seen for over two millennia as a native Chinese rival to the indigenous Taoist school. Debates and rivalries between the two ways of acting in the world were common. Eventually, many came to see them as compatible, and practice of both traditions by the same family or person is common. Still, each has its distinctive tone.

Confucianism, which lacks priests, has been called an ethical system, rather than a religion, but it can also be seen as a movement that instilled religious insight and authority within key social groupings: family, school, and state.

Dates, Dates, Dates

The sinologist A. C. Graham argued persuasively that the text of the _Daode Jing_ probably became important only _after_ Zhuangzi, the second great sage of Taoism, died (ca. 295 B.C.). Many scholars in China, on the contrary, have reverted to the traditional dating, placing Laozi before Confucius. We are convinced of the late emergence of the _Daode Jing_ and, thus, regard Zhuangzi as the _first_ sage of Taoism.

On the Path _____

A. C. Graham is the author of a number of important works on Taoism, notably _Disputers of the Tao: Philosophical Arguments in Ancient China_ (Open Court, 1989) and _Later Mohist Ethics and Science_ (School of Oriental and African Studies, 1978).

The interpretation of the _Daode Jing_ is complicated by its poetic beauty and brevity. There are now more than 100 different translations of the _Daode Jing_ and closer to 2,000 commentaries in Chinese. Traditional views are that Laozi invented or discovered Taoism and inspired the second sage Zhuangzi. In this view, Zhuangzi merely expressed the doctrine in more extended parable and story form. There was no substantive difference in doctrine between the two. Until recently, scholars mostly thought the religion was a distortion of the philosophy, but some now argue that the text emerged first from a religion that worshipped a legendary figure known as the Yellow Emperor, or Huang-ti, along with Laozi. The religion is known as Huang-Lao. (For more on religious Taoism, see Chapter 8, "Branches of the Tao.")

Tao Then, Tao Now

Many have wondered how anyone could combine Taoism and Legalism—the strict ideology of the repressive Qin period. But Laozi's *Daode Jing* famously includes a lot of political advice, particularly in the latter half of the book. The first commentary on the Laozi was written by a Legalist, Hanfeizi. (A side note: It's important to remember that the distinctions between such schools of thought as "Taoist" and "Legalist" was invented long after the original thinkers were history.)

A review of all the possible interpretations of sequence and influence is well beyond the scope of this book. Here's a short summary of where we think all this date debating leaves us though: Our point of entry to Taoism will be more philosophical than religious, and we believe this approach is justified because we agree with Graham that the *Zhuangzi* introduces Laozi into Chinese philosophical discourse. (As we'll see later, it's also doubtful that Zhuangzi wrote more than a small part of the book *Zhuangzi*. Zhuangzi himself probably never encountered the *Laozi* book—his later "editors" almost certainly did.)

Translation: Whatever its dates and origin, *Laozi* first meant to Chinese philosophy what the school of Zhuangzi first found of interest in it.

On the Path

An ancient story holds that Laozi was the keeper of the imperial archives. Having already instructed Confucius and saddened by his country's refusal to follow the path of virtue, he decided at the age of 80 to leave China. Before he made it out of the country, a border guard stopped him and refused to let him pass before he left a written legacy of his wisdom. Hastily, Laozi set down the 5,000+ Chinese characters we know as the *Daode Jing*. Then he made his way across the border and eventually set about instructing the Buddha! Or so the legend goes.

Let's Meet Zhuangzi

A similar, but not as impenetrable, mystery surrounds the other great figure of Taoism. The sage Zhuangzi, whose historical existence no one questions, probably authored only parts of the first seven chapters—the so-called Inner Chapters—of "his" book. The others were written either by followers or thinkers of related but different theoretical orientations.

Tradition treats Zhuangzi as following Laozi, both literally and figuratively. We know of Chuang-Tzu's life only what we can surmise from the text, which hardly confirms the view of him as Laozi's disciple.

We can be far more certain of Zhuangzi's frequent association with Hui Shi, a prominent representative of the ancient Chinese School of language theory (the "School of Names"). Stories of the dialogues between Hui Shi and Zhuangzi are common throughout the *Zhuangzi,* and the second chapter of the *Zhuangzi* was clearly written by someone with firm control of the ancient Chinese technical terms of linguistic analysis.

The Original Taoist?

Scholars today are widely influenced by A. C. Graham's theory that the Zhuangzi school was responsible for Laozi's being regarded as a Taoist.

Zhuangzi's followers may have noted a compatibility in a way of reading the *Laozi* and points Zhuangzi had been making. The later sections of the *Zhuangzi* contain a number of stories in which Laozi is used as a fictional spokesman for a version of Zhuangzi's positions (not unlike the role Plato assigns to Socrates). The people who developed this material presumably read the *Daode Jing* as consistent with the doctrines they were putting in Laozi's mouth, and thus shaped the philosophical interpretation of the book.

There is also good reason to assume the middle chapters of both the *Zhuangzi* and the *Laozi* were being written while these groups were in friendly contact. (The two schools appear to have shared themes, phrases, examples, and so forth.) Graham speculated that the text itself might have been anonymous when this occurred and that Laozi was chosen as the author because a traditional story referred to him as Confucius's teacher! We'll probably never know the truth.

The best course is probably to approach the *Zhuangzi* without assuming that its author "followed" or inherited Taoism from Laozi, as a disciple would be expected to "follow" a master. The influence is more likely to run in precisely the opposite direction. Zhuangzi was the original inventor of his doctrine, and Laozi was associated with it because it had some similar themes. The most important difference between them was that the *Laozi,* though it has a linguistic theory, does not use the technical language of the "School of Names."

The more likely candidate as Zhuangzi's mentor or philosophical colleague and friend may be the dialectician Hui Shi (370–319 B.C.). When Hui Shi died, the grieving Zhuangzi described him as the person on whom he had "sharpened his wits."

> **CAUTION**
>
> **Taoist Tip-Off**
>
> Zhuangzi shares both terminology and background assumptions with Laozi, the other major philosophical figure of Taoism, but the assumption that this requires him to have been a disciple of Laozi is unfounded.

Zhuangzi and the Language Thing

Zhuangzi was a philosopher of language. Surprised? Think about it. If the Tao cannot be (fill in the blank with word of your choice) in language, the explanation must lie not only in the nature of tao, but also in the capacity and role of language. Like his buddy, Hui Shi, Zhuangzi was deeply engaged with the linguistic studies of the Later Mohists (sometimes called Neo-Mohists or Dialectical Mohists) as well as with the School of Names (which includes, along with Hui Shi, the famous Gongsun Lung, author of *White Horse Not Horse*).

The Dialectical Mohists, followers of Mozi, the Utilitarian critic of Confucianism, formulated a theory of language called "realism." They held that the world determined where to mark the distinctions between words. Language, they argued, can play its role (coordinating human behavior) best when it reflects objective similarities and differences. They ran into trouble, though, when they tried to spell this natural realism out in detail, and they had to acknowledge that tradition determined which similarities and which differences counted.

The Mohists called their study *bian* (distinctions) and assumed that philosophical and ethical disagreements reduced to our having different ways of using language to cluster and label things. A real-world–guided approach should give us an objective basis for settling such disagreements. Zhuangzi's friend, Hui Shi, undermined this confidence in bian and the possibility of agreeing on anything except that everything is relative. This sets the stage for Zhuangzi's approach.

How Tall Is Tall? How Big Is Big?

An important traditional figure from another group, the so-called School of Names, was Hui Shi, Zhuangzi's debating companion (and possibly his teacher). Hui Shi concentrated on comparatives and other terms with obviously relative frames of reference. So for example, "tall" does not have any fixed range. *Tall* for a giraffe is not *tall* for a horse. *Big* for a house is not *big* for an insect.

Generalizing this feature of relativism in language, Hui Shi apparently concluded that no distinctions or differences rested on external reality. All are projections of different perspectives. The appropriate conclusion, he thought, was to treat the world as an absolute *one*—to treat all things as evaluatively equal and analyze from there.

The Limits of Analysis and Language

Zhuangzi, despite his obvious affection for Hui Shi, saw a flaw in this argument. If all judgments about what is one or two depend on one's perspective, then from what perspective can we judge that everything is one? Hui Shi, he observed, had drawn a "real" conclusion from relative premises. We should, Zhuangzi argued, simply stop trying to talk about ultimate reality … since we "know" only perspectives.

Other thinkers were arguing against language from different points of view. One (Shen Dao) argued from the concept of a natural "way." Knowing in ancient China meant knowing a tao—a way of guiding behavior. Each rival tao is a possible way we might act in the future and use the way to guide our action. Most agree that the way they advocate is natural. Shen Dao noted that there was exactly one way that the world went in the past, and, despite all the possibility, there is exactly one way it will go in the future. He called that actual, natural way, the Great Tao. "Even a clod of Earth cannot miss the Great Tao." So we can abandon knowledge and language and cease to bian and make distinctions of right and wrong. We will effortlessly follow the Great Way.

Tao Then, Tao Now

Zhuangzi enjoyed debating with Hui Shi because he was thoughtful enough to be worth refuting. Still, Hui Shi proved a soft target for a dialectician of Zhuangzi's caliber.

Both conclusions bump into a paradox that was illuminated by the Later Mohists. They amount to saying "give up language" or "language is defective." But saying either thing turns right back on the speaker. "Language is defective" is defective! "All language distorts the Tao" distorts the Tao!

In other words: Zhuangzi had to find a way to keep Hui Shi's linguistic insights *without* getting caught in the anti-language paradox. How?

Zhuangzi: Skeptical Relativism

Traditionally, scholars have contrasted a mystic (Zhuangzi) with a logician (Hui Shi). However, Hui Shi's theses are about language and semantics, not logic. So if we resist reading Zhuangzi as simply "following Laozi," a new view of the dynamic between Zhuangzi and the School of Names emerges.

Hui Shi was actually the mystic, an erudite, enthusiastic, loquacious, but somewhat confused and starry-eyed semantic dilettante. Zhuangzi, in contrast, appears as a language theorist par excellence.

The rediscovery of the Later Mohist analysis confirmed that Zhuangzi was deeply influenced by these various reflections on language. He appreciated an insight (also found in the *Laozi*) that language shapes our attitudes, including our patterns of distinctions, valuations, and desires. We come to regard our acquired ways of distinguishing and desiring as "natural" or "obvious." The *Daode Jing* finds this process of knowing via language a form of social control of our natural spontaneity and suggests we should avoid learning language—and avoid "unnatural" desires and their consequences.

This combination led Zhuangzi to a nuanced skepticism and *pluralism*. Translation: We *can't ever be sure* we have the right perspective. There are many perspectives on the way to categorize, desire, and live. Each depends on prior commitments that can be elaborated and developed endlessly; each "works" within its own evaluation of consequences. Humans view things and live within these perspectives.

Humans, the old saying goes, are in Tao as fish are in water. In practice, this means that we depend on an endless, unarticulated, presupposed tao; we must simply take it for granted in acting.

Zhuangzi's skeptical *pluralism* is beautifully reflected in his philosophical style, making most philosophical discussion take place in dialogues between representatives of radically different perspectives (including nonhuman ones) and then refusing to draw a conclusion.

Spoken and Unspoken

In philosophy, **pluralism** is the belief that no single way of explaining the world can account for everything.

One advantage of this approach was that it did not commit Zhuangzi to any (self-condemning) anti-language conclusions. Guidance by language is natural. Zhuangzi, of all people, could appreciate the beauty of language and its ability to create new worlds and possibilities. At the same time, he could incorporate the distinctive Taoist suspicion of conventional wisdom. What's most important, Zhuangzi could also dismiss the pretensions of contemporary "sages" who wanted to impose their own tao on everyone. Given that we cannot find an ultimate standpoint to resolve the different perspectives, we should live ours and allow others to live by theirs.

Yeah, but What Did He Believe?

Skepticism isn't exactly a satisfying result. What advice, many new to Taoism ask, can a pluralist skeptic offer us?

Exactly what philosophical position of his own Zhuangzi offers is a question open to endless and fascinating examination. We tentatively offer a three-part proposal for the distinctive "positive tao" Zhuangzi could offer us as "flowing" out of his perspective on perspectives.

1. **Be open to new ways and flexible in incorporating them in your own way of life.** Zhuangzi was fond of talking with freaks, people who had been mutilated as punishments for violating some official code or other.

2. **Understand both the usefulness and the limitations of convention.** Despite his suspicion of conventions, Zhuangzi observed that since they allow us to communicate and coordinate our actions, they are useful—and that is all we can ask. Following conventions, including language, is (despite what Shen Dao said) natural for humans.

3. **Cultivate skill to the point of spontaneous "flow."** One of the distinctive themes in the *Zhuangzi* is the joy in mastery of some tao—whether it is butchering an ox, catching cicadas, making wheels, playing a zither, or debating. Satisfaction and a feeling of intimate connection with the world can be had from the exercise of these acquired skills.

We have to take each of these pieces of advice with a grain of salt … because each pulls in a slightly different direction. If we are completely open to new ideas, we may never cultivate skill. Conventions may enjoin us from certain discussions or cultivating certain skills. We can't completely let go of the skeptical hesitation because that often chokes off spontaneity and, as Zhuangzi himself notes, no matter how much skill we acquire, there will always be things we cannot do well. ("Knowledge," Zhuangzi once noted, "is endless; life is limited. To pursue the endless with the limited is dangerous.")

Especially in view of his detached, fantasy-dialogue style of writing, the safest conclusion may be that Zhuangzi was a skeptic who accepted an implicit real context. What does that mean? There *may* be an absolutely right way, but we have little chance of finding it in our lifetimes. We can never decisively rule out the possibility of finding a better way of doing something.

A New View of Laozi and Zhuangzi

So where does Laozi fit in all this? Well, we suppose that what appealed to followers of Zhuangzi was Laozi's related theory of language. Though he didn't use the technical terms of linguistics, Laozi taught that words came in pairs of opposites. When we use them, we learn to divide things as our teachers, parents, peers, and others do. With these distinctions, however, we also learn to react in socially approved ways, gathering things we call beautiful and discarding those we call ugly. This leads us to action—wei. Laozi advocated abandoning the entire edifice of knowledge and action, resulting in his famous theory of Shen Dao.

The *Daode Jing* attributed to Laozi also promoted a notion of *reversing* values. Wherever the dominant (especially Confucian) value was one thing, Laozi would recommend looking at matters from the opposite point of view. Where convention valued being yang, i.e., dominant, male, strong, on top, aggressive, active, penetrating, Laozi advocated being yin, submissive, female, weak, taking the lower position, passive, receptive. In learning to value the opposite, we come to the realization that ours is not the obvious or "constant" value.

Spoken and Unspoken

Reversing values in Taoism may involve reference to yin and yang, the basic forces regarded as making up the natural world. They suggest an organic creation model of nature—creation by the interaction of opposites—and stand for a cluster of opposites: moon and sun, wet and dry, cold and hot, female and male, passive and active, and so on. Laozi and Zhuangzi appealed to yin and yang (sparingly) to illustrate key points. For more on yin and yang, see Chapter 5, "In the Flow: Key Concepts."

Laozi had his own kind of skepticism and pluralism, too. He said that any tao that could be used to guide us (to "tao" us) would not be a constant one. It would be made up of names, and no name is constant. However, Laozi tended toward a distinctive kind of primitivism. He seemed to favor a social ideal of small villages, presumably with no language, with villagers "knotting cords" rather than using numbers and so satisfied with their simple life "they would not even travel to the next village."

The *spirit* behind this primitivism, however, is one the followers of Zhuangzi could appreciate. Laozi's point was that the focus on learning to be "discriminating" leads to a chronic dissatisfaction; we become *so* discriminating that we cannot enjoy anything but the best wine, the most elite movies, the rarest paintings, and so on. Acquiring such sophistication is a kind of unnatural bondage. To the Taoist, there is a profound appeal in the idea of "returning to the child" who finds excitement in everything.

Followers of Zhuangzi could indeed find good reasons to think of the *Daode Jing* as a lead-in to the more sophisticated and mature views of Zhuangzi. So even in our revised story, Laozi fits in before Zhuangzi—but not, as in the tradition, because Zhuangzi studied Laozi, but because the teaching attributed to Laozi resonated with the sophisticated conclusions of the *Zhuangzi*.

What Does It Mean to Practice Taoism?

"To regard the fundamental as the essence, to regard things as coarse, to regard accumulation as deficiency, and to dwell quietly alone with the spiritual and the intellect—herein lie the techniques of Tao of the ancients …. They built their doctrines on the principle of the eternal nonbeing, and held the idea of the Great One as fundamental."

—Zhuangzi

Ultimately, the revolutionary insight into Zhuangzi is that we can approach him without imposing our own (probably inaccurate) historical assumptions on what he is trying to do. The revolutionary insight about Laozi is that we may gain something by consciously viewing him through the work of Zhuangzi.

In other words, the correct Taoist reading of Laozi may well depend on getting Zhuangzi right.

The Least You Need to Know

- Little is known of Laozi (also known as Lao-Tzu), the presumed author of the *Daode Jing*.
- Recently, some scholars have argued that the *Daode Jing* probably became important only *after* Zhuangzi, the other great sage of Taoism, died (ca. 295 B.C.).

◆ Zhuangzi was a brilliant philosopher of language who was skeptical of the idea that debate and analysis could definitively resolve philosophical issues.

◆ For many years, the word *Taoism* referred to the theory of Laozi and Zhuangzi, with Laozi as the "obvious" defining figure.

◆ In recent years, many have concluded that the correct Taoist reading of Laozi may well depend on getting Zhuangzi right.

Chapter 3

All About Laozi

In This Chapter

◆ Questions and answers about Laozi

◆ The importance or nonimportance of language

◆ Knowing when to stop

In this chapter, you will get a brief introduction to the *Daode Jing* and its mysterious author, Laozi.

Six Questions About Laozi and the *Daode Jing*

An alternate title to this chapter could be "What We Don't Know for Sure." Not knowing is certainly a fitting approach to Laozi's book, which is among the most translated, and deeply contradictory, in all of human history. (It has been claimed that the *Daode Jing* has been translated more often than any book, other than the Bible and the Bhagavad-Gita. Who knows if that's true or not.)

In this chapter, each of the points we ask you to consider about Laozi begins with a query. While we're addressing things that people may tell you that they know for sure about the *Daode Jing,* they may well have another dimension beyond the supposed certainty. We're going to find insoluble puzzles in those views. Accordingly, we're framing each key point in the form of a question, rather than a statement. This "skeptical" approach fits (we think) with the tone of the teachings in question.

Was There Really a Laozi?

As noted earlier, people disagree on this point. So we're off to a good start.

There's some small possibility that Confucius really had a teacher named Lao something or other. If there was such a teacher, he almost certainly did not write the *Daode Jing*. Still, he would count as the original Laozi, and we could then cease to care about (or at least abandon the prospect of discovering) his doctrine. Historians guess, however, that that part of the legend of Laozi may have been based on other people, too—and some of them may have been real even if the stories were false.

But who cares? What people really care about is the identity of the author of the *Daode Jing*. Was there a single or dominant author of the core ideas? We doubt it.

Universal Principles

"[We are] quite certain that Lao Tzu the sage did indeed walk the earth once upon a time in ancient China. But let us for a moment suppose the opposite. What if Lao Tzu did not exist and the truth expressed in *Tao Te Ching* was the work of more than one person? Would that not shake the very foundation of our beliefs? The answer is an emphatic no, if we are true practitioners of Taoism. We call ourselves Taoists precisely because we follow the Tao rather than any one particular individual. We all seek the universal principles, the patterns that exist in all things, and the basic truths in daily lives."

—From "Tao Living: Lao Tzu" (www.taoism.net, 1999)

Spoken and Unspoken

We are using *Daode Jing* and the *Laozi* as alternate titles—reflecting ancient practice. *Jing* simply means "canon" or "classic." *Daode* is a compound of Tao (ways, guides, instructions) and de (virtuosity, excellence, virtue). The compound became the Chinese word for "ethics," but the text uses only the separate characters.

We can approach the *Daode Jing* with seriousness and respect whoever the author(s) were. This means that in reading it, we are not pretending to reconstruct the whole philosophy of a historical individual, but trying to extract the best, most coherent guidance from the text. If you get too distracted by the historical puzzle of authorship, you run the risk of missing the consistent messages of the *Laozi* (another title for the *Daode Jing*), which so many have found enlightening through the centuries.

Here's an interesting side note. A common theory of the name is that it is the names of two separate parts of the book—the first beginning with the word *Tao* and the second with the word *de* (virtuosity). A Han manuscript has the parts reversed, suggesting that the text was commonly transmitted separately. A later discovery confirmed the traditional order, however. The earliest commentary on the text simply referred to it as the *Laozi*—hence our double name for this beloved canon.

We use both titles to remind us that we're taking the text to have some valuable teaching for us—as a person might. We do this without worrying about who the person was. We read the text, that is, as the students of Zhuangzi who first appreciated it did. The best attitude for reading this text might be expressed like this: "It seems to get *something* right—so let's figure it out."

> **CAUTION**
>
> **Taoist Tip-Off**
>
> The *Daode Jing* is filled with seemingly contradictory pronouncements. For instance:
>
> "Those who speak, do not know."
>
> "If 'twisted,' then 'straight'; if 'worn out' then 'new.'"

Is His Book Religion or Philosophy?

Here's one answer: It's a philosophical work that has launched one of the world's great religious traditions—Taoism. It has been argued that centuries of religious interpretation and dogma have obscured the work's philosophical foundations. It has also been argued that extended philosophical debate about the meaning of the *Daode Jing* deprives the work of its vital spirit.

Religious interpretations tend to dominate most translations of the *Daode Jing* and credit it with authority because of the (semi-divine) status of the author. This reinforces the notions that Laozi discovered Taoism and that Zhuangzi learned it as a religious disciple would. Religious interpretations avoid or obscure the theory of language in the work and blame all the obscurity on "tao."

A philosophical interpretation reads the text in the context of the ancient Chinese philosophical disputes about which tao is the correct guide to life. It avoids importing familiar Christian concepts to translate the doctrines, for example, heaven (for nature), eternal (for constant or reliable), and spirit (for life energy). And when the text suggests that language has a problem expressing correct tao, philosophers are likely to wonder what theory of language helps explain the passage as well as what theory of tao does.

Philosophers, in short, assume that Taoism joins the dispute about what tao to follow and that it has some philosophically helpful insights into that dispute … and whether its resolution is possible or not.

Is the Language of the *Daode Jing* Worth Considering?

The *Daode Jing* presents a most elegant expression of the underlying structure of the ancient Chinese theory of language. We can call this a contrast theory of language.

All terms come in pairs of opposites or complements. We learn them together because when we master one, we master how to use its opposite at the same time. There is only one distinction for each pair. The second chapter of the *Daode Jing* offers a classic expression of this view.

> ### Tao Then, Tao Now
>
> That the social world knows to deem the beautiful as "beautiful" simply creates the "ugly."
>
> That the social world knows to deem worth as "worthy" simply creates "worthlessness."
>
> Thus "exists" and "not-exists" mutually sprout. "Difficult" and "easy" are mutually done. "Long" and "short" are mutually gauged. "High" and "low" mutually incline. "Sound" and "tone" mutually blend. "Before" and "after" mutually supervene.
>
> Using this: Sages fix social issues without deeming; administer a "no-words" teaching.
>
> —*Daode Jing*, chapter 2

The *Laozi* uses this theory to advocate the idea that we should give up language—stop making distinctions. This reminds many of the doctrine of Shen Dao that we discussed in Chapter 2, "Laozi and Zhuangzi." It did the students of Zhuangzi also, and they wrote Laozi into the history of ideas leading to Zhuangzi, placing him between Shen Dao and Zhuangzi. Why?

As you recall, Shen Dao noted that while there were many possible taos advocated by various thinkers, there was exactly one way the world was and will actually go in the future. He called this total history of the world the Great Tao. It fits the requirement of moralists that their tao should be natural—the actual is necessarily natural. So we can follow the Natural Tao without having to study or learn from Confucius or Mozi or any of the rival "hundred schools" of competing taos. Shen Dao's slogan was "abandon knowledge; discard self." "Knowledge" meant knowledge of some moral tao or way of doing something. You need no knowledge of tao (guides) to follow the Great Tao. "Even a clod of earth can not miss the Tao," he concluded.

So Shen Dao gave up distinction (he abandoned "this"/"not this" and "right"/"wrong"). He made no judgments and just floated on reality like a leaf on water. His is an expression of a familiar tendency to fatalism (the idea that you can't change things) in Chinese religion.

Beyond "What Will Be Will Be" (with Apologies to Doris Day)

The Zhuangzi account criticizes and distances itself from the passive fatalism of Shen Dao. The narrator says, "[Shen Dao's] is a tao (guide) that is not a tao (guide)" and characterizes it as a tao (guide) for the dead, not for the living. The point is that "what will be will be" has no implications for action. Whatever we do will accord with Great Tao, but knowing that does not help us decide what to do!

The history suggests that the slogan "abandon knowledge" appealed to Laozi but not the fatalism. He found a *different* reason to abandon knowledge. It was this: Knowledge, particularly of distinctions guiding behavior, was seen simply as a way for society to control people, to shape and distort their natural propensities and happiness. Language, in this view, only gives us new desires for the things we learn to distinguish. It makes us strive and compete for those things marked as valuable by society and thus ends in unnatural conditions such as strife and war. Humans left free of socialization by these schemes of knowledge and names would, the *Daode Jing* suggests, live peacefully and in tranquility in small, primitive villages.

Zhuangzi implicitly diagnosed deeper problems and a paradox in Shen Dao's views. The problem is that using language is utterly natural for humans—as natural as the twittering of birds. Further, since Shen Dao tells us to do something, his slogan becomes a bit of guiding knowledge! So if we follow it, we disobey it. Laozi, however, not only tolerated this paradox—he replicated it! Why? Here's one answer: because it does not arise from the fatalistic notion of Great Tao. Instead, it arises from the anti-language conclusion of "abandoning distinctions."

On the Path

Why would Shen Dao teach that we should "discard self"? Taos in ancient China were often identified by a main word. Yang Zhu advocated egoism—where the main word in the guidance is *wo* (self). Shen Dao reminds us that even selfishness is a tao. If we abandon knowledge, we don't become selfish.

We can understand Laozi, then, as accepting the paradoxical "abandon knowledge" spirit of Shen Dao while rejecting his fatalism. Laozi reproduced a version of the paradox in the first line of his *Daode Jing*, which, as we've seen, can be translated as: "No tao (guide) that can tao (guide) is a constant tao (guide)."

That famous opening line is followed by a less noticed parallel that may be translated as follows: "Any name that can name is not a constant name." Here, we encounter in the philosopher Laozi, someone who is deeply skeptical of the reliability of what might be called a "discourse tao." This skepticism rests on the conventional (and, therefore, changeable) nature of language.

The (often-ignored) philosophical implications of the opening lines of the *Daode Jing* are worth considering closely. One can understand Laozi as saying that no instruction

based on discourse will guide reliably in all circumstances … because the terms used do not and cannot mark actual distinctions reliably. This contrast of the natural (what can be counted on to happen) and the conventional (what people try to impose on situations) pervades the text.

Toward Authenticity in Daily Life

How does this line of thought lead Laozi to the "abandon knowledge" conclusion? Well, the motivating force behind this idea is the goal of freedom from social control.

Laozi treats (prescriptive, instruction-focused) knowledge as based on language. Accordingly, he sees most knowledge as a maze of arbitrary, historically "accidental" social systems of making distinctions, guiding desires, and acting. Laozi then justifies the "abandon knowledge" as a way to recover our natural, authentic, spontaneity.

What Do the Teachings of the *Daode Jing* Say About Human Desires?

Artificial desires, according to Laozi, increase strife because …

- ◆ Social structures expand the number of desires.
- ◆ Our acquired desires are more competitive than our natural ones.

This is a profoundly pragmatic approach that we feel is worth appreciating on its own terms, not because it supports any mystical practice.

Consider our desire for rare things. That they are rare gives them no value to an individual alone. The object in question is only valuable if someone *else* wants it. It has only social value. Socially instilled desires motivate a thirst for status and power. Our natural desires, for example, for food, drink, and sex, Laozi would argue, are few and simple and align with the spontaneous processes of the universe.

Tao Then, Tao Now

"The philosophical system of Taoism stems largely from the *Tao-te-Ching* …. The Tao, in the broadest sense, is the way the universe functions, the path taken by natural events. It is characterized by spontaneous creativity and by regular alterations of phenomena (such as day following night) that proceed without effort."

—*The Columbia Encyclopedia, Third Edition* (Columbia University Press, 1993)

What Is Negative Knowledge?

The *Laozi* itself advocates a tao—it offers us lots of advice about how to live. Doesn't that contradict the spirit of the opening line?

One way to avoid blatant contradiction is to think of the advice as a scheme of negative knowledge. Human beings (particularly those influenced by Confucianism) normally value activity, dominance, the upper position, strength, and upstanding rigidity. Laozi urges us to see the value of passivity, weakness, the lower position, and receptive yielding. Laozi values dullness over brilliance, ignorance over knowledge, lacking over having, and so on. This negative knowledge is offered to show us that there can be wisdom in reversing the value scheme of conventional wisdom.

This idea of reversal in the context of the contrast theory of names links up easily with yin-yang, sexual reproduction cosmology that is familiar from the *Yi Jing* (*I Ching*). Laozi emphasizes the importance of the female and "draws sustenance from the mother." He treats the female as the "valley of the world." Further, yin-yang also metaphorically explains the importance of water with its connection to moisture, the lower position, passivity, and overcoming through yielding.

On the Path

On the metaphysical side, where we normally value having and being, Laozi points to the utility of lacking and nonbeing. He stresses the usefulness of the emptiness in a cup, a room, the hub of a wheel, and so on. The knowledge we gain from these "reversals" of ordinary value may be called "negative knowledge." It consists in seeing that the conventional ways of using terms to guide us can be reversed. They are not constant.

Confucians criticized the "scheming methods" and the disingenuous tone of some of this "negative" advice. Laozi, they charge, urges us to act submissive in order to dominate. He talks, for instance, of keeping people ignorant, so they can be ruled more easily.

Actually, we believe the point of this "negative" approach to wisdom is simply to get us to see the unreliability of formulated advice. If the opposite advice often makes as much sense, you shouldn't trust the obviousness of "conventional wisdom." The moral of the reversal is not simply to replace one moral scheme with another. It calls into question the whole idea of having a scheme in the first place, and, therefore, calls into question the wisdom of any similarly artificial, linguistic, and unnatural tao.

Laozi's position might well be that conventional distinctions (taos) make people's lives more complicated and troublesome. Best, perhaps, to forget all distinctions—not learn a different, rival set.

Laozi and Religious Feminism

Still, like most readers of the *Daode Jing*, we are reluctant completely to ignore the often beautiful "negative" advice given in the text. It often points to the value we assume for expressing it. Further, its special charm and uniqueness in being a radically feminist religion should not be so easily abandoned.

It's important to be reminded from time to time that we have no serious religious basis for assuming God is a man. The peace message and the ecological consciousness in the text surely is not simply a device to make us skeptics; it still has value—in that it reminds us of how our own modern values and preconceptions might lead us to a world far from home and natural comfort.

What Does Laozi Offer in Place of the Scheme of Names?

If names don't work, what does? What exactly does Laozi point to? What could the (implied) next level of knowledge be?

Tao Then, Tao Now

"How do I know the social world's condition? With this."

—*Daode Jing*, chapter 54 (These are the final lines of the chapter.)

The *Daode Jing* formulates no answer. Part of the genius (and enduring appeal) of Laozi's masterpiece is to leave such questions up to the reader. It is likely, though, that Laozi intended us to reflect on the very process of proposing rival daos (ways of doing things) for the purpose of guidance, and to open ourselves to the possibility of moving intuitively from question to question in life. We just do it from here, from this … not from some grand view of the whole universe.

The *Daode Jing*'s thrust seems to be relativist or skeptical. To say that there is no constant dao is to say that any dao will rest on some scheme of background distinctions and attitudes. This is an extremely important and at the same time remarkably elusive point. So here it comes again.

On the Path

The *Daode Jing* holds that all standards consist of distinctions and attitudes, and that these distinctions and attitudes are themselves subject to revision on subsequent reflection.

So we may decide that Laozi's point is either that there is no way—or there are many ways—of asking and answering ultimate questions about the right way to live. Or if we choose to emphasize the religious, rather than philosophical, approach, we may decide that his ultimate point simply cannot be uttered.

Can This All Be Boiled Down to a Single Sentence?

We'll give it a try: *Laozi was skeptical about the way human beings choose to divide up reality for purposes of acting on it—and would have preferred the approach "Just act!"*

In fact, using this, we can see a philosophical role for the religious or mystical reading that most popular translations of the *Daode Jing* highlight.

> **Tao Then, Tao Now** _____
>
> "The guide of nature: Is it not like a taut bow?
> That which is high, it represses;
> That which is low, raises up;
> That which has abundance, pares back;
> That which is insufficient, adds to it.
> The guide of nature is to pare back abundance and add to the insufficient.
> If it's the guide of humans, then it's not like that!"
> —*Daode Jing*, chapter 77

The point of Laozi's analysis of (supposedly) effective action-guiding human distinctions is that there really are none. This skeptical response is practically indistinguishable from the mystical response. "There is no ultimate criterion of rightness" and "There is an ultimate criterion that cannot be spoken" are, for all practical purposes, probably the same thing.

Laozi's skeptical overtones emerge in his occasional celebration of "ignorance" or "dullness." His point is simple: There is, perhaps, the greatest wisdom in knowing your not-knowing—and knowing when to stop.

Let's stop right there.

The Least You Need to Know

- We prefer to consider *Laozi* as a text speaking to us, rather than a semi-divine person writing the same advice. This preserves the value of the text without relying on any controversial theory of authorship.

- Centuries of religious interpretation and dogma may have fit the spirit of the *Laozi*, but these elements obscure the (fascinating) philosophical foundations and detail of the *Daode Jing*.

♦ Whichever viewpoint you prefer, you should consider joining the generations of readers who have read, absorbed into their lives, and contemplated with pleasure the poetic, metaphysical, shocking, and soothing text known as the *Daode Jing*.

♦ Laozi doubted we could find any fully correct way to divide up reality or to live. Better to stay in your village than go to war to convert others.

The Other Book: The *Zhuangzi*

In This Chapter

- ◆ An introduction to Zhuangzi
- ◆ Core principles of his teachings
- ◆ Stories and parables that will make you want to learn more

Many people who claim to know nothing of Taoism are nevertheless familiar with its two most famous sayings. The first saying is the one holding that a journey of a thousand miles begins with a single step; this, as we have seen, is attributed to Laozi. The second saying is a brief and famous parable involving a man who dreamed he was a butterfly. (Or … did he?)

In this chapter, you will learn about the remarkable man who formulated that teaching. His name was Zhuangzi. (The name is often rendered as Chuang-Tzu.) Although he died more than two millennia ago, one is always tempted to speak about him in the present tense, because he was—and remains—among the greatest teachers in human history.

Meet Zhuangzi

Zhuangzi is, with Laozi, one of the two defining figures in Chinese Taoism. His teachings have had an incalculable effect on Chinese thought. The standard history records that Zhuangzi lived in the region now called Honan between perhaps 370 and 286 B.C.

Despite the book's name, scholars are not convinced that it contains writings attributable solely to Zhuangzi. It seems likely that the sage in question is responsible only for parts of the first seven chapters of the *Zhuangzi*. These are the so-called *Inner Chapters*. The remainder may well be complementary material provided by Zhuangzi's students or the followers of similar traditions.

The "second book" of Taoism is an often irreverent, oddly compelling hodgepodge of elements. It contains extended observations on philosophical questions, stories, allegories, and chunks of earlier myths and teachings. It also contains a startling number of jokes and tongue-in-cheek explorations of Taoist principles. Many passages evoke, at least for the Western reader, some transcript of a surrealistic vaudeville routine that uses as its punch line the meaning of life.

A Sage Who Delights in Messing with Your Mind

One suspects that if Zhuangzi had lived in modern times, he might well have composed material for the *Monty Python* boys. Consider the following passage from one of the Inner Chapters:

What I Want to Say

"Now, I want to say something here. I really can't tell whether what I want to say matches the category of the things other people say or it doesn't. But—whether it matches the category of their sayings or it doesn't, it's clear that it must match *some* category. So, at least in that respect, it is basically the same as those statements other people make. All the same, let me say what I want to say.

"Things begin. There is a point before this beginning, 'not-yet-beginning-to-begin.' There is a point before this 'not-yet-beginning,' 'not-yet-beginning-to-begin-not-yet-beginning-to-begin.' There is something. There is nothing. There is 'not-yet-beginning-to-be-nothing.' There is 'not-yet-beginning-to-be-not-yet-beginning-to-be-nothing.' All

---

of a sudden, there is nothing. But I really can't tell, when dealing with this 'nothing,' which is actually something and which is actually nothing.

"There now: I've just said something.

"But I really can't tell whether or not what I've said has actually said anything or whether it hasn't said anything at all.

"Nothing in the world is bigger than the tip of an autumn hair, and Mount Tai is small; no one lives longer than a doomed child, and Pengzi died young. Sky and earth were born together with me, and the myriad things and I are one. Now that we are all one, can I still say something? Already having called us one, did I succeed in not saying something? One and saying so makes two; two and one make three. Proceeding from here, even an expert calculator cannot get to the end of it, much less a plain man. So, if we take the step from nothing to something, we arrive at three, and how much worse if we take the step from *something* to something.

"Better to take no step at all, and instead leave it all alone!"

Translation, Please?

Sorry. That's pretty much impossible. But let's place ourselves in Zhuangzi's philosophical shoes. He's attracted to an anti-conventional, liberationist idea of natural behavior, and to the idea that language constrains it, socializes it to "fit" what society wants. But he's also aware that any blanket condemnation of language generates a paradox. How, then, can he express himself?

To get closer to his meaning in the passage in the text box, imagine Zhuangzi using the opportunity to pose some interesting questions. It might sound something like this:

Taoist Tip-Off

Because Zhuangzi often places his teachings within a context of satire and parable, it is often quite difficult to know precisely what he is getting at. He often intends to confuse and baffle his listeners and readers as a means of loosening up their hardened preconceptions.

> "All language distorts reality. But saying that doesn't go far enough. In fact, even the statement 'All language distorts reality' distorts reality, because such a statement must use narrow words and distinctions to get its point across, and must be made from a limited personal perspective—while the Tao has no limit, and no single narrow perspective!

In fact, even the sentence I spoke just a second ago—the one that explained to you that the sentence 'All language distorts reality' must be made from a limited, rather than infinite perspective—even that sentence distorts reality, because it too ... well, you get the idea. It's a limited tool, language, and it can only be used to convey a meaning that is rooted in a given context. But the Tao transcends all limited contexts!"

What can anyone say to follow that?

Is It All That Dense?

Admittedly, Zhuangzi can sometimes be a little challenging, but he is one of the most accessible philosophers ever to write. He was the first author to have a comic book edition of big chunks of his book. He can be daunting at times, but he expresses his views in story style that everyone can understand in *some* way. The problem is, the main ideas are often presented in different ways, and we can never be sure who got it right. Maybe that is the point. For an example, consider his famous parable of the butterfly.

Dreaming a Life

Once Zhuangzi dreamt he was a butterfly, fluttering buoyantly; a butterfly, fully content being himself. He knew of no Zhuangzi! Suddenly, he awakened. And plain-old Zhuangzi doesn't know if he's Zhuangzi who just dreamt a butterfly or the butterfly dreaming he was Zhuangzi. Zhuangzi or a butterfly? There must be a distinction. This is how things change.

That which seems so very real to us as we read a book with an orange cover and black type on its white pages—is it real, after all?

Notice that a butterfly is a creature that flutters about from place to place; it follows the wind. Notice, too, how Zhuangzi ends the story. Which is it? There must be an answer! If we could answer it, then …

Zhuangzi really doesn't give us any answers; instead, he leaves us to ponder. (This makes him less convenient as a religious founder than Laozi.)

Zhuangzi and Laozi

The exact relationship between Zhuangzi and Laozi is a story that is retold with each new discovery. The traditional story was easier. Zhuangzi was a religious disciple of Laozi, who was a religious mystic. Recent discoveries have confirmed the doubt that there never was a Laozi and Zhuangzi probably lived and died before anything like the book we call the *Laozi* took shape.

Seven Big Points from the *Zhuangzi*

Here are seven key ideas from the *Zhuangzi* that come up again and again. If you take the time to become familiar with them, you'll probably find reading the *Zhuangzi* an easier and more rewarding experience.

Tao Then, Tao Now

Zhuangzi's role in the rise of Taoism has been compared to that of St. Paul in the rise of Christianity. The comparison has its problems, however. Many Taoist scholars and practitioners regard Zhuangzi's work as having deeper insight than the primary text of Taoism, the *Daode Jing*.

Keep Language in Its Place

As we have seen, the anti-language thrust of Laozi's thinking led to paradox. Zhuangzi found a way to keep his irreverence of the doctrines of moralists without stumbling over the language paradox.

Language *is* natural! Humans use it to coordinate behavior, and, thus, language is one of the pipes of heaven. With this metaphor, Zhuangzi undercut the moralists, because each wanted to claim that only *his* tao was natural. Zhuangzi, on the other hand, argues that each is *equally* natural. Similarly …

Your Perspective Affects What Language Means

Language is filled with words that make sense only in context; for instance, *here, now, this, today, mine, above, small, you*. Words are about reality, but the reality the word *you* refers to in a book like this changes every time a different person picks up the book.

The same goes for terms like "good" and "beautiful" and "yummy." Different perspectives have ways of evaluating that pick out different things. The crucial first step in learning, Zhuangzi suggests, is appreciating that the other person might have a view as good as or better than yours. Her way of talking and acting is just as natural and just as convincing to her. In other words: Where you sit affects the show you see.

Relax: Death Is Part of the Deal

Zhuangzi notes that we "shoot out our 'Right!' 'Wrong!' judgments like bolts from a crossbow." With each one we take on a new commitment that binds us to some later response. Thus, we pass through life going from a position of open-minded wonder to learning, to comfortable knowledge, to fixed certainty, to prejudice, and, eventually to mental death. The mind and body grow old and die together.

We can't abandon or forget language; death is similarly inevitable. Ultimately, our lives appear meaningless. Life is limited. The possibilities of knowledge are unlimited. To live with the purpose of gaining perfect knowledge is clearly foolish. There is no accomplishment, Zhuangzi would argue, without defect! (This is a corollary to "There is no life without death.") However, Zhuangzi's view of death did not make him pessimistic. He taught that we could view death not as an end, but as a continuity of the transformation process that produces the joy of new life. Both are the transformation of one kind of thing into another. Zhuangzi accepted the implications of this acceptance of death. One story tells of him "drumming" after initially mourning his wife's death. He was celebrating her continuity as part of the universe.

Another story relates that when he was near death, his followers were discussing his funeral arrangements. One suggested that his body be left out in the open for a number of days so that it might be visited by more people; another follower objected that this would expose the corpse to being pecked away by birds of prey. Zhuangzi retorted that if his body were buried, he would be eaten by worms; if his body were left out in the open, he would be eaten by birds. What reason, he wondered, did we have to deprive the birds and feed the worms? (Read more on this topic in Chapter 14, "What Taoism Teaches About Life and Death.")

Beware of "Cosmic" Philosophy

When we face our mortality and the limited contextual nature of our judgments, it's natural to seek a larger perspective so that we can make a better judgment. That's acceptable, but we can never hope to find an absolute perspective—the view of the universe (or of God, or from nowhere). The cosmos does not make judgments, does not use language, and has nothing to tell us. A judgment made from the view of the cosmos would be irrelevant to us when we're discussing what to do.

So Zhuangzi rejected the attempts of Confucians and Mohists to "speak for nature." Those who pretend to evade the contextual dependence of language in judgment by advocating intuition don't solve anything, he argued. If our intuitive heart or mind tells us to do something, we still have to decide whether to follow it or to follow the desires of our other, equally natural organs!

Remember the Virtue of Flexibility

We can't escape in the other anti-language direction either by becoming mystics, or withdrawing from all judgment, or intoning something along the lines of "all is one." In doing that, we are still making judgment—a judgment not to make a judgment or a judgment that judgments are wrong.

There is, as Zhuangzi never fails to remind us, no perspectiveless perspective.

Embrace Skill

Zhuangzi celebrates the notion of self-transcending skill. In his view, highly honed skills reach a stage where we lose ourselves in performance and "become one with" the world in which we act. During such performances, we seldom think about the rules we learned as acolytes. We feel ourselves "pulled" by the activity, not as someone making decisions or deliberating. These discussions are the most frequent places where we find mystical talk in the *Zhuangzi*.

We can achieve this absorption in performance in any activity and any tao of that activity—dancing (classical or modern), skating (racing or performance), playing music (jazz or heavy metal), butchering, chopping, constructing a logical argument, lovemaking, skiing, using languages, programming computers, throwing pottery, knitting, cooking, and so on. At the highest levels of skill, according to Zhuangzi, we reach a point where we seem to transcend our own self-consciousness. Our control over our own actions begins to feel like control from the natural structure of things.

We should never confuse this absorption in action with cosmic enlightenment. No matter how much we hone our skills, we always come to "hard places" where we have to hesitate and focus on the problem, marshalling all we have learned for this new and unique situation. Then we return to the flow.

Tao Then, Tao Now

Zhuangzi's ecstatic portrayal of skill must be balanced by his awareness that there is no perfection without defect. Any mastery, Zhuangzi notes, must leave something out. In particular, to master any skill is to ignore other skills as this practice may involve a loss of balance and necessitate loss of balance in life. Zhuangzi remarks that masters are frequently not very good teachers. All too often, they fail to transmit their mastery to their children or to their disciples.

(To learn more about Zhuangzi's view on learning skills, refer to Chapter 13, "What Taoism Teaches About Skill.")

Beware of Foolish Conformity

Many thinkers in the history of thought leading to Taoism were skeptical of tradition and convention. Zhuangzi is no exception. However, his view is moderated by an awareness that conventions (the common practices) are useful because they make communication possible. And that's all we can ask of them.

So it is okay to conform, but we should remember we do so for a pragmatic purpose, not from a conviction (for instance) that our ethnic group is better or more civilized than another. We must never accept convention for its own sake. "Those who search for absolutes or perfection are on the wrong side of the choice about conventions." Zhuangzi often points out that a perfect man would be totally wrong by any conventional light. We couldn't even understand or follow him. Free from any dependencies, his judgments are really of no use to us. Better to rest in the temporary and useful than to waste our short lives seeking a perfection, which, for all we can tell now, is stupid or meaningless.

Zhuangzi and Confucius

Like many Taoist writers, Zhuangzi frequently poked fun at Confucius and his followers for their heavy emphasis on notions of duty and correct behavior. He also sometimes used Confucius as a positive model in his stories (partly because Confucius was more "Taoist" than any of Confucianism's later thinkers). Confucianism was an extremely rigid and disciplined school that focused on winning virtue, notably by following a written book of established customs and rituals (*The Book of Li*) and by showing obedience to one's parents, elder brothers, husbands, and conventional rulers.

The Taoist tradition always had an anti-social, anti-conventional bent. The blind acceptance of conventional duties and commitment to conventional conformity for its own sake would distract us from Taoist goals.

What are these? Any list would include the kind of reflection that could prompt us to enrich our lives by flexible openness and toleration of other points of view. Zhuangzi would argue that we should stay conventional enough to be able to communicate and get things done, select and practice a tao to a satisfying level of skill, and accept that death and deficiency are inevitable.

Zhuangzi viewed the pursuit of self-realization as a deeply personal journey that transcended the political and social duties so important to the Confucian tradition. Coming to peace with yourself while simultaneously seeking widely for new insights, practicing to cultivate your skills, and accepting limits, he would maintain, is what truly requires clear focus and continuous, attentive action.

Zhuangzi Turns Down a Job Offer

Zhuangzi appears to have been deeply suspicious of social institutions and political movements. Late in his life, after he had established a reputation as a sage, we are told that he was asked to take a leading role in the government by the king of Chu. The king sent two envoys to Zhuangzi to attempt to convince him to take on the role of prime minister.

The envoys found the sage fishing at the banks of a river. When they approached him, introduced themselves, and posed the king's request, he barely looked at them, but instead stared at the river. After a pause, he said to them, "I have heard a story that in the king's temple, there is a huge tortoise who lived to the age of 3,000 years, and was then killed and worshipped. Please tell me which path would be the better for that ancient tortoise: to be put to death so that he might be worshiped, or to continue living, crawling about in the mud?"

"Well, it would be better for the tortoise," the envoys of the king replied, "if he were left alive to crawl in the mud."

Zhuangzi smiled and said, "I would prefer to be a tortoise who crawls about in the mud."

The envoys carried Zhuangzi's answer back to the king, and the old sage continued to live the life of a hermit.

Four More Lessons from Zhuangzi

Here are four more teachings from Zhuangzi to ponder. If they inspire you to read his book from beginning to end, this chapter has done its job.

Limitations

You can't talk to a frog in a well about the ocean; he can't see beyond the hole above him. You can't talk to a summer fly about ice; a fly knows nothing of winter. You can't talk to a scholar about the Great Tao; he's surrounded by his own learning.

Two Taos

Once a zookeeper told the monkeys he was caring for: "You'll get three bananas in the morning and four in the afternoon."

All the monkeys screeched in a rage.

"Okay, okay," the zookeeper said. "How about four bananas in the morning and three in the afternoon?"

Hearing this, the monkeys were content.

Knowing What to Do with Big Things

Huizi said to Zhuangzi, "I received from the prince of Wei the seed of a massive variety of gourd. I planted it, and there came forth a fruit so huge that it would require a five-bushel measure to contain it! If I had used such a gourd to hold liquids, it would have been far too weighty to pick up. If I had cut it in half and tried to turn it into ladles, the shape would have been all wrong, and those gargantuan ladles would have been too flat for any practical use. There was no denying that this was a huge thing, but for all its size, I couldn't find anything useful to do with it. So I dashed it to bits."

Zhuangzi replied: "Your problem is that you don't know what to do with big things."

He continued: "Once there was a man in the Song dynasty who knew how to make a balm for chapped hands; he came from a long line of silk-washers, you see. One day, a stranger who had heard about the balm showed up and offered the man a hundred ounces of silver for instructions on how to make it.

"At that, the silk-washer called together his family and said, 'For years, we have had to scrimp and save as silk-washers, and now we can get a hundred ounces from this man in a single day! Let's take him up on his offer.'

"And so the stranger got the instructions. Later, this same man met with the prince of Wu. The prince told him that the kingdom was in trouble, and a major naval battle was going to take place—at the beginning of winter.

"As it happened, the prince's enemies were routed. [Note: This was because the balm kept the hands of the prince's troops from turning raw in the bitterly cold sea air.] The stranger who had visited the silk-washers was rewarded with a piece of royal territory.

"So: the properties of the balm that prevented chapped hands did not change at all. In one situation, however, it won someone a title of nobility; in another, it was an everyday comfort to a group of silk-washers.

"Now I want to talk to you about that five-bushel gourd of yours. Why couldn't you have turned it into a raft, and used it to navigate the waters here? All you could do was complain of its dimensions. Too flat! I believe it is your mind that is too closed."

The Sages of Olden Times

The sages of olden times did not grasp the after-life and were not terrified by death. They came without joy and made their exits without putting up a fuss. They came simply and left simply. They did not lose sight of their origin, ask their destination, or set themselves against enemies in order to make their way through life. They accepted life gladly as it was apportioned to them. They accepted death, too, as it was apportioned to them without resistance. When they left, they departed and were fully away. They did not set their minds against the Tao. They did not attempt, by means of their own mental struggling, to push the Tao forward or backward. They were the ones who were truly human.

The Least You Need to Know

◆ Zhuangzi is the main source of Taoist philosophy. He cultivated a style that expressed his substance as well as any direct statement. He seldom gave definitive answers to the fundamental questions.

◆ Zhuangzi's philosophy was informed by a sophisticated theory of language that accepted both its naturalness and its semantic inconstancy. This theory accepted that language rests on context.

◆ From his skeptical viewpoint, Zhuangzi's advice is provisional—be tolerant and flexible and yet cultivate some fulfilling tao to the point of satisfying flow.

◆ Accept that there are limits (for instance, death) and yet find meaning in everyday activities.

◆ Zhuangzi has no political philosophy and makes fun of those, like Confucians, who take political duties, loyalty, and goals of unifying the empire seriously.

5

In the Flow: Key Concepts

In This Chapter

- ◆ What does de (or te) mean?
- ◆ Are wei/wu-wei opposites?
- ◆ Learning about shi-fei
- ◆ Introducing the concept of ming
- ◆ Explaining chi

Besides *tao*, which has already been covered in-depth, there are five terms you should be familiar with in order to support a basic understanding of Taoist thought and practice. All five are usually expressed by means of Chinese terms. Unfortunately for people who don't speak Chinese, these ideas are often quite difficult to translate with a single English word.

In this chapter, you will get the full rundown on all five ideas as well as examples of their use and some insights on their implications.

De (or Te)

The middle syllable in *Daode Jing* has been rendered into English in a dizzying number of ways. "Virtue" is probably the most common translation, although this usage is prone to a number of misinterpretations. (See the following "Whatever You Do …" section.)

Spoken and Unspoken

De (or **Te**) encompasses a broad range of English meanings, including virtuosity, virtue, integrity, action, and power. It's pronounced *duh*.

Translation: virtuosity, virtue, integrity, action, and power.

In-Depth

The character *de* is a complicated combination of an eye, a heart, and a path. Its core meaning is the ability to follow a path (a tao). Taoists speak of de as "tao internalized." When we internalize a tao, it gives us a way to do things well; it entails a kind of power. Doing well includes doing elegantly and reacting appropriately to the details of the situation as you execute your tao. This "power of accomplishment" feature leads to extended uses for things like the following within the character de:

- Charisma
- Life
- Conscience-directed action
- The power of action worthy of imitation
- Impersonal supernatural power
- Natural capacity
- Natural empowerment
- Identity or selfhood
- The distinct personal characteristics and aptitudes of a given person

That's a lot to take in, but if you read through the list of concepts once or twice, you'll begin to get a sense of the broad and powerful idea behind the word *de*. If we had to pick a single brief translation, it might be the popular Taoist formulation "Dao within." Some de is innate (your natural abilities), and some comes from practicing a tao (skill acquisition).

Quotes of Note

Here are some thoughts on de to contemplate. Take a close look at them until understanding of this concept becomes part of *your* virtuosity.

> "Your name or your self—which is closest to you?
> Your self and commodities—which counts as more?"
>
> —*Daode Jing*, chapter 44 (Hansen translation, 2001)

> "Like karma, *te* is the moral weight of a person, which may be either positive or negative. In short, *te* is what you are."
>
> —Victor H. Mair, in the afterword to *Tao Te Ching: The Classic Book of Integrity and the Way* (Bantam Books, 1990)

Whatever You Do ...

… don't mistake the word *de* for excellence (as many mistakenly do when accepting the word *virtue* as the correct translation). De is not a virtue to be contrasted with a vice. It is that which enables a person to execute a tao (for instance, instruction, the composition of a musical score, the performance of a role in a play, the completion of a dance routine) in a real situation. Hence the idea of excellence of virtuosity.

Cool Facts

As you learned in Chapter 2, "Laozi and Zhuangzi," the *Daode Jing* is divided into two halves; one is labeled Dao and the other is labeled De.

The De section of the *Daode Jing* is somewhat longer than the Dao section. Ancient manuscripts found in a ruler's tomb from the Han era had the De section before the Dao section—probably reflecting the greater interest among the ruling class in politics. In the most traditional text, the Dao section comes first. This order was confirmed by a later archaeological discovery of a selection from a still earlier version of the text.

Wei and Wu-Wei

Think of the sequence in *Forrest Gump* in which a feather floats effortlessly above the varied landscape of the city and lands in precisely the right spot. Think of Peter Sellers as Chauncey Gardiner in *Being There* doing absolutely nothing … and capturing the attention of the most powerful people in the country. Congratulations. You are now thinking about the paradox of *wei* and *wu-wei*. These are translated respectively as "action" and "lack of action" (also "doing" and "nondoing").

In-Depth

Several other ancient terms had the same sound and are related in meaning: *wei* (to call), and *wei* (to be, constitute).

In the sense that we're discussing, the word *wei* has three important uses in ancient Chinese:

1. It is used a little like "believe" in English except that we "wei" objects and "believe" sentences. When we wei something, we give it a name, categorize it, assign it to a role in our tao, and act toward it in a certain way.

2. It is used to describe the action of making or converting something to a different category. To imagine the relation, think of the old English phrase "What time do you make it?"

3. It is used (with a different tone in modern dialects) to mean "for the purpose of." This is clearly linked to the first two uses, since acting on a thing's classification is usually the same as acting deliberately and purposively. All three meanings figure in Laozi's doctrine of wu-wei, which can be understood as lacking or avoiding all three of the activities just described. Wu-wei is part of the general attack on names, distinctions, and conventional knowledge. Usually, to wei is to apply some conventional distinction and treat an object according to a social tao.

The wu-wei position, however, conceals a familiar kind of paradox. Merely to utter this advice about wu-wei is to perform some kind of classification. We identify some actions as the "bad" wei actions and others as the "good" (natural or spontaneous). Laozi formulated this paradox in a famous slogan ("wu-wei and yet wu-not-wei") that has puzzled interpreters for centuries. It has given rise to numerous interpretations.

Potent Quotes

Confused? Consider the following observation about wu-wei and see whether the issue becomes any clearer:

> "[Wu-wei] is the practice of going against the stream, not by struggling against it and thrashing about, but by standing still and letting the stream do all the work. Thus, the sage knows that relative to the river, he still moves against the current. To the outside world, the sage appears to take no action—but in fact he takes action long before others ever foresee the need for action."
>
> —From "Taoism, the Interfaith Center of New York" (www.interfaithcenter.org/taoism.html, 2001)

And here's a famous passage from the *Daode Jing* that addresses essentially the same issue—the ideal of (somehow) taking perfect action without acting:

> "If you can empty your mind of all thoughts
> your heart will embrace the tranquility of peace.
> Watch the workings of all of creation,
> but contemplate their return to the source.

> "All creatures in the universe
> return to the point where they began.
> Returning to the source is tranquility
> because we submit to Heaven's mandate.

> "Returning to Heaven's mandate is called being constant.
> Knowing the constant is called 'enlightenment.'

Not knowing the constant is the source of evil deeds
because we have no roots.
By knowing the constant, we can accept things as they are.
By accepting things as they are, we become impartial.
By being impartial, we become one with Heaven.
By being one with Heaven, we become one with Tao.
Being one with Tao, we are no longer concerned about
losing our life because we know the Tao is constant
and we are one with Tao."

—From the *Tao Te Ching*, chapter 16 (J. H. McDonald translation, www.wam.umd.
edu/~stwright/rel/tao/TaoTeChing.html#1, 1996)

Whatever You Do ...

… don't mistake wu-wei for simple laziness. Instead, think in terms of relinquishing
pointless struggles and doing away with heedless, delusional, and inefficient approaches
for undertaking whatever task is at hand.

Cool Facts

Wu-wei means responding completely, authentically, and spontaneously to the emerging
circumstances of one's environment—without employing what some Zen teachers call a
"grasping idea" or "monkey mind." (Think of the chattering overwrought primates at the
local zoo—or the local anchor desk—and you'll get the idea.)

In his book, *The Tao of Pooh*, author Benjamin
Hoff makes a persuasive case that A. A. Milne's
classic "silly old bear" frequently embodies the
principle of wu-wei (see Chapter 21, "The Tao
and Pop Culture").

Spoken and Unspoken

A typical modern dictionary entry for **shi** might be yes, right, or the verb "to be." (Modern English speakers use "to be" in far more grammatical contexts than modern Mandarin speakers use shi.) The definition for **fei** might be wrong, bad, non-, or without. In modern Chinese, fei functions more as "non-" than as "is not."

Shi-Fei

Zhuangzi, whose teachings you learned about in
Chapter 3, "All About Laozi," has a tendency to
abandon the notion of wu-wei and to emphasize
instead the similarly paradoxical notion of *shi-fei*.

Translation: this/not this (also as right/wrong or
being/nonbeing).

In-Depth

Whenever we apply a label, we have to pick out what is "this" (the label) and what is "not this." (Or if we look from the label's point of view, the label tags "this" and "not that.") From the point of view of mastering the language and relative to the label, this naming is also "right"—the right thing to call by this name. The rest is "wrong." Or this "is (label)," and the rest "is not (label)." This is the version of the contrast theory of language used outside the *Daode Jing*.

All judgments, thus, are shi-fei judgments—and to abandon judgment is to abandon shi-fei. Shen Dao argued we should abandon shi-fei.

Zhuangzi speaks of an "axis of taos" from which the possibilities of shi-fei assignments are endless. That is to say: *Anything* could be classified as a shi and *anything* as a fei. From the axis itself, however, no judgment can be made! Once one is made, we step off the axis and have a commitment that guides and constrains all further shi-fei judgments down that path.

Potent Quotes

Consider the notion of the axis of taos as you ponder the following insight on the making of distinctions:

> "For Chuang-tzu, the making of distinctions, such as between 'right' and 'wrong,' is utterly futile since all possibilities are possible, depending on one's situation or viewpoint. In chapter 2 of the *Chuang Tzu*, 'On the Equality of Things,' a chapter which emphasizes language and its inability to accurately define reality, Chuang-tzu describes a dispute between 'Master Timid Magpie' and 'Master Tall Tree.' Master Tall Tree says, 'Suppose that you and I have a dispute. If you beat me and I lose to you, does that mean you're really right and I'm really wrong? If I beat you and you lose to me, does that mean I'm really right and you're really wrong? Is one of us right and the other wrong? Or are both of us right and both of us wrong? Neither you nor I can know, and others are even more in the dark. Whom shall we have decide the matter?'"
>
> —From "The *Chuang Tzu* Within Its Historical Context," by Susan S. Martin (University of Minnesota, zhuangzi.homestead.com/papercontents.html, 2000)

Whatever You Do ...

... don't assume any parallels between Western concepts of "being" and the use of shi-fei to mean "is." This is the "is" that links a predicate to a subject, not the one that means "exists" (as in "God is"). The counterpart of "being" in Chinese is the *you-wu* pair.

Cool Facts

Shi-fei fills the space in Chinese philosophy occupied by the Western concept of "judgment."

The shi (in shi-fei) can refer to an object or an action—the right object to use (the right cap to wear) or the right behavior (a proper bow).

Taoist Tip-Off

Thinking of any ancient Chinese term as corresponding to the English verb "to be" is dangerous.

Within Confucianism, this kind of dispute motivated the doctrine of "rectifying names." The "correct" answer reflects a correct interpretive performance of the ceremonies in question—*this* is the behavior prescribed in *this* situation. Modeling was the way Confucius would have rectified names and objects; doing the ceremony correctly was the correct way to teach the proper use of the words in *The Book of Ritual*. Zhuangzi and Laozi were deeply suspicious of this approach. How did the Confucian rectifier being "modeled" know which object to use? Which action to perform?

Ming

What exactly happens when you call an apple an apple? Have you captured the nature of the object you're talking about? How do we convince ourselves that we have selected the "real" name for anything? Is there such a thing as a "real name"?

Translation: names or labelings.

In-Depth

Ancient Chinese language theories called all words *ming*—names. This is presumably because all words pick out a part of reality for purposes of action.

Adjectives (fluffy) and common nouns (cat) have a scope—they "pick out" a range of reality and exclude the rest. As a result, words are "names" of a certain "range of stuff."

For example, learning a name for X means learning how to make a distinction between X and non-X. We cannot claim mastery of the word "cat" if we make a habit of calling spiders "cats."

As a result, we learn X and not-X together as a single, socially shared way to make a distinction. (Refer to the preceding "Shi-Fei" section.) But to actually experience the animal under discussion (to hear a purring noise and feel soft fur passing along one's leg) is something quite different.

Cat—not-cat. Furry—not-furry. Laozi implies that in learning to apply these distinctions and classify things in one way rather than another, we are being socialized into an inherited social design. Taoists are intrigued by the possibility that we could carve up the world in far different ways (taos) than we do in conventional language. Who knows how well we could live with a different carving?

These kinds of questions about the nature of language appear to have been common in ancient China. What Laozi adds is the insight that the names not only train us in making distinctions, but *shape and govern our desires and actions*. When we acquire a "sophisticated" taste, we find ways to limit our desires to a much smaller slice of the experience in question (leaving the rest to plebeians, we may think smugly to ourselves!).

But the joke is on us. The distinction is arbitrary in that it could have been drawn in innumerable other ways. We're being manipulated into spending more money and working harder to acquire those "rare" things. Best to stay plebeian!

Potent Quotes

What narrow range of experience have we (perhaps arbitrarily) distinguished from the rest of creation? What were the consequences of those distinctions? While pondering those questions, consider taking a moment to explore the following insight on ming:

> "The Tao that can be spoken of is not the enduring and unchanging Tao. The name that can be named is not the enduring and unchanging name."
>
> —*Daode Jing*, chapter 1 (Legge translation)

Here's an important passage from the *Daode Jing* on names and naming:

> "That the social world knows to deem the beautiful as 'beautiful' simply creates the 'ugly.'
>
> "That the social world knows to deem worth as 'worthy' simply creates 'worthlessness.'
>
> "Thus 'exists' and 'not-exists' mutually sprout. 'Difficult' and 'easy' are mutually done.
>
> "'Long' and 'short' are mutually gauged. 'High' and 'low' mutually incline.
>
> "'Sound' and 'tone' mutually blend. 'Before' and 'after' mutually supervene.
>
> [Pro-sage commentary]
>
> "Using this: sages fix social issues without deeming; administer a 'no words' teaching."
>
> —*Daode Jing*, chapter 2 (Hansen translation)

Cool Facts

The focus on the "unchanging name" that appears in the first chapter of the *Daode Jing* provides an interesting parallel with the focus on the passage beginning, "In the beginning was the Word" that appears in the first chapter of the Gospel of John (see Chapter 15, "The Tao and the Judeo-Christian Tradition").

Qi (or Chi)

There's an old Taoist saying: "A fool breathes from his throat; a sage breathes from his heels." It's physically impossible, of course, but just as an experiment, do it anyway. Right now, sit up straight (or better yet, stand up) and take a deep breath that originates from your heels.

Feel that? That's *qi*.

Translation: air, breath, energy, power of life.

Spoken and Unspoken

Qi is vital energy or breath. It's also spelled **chi**.

In-Depth

Taoist practitioners believe that human life is sustained not only by water, food, and sleep, but also by an accumulation and balance of energy through the body. This energy is deeply rooted in personal activity, outlook, breathing patterns, and openness to accessing the flow of universal energy. This energy is known as *qi*. (The same term is also frequently spelled *chi*; in either case, you pronounce it *chee*.)

The English word *spirit*, if it's understood as having an intimate relationship with the concepts of breathing and power, represents another good parallel for the Chinese word *qi*. (Spirit derives from the Latin *spirare*, which means "to breathe"; compare the words *inspiration* and *respiration*.)

Potent Quotes

Re-energize yourself! Breathe in the following energizing insight on qi:

> "One who is filled with the Tao
> is like a newborn child.
> The infant is protected from
> the stinging insects, wild beasts, and birds of prey.
> Its bones are soft, its muscles are weak,
> but its grip is firm and strong.
> It doesn't know about the union
> of male and female,
> yet his penis can stand erect,
> because of the power of life within him.
> It can cry all day and never become hoarse.
> This is perfect harmony."
>
> —*Tao Te Ching*, chapter 55 (J. H. McDonald translation, www.wam.umd.edu/~stwright/rel/tao/TaoTeChing.html#1, 1996)

Traditionally, Taoist practice distinguishes between various types of qi. Here we list some of the properties of the five types of chi as their names imply:

> "Water: runs downward, liberal.
> Wood: grows upward, enduring.
> Fire: spreads in all directions, radiant and hot.
> Metal: pierce inward, sharp and pointing.
> Earth: attracts and concentrates, stable."
>
> —From "Chinese Astrology and Feng Shui" (fengshui.freewebsites.com/ wuxing.htm)

Qi figures prominently in the discipline known as *feng shui*. Consider the following (brief!) explanation of this popular practice:

> "Allowing qi to meander into every room brings benefits to the occupant of that room. Positive qi is called *sheng qi*. *Sheng* means generating. So it stands to reason that if we want to attract well-being and prosperity we have to create a harmonious space filled with *sheng qi*. However, man-made objects or nature not only block essential qi if they face our front entry or windows but they become secret arrows of defective qi."
>
> —From "Opening the Door to Qi," by Siou Foon Lee (www.fengshui-innovations. com.au)

For more on the ancient discipline of feng shui and its conception and use of qi, see Chapter 8, "Branches of the Tao."

> "Chi can be translated as air, breath, or energy. It cannot easily be seen, but yet easily felt. It is the momentum life-force in the universe. Without it, there would be no life. It animates us and other life forms. It determines the health of an individual. If you are lacking or have stagnant chi, you will feel ill. Without chi you will die."
>
> —From "Internal Art: The Way of Self-Cultivation" (members.tripod.com/ internalart/main.htm)

Whatever You Do ...

… don't get distracted by the variant spellings *qi* and *chi*. They mean exactly the same thing. If we were speaking Cantonese, the same character would be written and pronounced *hei*.

Cool Facts

Traditional Chinese medicine regards the blockage of qi circulation in the human body and the inability to access qi from the universe at large as the primary causes of disease.

The notion that qi is everywhere finds a close parallel in the finding of contemporary physicists that matter and energy are intimately linked (see Chapter 18, "Einstein, Meet Laozi").

So there you have it: de, wei/wu-wei, shi-fei, ming, and qi. By now you've got a good start on understanding five key Taoist terms that are notoriously difficult to express in English. There are more, of course … but these will do for a start.

The Least You Need to Know

- De (or te) may be understood as "virtuosity" or "the Tao within."
- Wei/wu-wei may be understood as "action/inaction" or "doing/nondoing."
- Shi-fei may be understood as "this/not-this" or "being/nonbeing" or "right/wrong," but it remains an exceptionally difficult concept to convey briefly in English.
- Ming may be understood as "names."
- Chi may be understood as "vital energy," "breath," or "life force."

Chapter 6

All Down in Black and White: Yin and Yang

In This Chapter

- ◆ A gap in Western thought
- ◆ The yin-yang symbol
- ◆ What it represents

In this chapter, you will learn about the principle of alternation and harmony that serves as the foundation of Taoist thought. This principle finds its most common expression in the yin-yang symbol.

The Thesaurus and the Chasm

A writer we know told us about a lesson he learned while preparing an article on Eastern philosophy.

He was trying to find a synonym for the word *paradox*. Because he was working on a computer, he knew he could rely on the digital thesaurus in his word processing program. This function had helped him many times; all he had to do was make a few keystrokes and the computer would show him at least half a dozen ways to express any given idea. So he highlighted the word *paradox* and activated the thesaurus function.

Nothing usable came up.

The problem was, the idea he was trying to find a way to express was the *Eastern* conception of paradox—the one that accepts apparent contradictions and sees each phenomenon as containing some element of its opposite. The words the computer sent back made it clear, though, that the thesaurus was more interested in paradox as a mistake or as a logical inconsistency—as something to be rooted out, rather than accepted or worked with.

A chasm between Eastern and Western ways of approaching this idea was apparent.

> **Tao Then, Tao Now**
>
> Complementary opposites are at the heart of the ancient yin-yang symbol. Dark cycles through light, and light cycles through dark; a seed of light lies within the dark, and a seed of dark lies within the light. A similar sense of paradox is evident in many of the sayings of Taoism. The *Daode Jing* advises us that "True things appear perverse" and "The 10,000 natural kinds carry Yin and embrace Yang."

We tried the experiment ourselves. Here are the words that the computer, when asked to give a synonym for the word *paradox*, came back with:

- Absurdity
- Inconsistency
- Irony
- Contradiction
- Contradiction in terms
- Illogicality
- Impossibility

A search through an old-fashioned, printed thesaurus yielded much the same result.

One conclusion: The English language, as well as the Western mind, apparently has a blind spot. When asked to consider the possibility that things may contain, rather than exclude, some part of their opposites, or that entities set in opposition can support, rather than conflict with, one another, our minds seem to blow a fuse.

Taoists, as we have seen, do not necessarily tolerate contradiction. Laozi, in fact, frequently lands himself in paradox, but Zhuangzi avoided it; Confucians have criticized Laozi mercilessly for this error.

However, the contrast theory is not a logical contradiction. It is an awareness of the role that contrast (especially of opposites) plays in all languages. This view of language as paired and self-perpetuating opposites in play is neatly encapsulated within the famous *yin-yang* symbol, in which the dark section is not utterly dark, nor the light section utterly light. The two elements work together to make up the whole.

Spoken and Unspoken

The terms **yin** and **yang** originally referred to the dark and sunlit sides of a mountain, respectively. The image is worth mulling over closely. The shadowy and sunny sides of the mountain combine to make a unified whole; they are not separate and do not struggle with one another. Furthermore, the very perception of both "dark-side-of-the-mountain-ness" and "light-side-of-the-mountain-ness" is made possible by a powerful source of constant energy.

The yin-yang symbol.

The principle we're talking about applies to *every* element of experience we may choose to examine. Philosophical Taoism itself, for instance, which emphasizes spontaneity and observance of the patterns of nature, may be seen as a complement to the hierarchically oriented, etiquette-driven Confucian system of thought.

Or think of a single human being. We come into existence because of a combination of masculine and feminine elements. No man is so "macho" that his cells do not owe a debt to his mother's DNA.

> **Tao Then, Tao Now** _____
>
> While the contrast theory is integral to early Taoist theory, yin-yang theory, though compatible, was not a central part of the early philosophy. Classical thinkers barely mentioned the originator of yin-yang cosmology, Zou Yan. The *Laozi* uses the terms yin and yang only once in passing in only two of the Inner Chapters of the *Zhuangzi*. Yin-yang was most prominent in the *Yi Jing* (*I Ching*, or *Book of Changes*). The association of yin and yang with Taoist ideas actually stems from the most influential early commentator of the *Daode Jing*, Wang Bi, who wrote after the fall of the Han dynasty. He treated the *Yi Jing* and the *Daode Jing* as a single system.

Why We Have Trouble with This

In the West, we are, broadly speaking, used to thinking of things as on or off, black or white, good or bad, and up or down. The baseball team is doing badly. They're skunks! Next season, the baseball team wins the World Series. They're heroes! First, there was a bad team. Then there was a good team. Case closed. We tend to make large assumptions and generalizations like these, and derive from those assumptions and generalizations a conclusion about the way life "really is" at any given moment.

Is there a deeper way of looking at the universe and our position in it? Does a poor team's "skunkitude" bear any relation to its later triumph in the World Series? The Taoists would answer "Yes" and would begin their explanation by looking at the ancient symbol you saw just a moment ago. The principles of yin and yang, they would maintain, are essential to any thorough understanding of life and change.

> **On the Path** _____
>
> The terms *yin* and *yang* are of ancient derivation; they reflect the principle that each perceived opposite contains some element of its contrary. Taoism emphasizes that even apparent disunity is part of a unified, self-renewing whole. As Zhuangzi puts it, "Everything can be a 'that,' and everything can be a 'this.' Therefore 'that' comes from 'this' and 'this' comes from 'that'—which means 'that' and 'this' give birth to one another. When there is no more separation between 'that' and 'this,' we call this being at one with the Tao."

Beyond Self-Contained Ideas

Taoism challenges us to think of the universe as a whole divided into parts by terms that are complementary. Individuals or particulars are but smaller divisions (usually marked not by the nouns, but by *measure* words). Taoism views time as a process, rather than as atomic events in causal relations.

This way of looking at the universe challenges us to accept processes rather than isolated events, paired concepts instead of self-standing ideas.

Yin

This side of the equation is traditionally associated with the following:

◆ Femininity

◆ Passivity

◆ The moon

◆ Yielding

◆ Cold temperatures

◆ Darkness

◆ Submission

◆ Completion

Yin is also strongly associated with the earth.

Yang

This side of the equation is traditionally associated with the following:

◆ Masculinity

◆ Activity

◆ The sun

◆ Advancing

◆ Warm temperatures

◆ Brightness

◆ Advancement

◆ Creation

Yang is also strongly associated with the sky and the constant order of nature.

The Two Together

Placing yin and yang together forms a circle—the *yin-yang symbol* of infinity and integrity that encompasses everything and pervades everything.

Spoken and Unspoken

The **yin-yang symbol** is the so-called "black fish, white fish" design that expresses the interrelationship of apparent opposites. It is also known as the tai chi symbol.

Both Produce One Another and Overcome One Another

"The essentials of the yin-yang school (of thought) are as follows: the universe is divided into … two principles which oppose one another in their actions, yin and yang. All the opposites one perceives in the universe can be reduced to one of the opposite forces. The yin and yang accomplish changes in the universe through the five material agents, or *wu hsing* [wood, fire, earth, metal, and water], which both produce one [an]other and overcome one another. All change in the universe can be explained by the workings of yin and yang as they either produce one another or overcome one another."

—Richard Hooker (www.wsu.edu:8080/~dee/CONTENTS.HTM)

Seven Cool Things About the Yin-Yang Principle

Here are seven key points about yin and yang. If you let them, they'll change the way you look at yourself and the world at large.

One Unified Whole

In Taoism, even apparent opposites actually express a fundamental and pervasive unity. You don't get day without night, and vice versa. You don't get front without back, and vice versa. You don't get male without female, and vice versa.

This is the principle that guides the cosmos, and it is also the principle that elucidates the problems of human life. Consider (to use an example of Taoist-influenced popular myth-making) the *Star Wars* films.

Darth Vader initially appears to be the most powerful and diabolical villain in the universe. Our hero, Luke Skywalker, seems to represent all that is true, good, and upright. And yet we eventually learn not only that Vader is Skywalker's father, but that Luke's own anger and negativity are his real obstacles. When Skywalker has an early vision of confronting Vader, he sees himself cutting off the villain's head. Yet when the head rolls to the ground, the black helmet magically evaporates to reveal Skywalker's own face.

Balance Is Everything

The universe, from the Taoist viewpoint, moves perpetually through its various stages as part of an ongoing process that is supremely balanced. In approaching any experience, we are asked not to pick one element over another and not to mistake the various expressions of balance as being in conflict with each other. Instead, we are asked to understand the ways in which they may be related to one another.

The *Daode Jing* is full of references to the resolution of such opposites in the pursuit of true balance. In one memorable passage it urges us to "blunt the sharp thing and untangle the knot."

Things Change

The yin-yang symbol is not static, not fixed; it seems to swirl, to incorporate movement and flux. It suggests that apparent opposites not only complement each other, but evolve into new forms. Look closely at the symbol, and you'll notice that as one element rises to the peak of its energy, it transforms itself into its counterpart.

Within Taoism, the acceptance of alteration is part of the way. When we look at a single event and see it as fundamentally divorced from any other event, we're engaged in a certain poignant self-deception. The Taoist accepts with wonder and reverence the principle of constant change.

Fritjof Capra captured this point in his book, *The Tao of Physics:*

> "One of the most important insights of the Taoists was the realization that transformation and change are essential features of nature …. The Taoists saw all changes in nature as manifestations of the dynamic interplay between the polar opposites yin and yang, and thus they came to believe that any pair of opposites constitutes a polar relationship where each of the two poles is dynamically linked to the other."

Thus, any experience must be seen not only in isolation, but also as yielding to another experience or phenomenon. For example, to use the image that the terms yin and yang originate from, a mountain on which the sun is shining does not remain with one side dark and the other side light all day long. Instead, there is a gradual transformation over the course of the day, and eventually the sunny side comes to be the shady side.

All things are in transition. Nothing endures, and yet everything continues.

Apparent Opposites Interact Spontaneously

Yin and yang follow each other continuously and without effort in the Taoist view. Here, as in so many other aspects of Taoism, the notion of spontaneity rises to a position of great importance. One might even go so far as to identify spontaneity as the guiding emphasis that brings yin and yang into contact.

Once again, Fritjof Capra captures the essence of the idea:

> "When we talk about the Taoist concept of change, it is important to realize that this change is not seen as occurring as the consequence of some force, but rather as a tendency which is innate in all things and situations."

Taoist Tip-Off _____

As old as the terms yin and yang are, one must bear in mind that they are labels for a principle that was essential to Chinese thought for centuries before these terms were coined. The I Ching, or Book of Changes, contains the first recorded reference of the words yin and yang, but it also makes many references to the same principle using other words.

Everything Contains Its Own Opposite

Because phenomena are constantly overlapping and change is always being manifested spontaneously, Taoists regard any phenomenon as containing the seeds of its counterpart. Thus, even apparently robust health contains some component of illness, and even illness contains some aspect of health.

If this seems like a strange concept, consider the process of inoculation against viruses. By making our bodies "sick" enough to develop healing antibodies, we actually make them "well" enough to fight off more serious attacks.

Look closely at the yin-yang symbol, and consider the extraordinary implications of the light dot residing within the dark component, and the dark dot residing within the light component.

Existence Arises from Pairing Off

The transformative relationship between yin and yang, in the Taoist view, is what gives rise to the process of life and death itself. This interplay makes possible humanity and, indeed, all other manifestations. As the International Chinese Medical Society observes at its website (www.tcm.ch/ETCM.html):

> "In the Chinese view, the human body [is] a microcosmos which reflects the relationships to be seen in the cosmos. They believe that the same energy which rules the universe and breathes life into nature also has a determining influence on man. Chinese philosophy regards man as part of the cosmos, embedded in the rhythms of the universe, a span between heaven and earth, between the poles of the two elemental forces in the universe, yin and yang. The principle of polarity is to be found everywhere in the universe ... for example, the earth moves and rhythmically changes its position in relation to the sun. This brings about the slow change from day and daylight through the dusk into the darkness of night .... The interplay of yin and yang brings about every change and every movement in the universe."

These are extraordinary implications indeed! It is easy to understand why the yin-yang principle has maintained its remarkably pervasive influence in Eastern culture through the centuries.

A Window on Everything

In the Taoist view, all phenomena can be analyzed according to the principles of opposites. In traditional Chinese medicine and science, this very much includes governmental systems, music, the human body, cycles of weather, and so on.

As the author Ray Wood wrote in his article "Kyushindo Tai Chi Chuan and Related Aspects" (University of Southampton, www.soton.ac.uk/~maa1/chi/philos/yin.htm):

> "As a theory, yin/yang is a view of the universe based upon centuries of experience and observation by the Chinese people. It should be noted that it is only a theory. However, it is an all-encompassing, yet flexible theory; at the same time, it is a simple tool that, once learned, can be used to explain any number of phenomena. Its qualities are not exclusive, but complementary and relative. Life is not black and white, but a scale of colors ranging from one end of the spectrum to the other, and always changing."

Some Final Thoughts

One could go on at great length about yin and yang, and many writers have. In this book, we've chosen to offer just a few basic insights on the way of looking at the world implied by the familiar yin-yang symbol. If you open yourself up to it, you will soon become convinced of its ability to make its own points to you as you continue to learn about Taoism.

Two Images

The final point we want to leave you with is an intuitive one. Take a look at these two images.

Two ways of looking at the world.

The figure on the left is how many observers have illustrated the Western concept of opposites. This is a view in which counterparts exist forever independently of each other, day is very different from night, and the intermingling of opposites is a logical error. The figure on the right is, of course, the ancient yin-yang symbol. This is a view in which duality is seen as impossible without both parts, day slowly emerges from night, and the intermingling of opposites is the way the world actually works.

Which model seems most useful? Which best reflects the reality of the world in which you live?

The Least You Need to Know

- Western thought and expression make it difficult for many of us to approach the notion that duality is impossible without both parts, an idea central to Taoism.
- The familiar yin-yang symbol expresses this idea of duality.
- The yin-yang symbol reflects the belief that the universe moves in cycles, that these cycles give rise to everything, and that all phenomena contain the seeds of their counterparts.
- The yin-yang principle offers a way of looking at the world that can be adapted to virtually any situation.

Chapter 7

Society and Nature

In This Chapter

- ◆ The natural ideal for living and maintaining relationships
- ◆ Treating Earth as a standard
- ◆ Adapting to cyclical change

In this chapter, you will learn how Taoism celebrates the idea of following nature's example in social matters. This is a particularly important idea, one that supports many points within the Taoist tradition.

The Natural Ideal

As you've seen, the early Taoists opposed the attempts of the Confucianists to control and order social relationships. Taoists believed that nature, and not artificially imposed hierarchies and codes of etiquette, should be the guiding model for human behavior. One might even say that the Taoists sought to pass along a vision of a society largely uncontaminated by social manipulations. Self-contradictory as this notion may seem at first glance, it eventually accumulated great influence in China.

Tao Then, Tao Now

"In Taoism's study of 'ultimate reality,' all disciplines of Taoism reflect what is truly 'real.' The only true reference point for Taoists that is not twisted or distorted by social influences is *nature*. Nature is the constant that Taoists use to model behavior."

—From the Center of Traditional Taoist Studies (www.tao.org)

Following are some key points on nature and society as found in the *Daode Jing* and the *Zhuangzi*. Some of them may remind you of the images you occasionally see, fleetingly, out of the corner of your eye. Even though you don't get a complete view at first, there is, in fact, something there.

As you review these ideas, you may find yourself initially baffled in considering how precisely to apply them. Then, perhaps unexpectedly, you may well encounter something of value for your home life, your workplace, or the larger community.

Listen to the Earth

What does it mean to use nature as a model? Consider the following.

The *Daode Jing* tells us in chapter 25:

> "Humans treat Earth as a standard.
> Earth treats the sky (*constant nature*) as a standard.
> The sky (constant nature) treats tao as a standard.
> A tao treats being so of itself as a standard."

Spoken and Unspoken

The phrase **constant nature,** as used in chapter 25 of the *Daode Jing,* is also frequently translated as "heaven." We prefer the rendering used here, because it emphasizes the absence of the western dualism (natural/supernatural). The term *tian* literally means "sky." Most philosophers seem to use tian in the sense of nature *with authority.*

The natural motions of the sky are the paradigm of "constancy." The sky is associated with the notion of father (with Earth as mother) because of this constancy. "Heaven" is often offered as a translation of "sky" since the word *tian* has moral authority—but most Taoists would disagree with this rendering; all moral authority comes from some tao.

Taoism, then, holds that the best way of acting always expresses itself as action inspired by the natural processes of the earth.

> "Be still like a mountain and flow like a great river."
>
> —Laozi

Where does one find these inspirations? They're everywhere—but they may be easiest to encounter once you take the trouble to spend some time alone in a forest, on a seashore, along a mountaintop, or in some other undisturbed place. Personal exposure to the natural environment supports a kind of spontaneous listening and an openness to intuitively correct "standards" that may not seem quite as obvious when one is trapped in rush-hour traffic. (With practice, one assumes, the rush-hour traffic can also be correctly understood as a manifestation of the Tao, but until sufficient practice has been conducted, a walk through a meadow will do just fine.)

So far, we've been talking about *solitary* exposure to nature, rather than about social groupings. That's because there's a long tradition of a meditative, direct, and personal experience of nature within Taoism, a tradition that serves as a foundation to all that Taoism has to say about effective interaction with society.

Translation: Consider watching the waterfall before you try to run the city council meeting.

> **Tao Then, Tao Now**
>
> "We reject hatred, intolerance, and unnecessary violence, and embrace harmony, love, and learning, as we are taught by Nature."
>
> —From the creed of the Western Reform Taoist Congregation

Struggling Against Nature Is a Recipe for Calamity

On the individual level or the group level, humans must not set themselves against natural changes and the forces that initiate them.

Zhuangzi uses a parable of a praying mantis to warn us against any undertaking that denies or attempts to obstruct the way things reliably take place. The mantis, we are told, stood boldly in the path of an oncoming chariot, waving its arms, imagining that its efforts alone could cause the huge vehicle to come to a stop. He had not the slightest understanding that the task he had set for himself was far beyond his own capacity. The result was not pretty—and it could have been avoided, had the praying mantis not put such an inflated value on his own ability.

The story has value for those interested in developing and maintaining harmonious social relationships. Its point is that we must not overestimate our own capacities, nor should we instantly set ourselves up against processes we can, with a little insight, understand, predict, and adjust for.

Instead of rushing out into the road, Zhuangzi seems to be suggesting, a certain passive observance of the situation at hand is worth considering. Intelligent restraint may well be the best guide when it comes to interactions with the outside world.

See Human Relationships as Cyclical

Remember the 1970s George Harrison song "All Things Must Pass"? It may well have been inspired by the following lines:

"A twisting wind does not end the morning;
A sudden storm does not end the day.
What makes these the case? The cosmos.
The cosmos can raise it, but cannot make it endure.
How much more is this the case with the human realm?"

—*Daode Jing*, chapter 23

Relationships go through cycles, just as all of natural existence does. The Taoist view is that, since one cannot expect to alter or put a stop to these cycles, one might as well accept them and adapt harmoniously to them.

Think again of that story about the passing of Zhuangzi's wife. When she died, he reacted emotionally at first, but then he set aside grief and ignored the traditional etiquette of mourning. His natural response—which would no doubt have been shocking to the Confucians of the day—was to sit on the floor, sing, and hit a small pan as though it were a drum.

Zhuangzi's justification for his unusual action shines a light on his deep understanding of the transient, changing nature of all human interactions: "I thought of her origin, and concluded that, to begin with, she was not born at all." He then reasoned that, since his wife had originally come from "nothingness," certain changes must have taken place to bring her into "somethingness." This, he realized, was evidence of a larger natural pattern of life and death. Zhuangzi reasoned further that such patterns were "like the sequence of the four seasons from springtime to fall, and from wintertime to summer." (Note that fall does not *directly* follow spring, nor winter summer; Zhuangzi subtly underlines the importance of a certain trust in the processes of nature to point themselves in the right direction.)

He finally decided that to wail or follow elaborate procedures for expressing his grief was "not in harmony with destiny," and so he took up the pan, beat it rhythmically, and started to sing.

Using this: No human relationship or connection can transcend transformation. One simply finds a natural middle point as the transformations unfold.

Return to the State of Uncarved Wood

The notion of "uncarved wood" (or in some translations, "the uncarved block") is a repeated image in the *Daode Jing*. This idea, so strange upon one's first contact with it, serves as a model for both self-discovery and effective social interaction.

What is uncarved wood? It is one's natural identity—the natural instinct one possesses before language, machinations, stress, exploitation, uncertainty, or socialization. It's the presence you sense when you take a deep, relaxed breath. It is *not* putting on airs or pretending to be something one isn't.

When you are like uncarved wood, the *Daode Jing* informs us, your demeanor becomes "unaffected" (chapter 15), you are "on the point of lacking desires" (chapter 37), and you act "as the world's valley" (chapter 28).

That last quote is particularly crucial for this chapter. This is because a journey through a valley, with hills rising on either side, serves in the *Daode Jing* as an important image for the Great Tao itself. To act as the *world's* valley, by means of personal simplicity and openness, means to act in accordance with the Tao in all situations, including social interactions.

So …

> "Visualize simplicity and embrace uncarved wood."
>
> —*Daode Jing*, chapter 19

And …

> "Mollify them with the nameless uncarved wood."
>
> —*Daode Jing*, chapter 37

This (deceptively) simple strategy of modesty, passivity, happiness, and self-knowledge, the *Daode Jing* informs us, is the best—and only effective—means of modeling virtue for society at large. Laozi, not unlike Jesus, counsels those who would be first to begin their efforts by humbling themselves.

Taoist Tip-Off _____

The *Daode Jing* warns that ambition for its own sake is not only ineffective, but counterproductive. If one must guide others, it suggests, then one should "guide by treating nameless uncarved wood as constant" (chapter 32). Although the Tao may appear small to some, none in the world of society can "treat it as a vassal," and "if fief-holding kings could embrace it, all the natural kinds would come to self-conformity" (chapter 32).

Transcend Socially Acquired Assumptions

Nature isn't just in a tree, a bush, or a river. Nature is in all of us. The question is, do we allow ourselves to encounter it? Or do we impose artificial restrictions and divisions?

There is a Chinese character, *qing*, that can be translated as either "affections, feelings, or emotions" or as "facts, circumstances, or reality." An argument may be made that, in early China, the character referred to a certain kind of input—namely, information relevant to following a guide or a way of doing things (dao).

Spoken and Unspoken

Qing is a term that, in ancient China, seems to have referred to input that is relevant to following a guide or a way of doing things (dao).

Zhuangzi, among others, developed the insight that the (inherently social) act of learning a language instills a kind of unnatural prejudice in our attitudes and, consequently, in our behavior. He did not argue that we should, or could, abandon language completely, but instead emphasized a kind of pluralism. He encouraged us to recognize that different languages, conventions, lives, and outlooks could produce sharply divergent guiding views, or qing.

For Zhuangzi, pre-social qing are seen as positive elements. After reading his works, one might be tempted to regard one's "true nature" as an inherent, pre-socialized identity—a qing that exists prior to any "pro-and-con" (shi-fei) judgments.

Of qing that arise from interactions with the social world, Zhuangzi warns, "Do not let such judgments harm yourself or multiply excessively."

To approach Zhuangzi's point about language and social influence, we might ask: What was our original, natural qing before we learned words, or used those words to make judgments?

Live Simply

Social prestige, pride in material possessions, fixation on rank and hierarchy—these, in the Taoist view, are profound distractions from the primary example of nature. In chapter 3 of the *Daode Jing*, we read …

> "Don't glorify the high-brow; cause people not to wrangle.
> Don't value limited commodities; cause people not to contemplate stealing.
> Don't display the desirable; prevent confusing the heart/mind of the populace."

Later, in chapter 53, we learn …

> "Wealth and commodities are excessive.
> This is called stealing.
> Exaggeration!
> Not a guide!"

That last line has also been translated along the following lines: "This certainly is not the way of the Tao!" Either way, the meaning is clear: Human hunger for wealth, position, and power is not in keeping with the great guiding process that sustains nature. This thing-lust and status-lust is instead a dangerous variety of reckless imbalance.

In his advice to leaders of governments, Laozi typically expounds a passive yet active approach. Set the right example, he seems to be saying; use the balance, simplicity, and self-sufficiency of the natural world as your model; understand that authority well exercised has no need of exaggeration for its own sake.

So …

> "I lack desires—and thus the people self-simplify.
> They become like uncarved wood."
>
> —*Daode Jing*, chapter 57

Taoism explicitly rejects the acquisitive materialism on which much of contemporary Western society is built. (For instance, in chapter 29 of the *Daode Jing*, we read, "Sages abandon superlatives, abandon extravagance, abandon expansiveness.") The question of exactly what form Taoist belief and practice might take for someone who lives in a contemporary, industrialized, consumer-driven economy is an interesting one. We do not pretend to have resolved it, but we have a sense that Zhuangzi would, if he were alive today, not be spending most of his time at the shopping mall, the hairstylist, or the cineplex. One might be more likely to find him walking through the local park or sitting quietly by the shore of the closest lake or ocean.

Don't Try to Control

> "Social affairs are highly reciprocal.
> Where you place a division,
> Thorns and briars grow."
>
> —*Daode Jing*, chapter 30

Human affairs are reactions to the situation presented by heaven and earth. What we do has a reciprocal feedback to nature. Confucians in the Han era used to look for portents in nature as if they were instructions; Taoists, on the other hand, sought a *way* to co-exist harmoniously with *all* of nature. The idea is not to segment out or manipulate our reactions to the world in which we find ourselves, but to react to each situation authentically.

In practice, taking sides usually means making an existing conflict between people worse. Applying force or violence usually earns one new enemies. Attempts to take over any situation, and remake it according to one's own limited understanding, tend to backfire.

Suppose, instead of combating enemies, you were attentive to the changing of the "seasons" in human relations. Suppose you simply were open to new opportunities as they

Tao Then, Tao Now

The supposedly "passive" outlook of the *Daode Jing* does not preclude it from taking stands on the right ways to govern people and conduct wars. For more on this often-neglected aspect of Taoism, see Chapter 19, "The Tao and Politics."

arose and acted appropriately? Of this approach, the *Daode Jing* says, in chapter 30, "This is called 'don't guide.' Practice 'don't guide' early!"

The passivity of the Taoists has often been misinterpreted. Near the end of the same chapter, Laozi urges his reader to "have effects, and treat it as inevitable; have effects, and avoid coercion." The kind of "effect" he is discussing is not purposeless, simply practical. It is based on reality, on the way things actually happen without manipulation.

Conform to the Natural Way

Philosophical Taoists recognized that nature did not give any guidance—that all guidance comes from some tao. But the influence of Shen Dao and Great Tao concepts still had widespread followings in Confucianism and popular consciousness. Religious Taoists tapped this desire for absolutes and responded to the uncertainty and cynicism of their time by imagining that a pervasive guide, essentially indescribable but clearly evident in its harmonious effects, exists as the motivating force of the natural world. Central to following this guide was their revised notion of wu-wei.

For those willing to embrace this revised wu-wei as a means of following the Way in the spiritual realm, religious Taoists believed there would also emerge a spontaneous model for harmonious interactions with others. Such relations would not be narrowly conceived in terms of "higher" or "lower" social rankings, but would build on an intuitive understanding of the transitions of the natural world. This open-ended, unaffected view of human life, they believed, was far more likely to provide a workable model for human happiness than the coercive power of any state, or the rigidly conceived social rankings of a hierarchy, or the rituals, recitations, and easy certainties of any previous intellectual system.

Real life, they argued, the life of the true person, followed the creative natural path, rather than the predetermined values of any group. For those willing to conform to the natural way, rather than the conceptions and preconceptions of others, true freedom—that is, self-conformity—was possible. And even more: This tendency toward self-conformity was inherent in all people. Left essentially to its own devices, the larger society could, like a pond or a forest, attain its own balance and maintain its own systems of effective functioning—without outside help. (Or would "interference" be a better word than "help"?)

> "The people, no one ordering them, self-balance."
>
> —*Daode Jing*, chapter 32

The Least You Need to Know

- ◆ The natural ideal advocates using the earth as a standard.
- ◆ It also advocates avoiding struggles against nature, seeing human relationships as cyclical, and returning to the state of uncarved wood.
- ◆ Other important nature-based notions include transcending socially acquired assumptions, living simply, avoiding attempts to control, and conforming to the natural way.

Chapter 8

Branches of the Tao

In This Chapter

- Religious Taoism
- Its history and development
- Some of Taoism's important traditions

In this chapter, you get an introduction to religious Taoism and learn about some of its most important legacies. These legacies are important, because certain aspects of religious Taoism have gained wide popularity in the West.

Religious Taoism

After the emergence of *philosophical Taoism* in China, a religious expression of Taoist principles, metaphors, and practice took root.

A word of warning: Matters get a little tricky here. This is because some people simply view religious Taoism as a continuation of ancient Chinese nature religion (but with new names and images); others see it as the direct or indirect evolution of principles in the *Daode Jing* and the *Zhuangzi* within the context of China's folk culture.

In other words, some dismiss religious Taoism as more or less irrelevant to an understanding of philosophical Taoism, and others see it as the practical culmination of that school of thought.

Spoken and Unspoken

Religious Taoism, which some scholars see as arising after philosophical Taoism, is a diverse set of traditions that makes extensive use of rites, priests, and temples; venerates Laozi and a figure known as the Yellow Emperor; and has strong connections with traditional Chinese nature religion and medical practices. It is not a codified and centralized religious system (like many forms of, say, Islam or Christianity), but rather a loose assemblage of beliefs and practices that can vary widely from place to place.

Spoken and Unspoken

Philosophical Taoism (or **classical Taoism**) focuses closely on questions of language, guidance, reality, the shortcomings of conventional moral thought, knowledge, and possibility.

Six Points to Ponder About Religious Taoism

However you understand it, there are six big points to keep in mind when approaching religious Taoism:

- **One.** It's been around for a very long time indeed. This means that even those who question its direct connection to principles of philosophical Taoism cannot easily dismiss the enduring cultural influence of religious Taoism.

- **Two.** It regards the *Daode Jing* and the *Zhuangzi* as sacred texts.

- **Three.** It's so diverse as to accommodate a breathtakingly wide variety of practices, emphases, disciplines, and denominations. Dozens of variations on rituals and blessings, for instance, exist in the various schools.

- **Four.** It was, and is, often practiced side-by-side with other religious traditions within the same household. (This, of course, contrasts sharply with the Western practice of "being" one religion rather than another.)

- **Five.** Many of its traditions, notably the use of the ancient oracle known popularly as the *I Ching*, certainly predate, and just as certainly complement, ideas in the *Daode Jing* and the *Zhuangzi*.

- **Six.** The healing arts (for instance, traditional Chinese medicine) are vitally important within this tradition.

On the Path

The vast complex of practices covered by the umbrella term religious Taoism reflects an ancient tradition with a pantheon of deities and an emphasis on the practices of alchemy, astrology, divination, and the medical arts. This tradition relies strongly on the principles of yin and yang and on the "five elements" (or "agents"): metal, fire, water, earth, and wood. It celebrates Laozi as one of the "Supreme Ones" and has, at various points in its history, emphasized the notion of physical immortality. Breath control and a system of meditative "internal alchemy" are usually seen as important tools for spiritual awakening within religious Taoism.

Everything You Always Wanted to Know About Taoist Sects

Important sects and movements within religious Taoism have included those in the following list. Please note that this is only a listing of *some* of the traditions within religious Taoism that have surfaced over the centuries. Note, too, that each individual entry comprises many strands of practice and observance.

- ◆ **"Celestial Masters" sect.** (Founded in the second century A.D.) Emphasized confession of sins and physical healing. Virtually extinct by the seventh century A.D.

- ◆ **"Old Southern Taoism" tradition.** (Period of origin obscure.) Promoted personal development as a pathway to health, long life, and even immortality. Note: It may be better to regard this school as a countermovement within Confucianism, rather than an authentic Taoist tradition, although it did influence later Taoist movements. Its influence had waned by the fourth century A.D.

- ◆ **"Great Revelations" sects.** (Active in fourth and fifth centuries A.D.) Advocated union with "Perfected Ones" or other deities by means of image-directed meditation, alchemical procedures, or recitation of texts.

Taoist Tip-Off

Don't assume that the core texts of philosophical Taoism are *all* that support religious Taoism. In addition to the writings of classical Taoism, religious Taoism reveres as sacred more than 1,100 separate titles in more than 5,000 volumes. Amazingly, most of these remain untranslated into English or any other Western language. Beijing's White Cloud Abbey possesses a large library of sacred Taoist religious writings.

◆ **"Teaching of the Tao" movement.** (Arose in the fifth century A.D.) Also known as "Organized Taoism," this broad and long-lived movement reflected the establishment of Taoist scriptures and practices into a form accessible to many levels of Chinese society. Taoism took on a more distinct national structure and was embraced by the imperial elite. Active until the twelfth century A.D.

◆ **"Golden Elixir" sect.** (Arose around the eleventh century A.D.) Promoted a process of spiritual awakening through "internal alchemy," or meditation.

◆ **"Orthodox Unity" or modern "Southern Taoism" sect.** (Active in the eleventh century A.D.) Emphasizes healing rituals and harmony of the human community with the cosmos. Claims (incorrectly) to be directly descended from clerics of the Celestial Masters sect. The sole surviving ancient Taoist liturgical movement, but *not* the only popular expression of Taoist practice in China.

◆ **"Completely Real" or modern "Northern Taoism" sect.** (Founded in the twelfth century A.D.) Emphasizes meditation and the internal alchemy tradition of the old Golden Elixir sect. Characterized by a strongly monastic outlook. A popular contemporary branch is known as "Dragon Gate" Taoism.

Legacies of Traditional Chinese Taoist Practice

A number of distinctive practices and disciplines strongly linked with the healing and divination traditions of religious Taoism have attracted the interest of people in the West.

Here's a brief overview of some of those legacies. They show off the extraordinarily broad application of Taoist principles in Chinese history.

The *I Ching*, or *Book of Changes*

This ancient book of divination centers around the interpretation of 64 hexagrams, each composed of two trigrams, or three-line combinations. Each line is either yin (broken, weak) or yang (solid, strong). Some lines are "moving" (about to become their opposite).

The practitioner "divines" each line and constructs the hexagram from the bottom up. The completed hexagram has a single character interpretation, as does each component trigram. One then reads the commentaries on the hexagram and on the moving lines. These stimulate an intuition about the action queried at the beginning of the process. The practitioner's "prodded" intuition provides the guidance or answer. The *I Ching* is still in use in China (and indeed, around the world) as a tool for self-discovery and guidance.

It is interesting that most forms of divination in the West take the form of fact-prediction ("You will meet a handsome man," "You will get rich," and so forth), whereas Chinese divination practices always focus on a practical question ("Should I date this woman?"

"Should I fly to Paris?" "Should I accept this job offer?" etc.). This reflects the different cultural views of the basic role of language and the mind. In the West, what matters is knowing facts—especially predictive ones. For China, what matters is what might be called "knowing-how" or "knowing-to"—practical wisdom.

The core structure of the I (the lines and trigrams and hexagrams) may be of prehistoric origin. The text itself and its commentaries came into prominence quite late in the classical period. Eventually, the symbols of the eight trigrams, each connected to a specific image from nature, were reverently juxtaposed with the yin-yang symbol to form a central image of religious Taoism. This symbol, shown in the following figure, came to be known as the Diagram of the Great Ultimate and was instrumental in the Confucian revival during the Song dynasty.

The Ba Gua (a.k.a. Pa Qua) symbol, or Diagram of the Great Ultimate.

Centering on Stillness

"Taoists believe that Tao has appeared in the form of sages and teachers of humankind—as, for example, Fu His, the giver of the Pa Qua (eight trigrams) and the arts of divination to reveal the principles of Tao. The Pa Qua is the foundation of the *I Ching* and represents the eight directions of the compass associated with the forces of nature that make up the universe .... Taoists do not focus on life after death, but rather emphasize practical methods of cultivating health to achieve longevity. Therefore, Taoism teaches people to enhance their health and longevity by minimizing their desires and centering themselves on stillness."

—From "Taoism: A Portrait," by Dr. Douglas K. Chung (origin.org/ucs/sbcr/taoism)

Although the *I Ching*'s origins will probably always remain somewhat murky, one estimate is that the earliest text layers of the oracle may date to something like a thousand years before the compilation of the core writings of classical Taoism.

Tao Then, Tao Now

The *I Ching* contains the first recorded usage of the terms *yin* and *yang*.

The counsels of the oracle are intended as guides to appropriate behavior for those who consult it reverently. The text may come across as vague, unconvincing, or even impossible to decipher to those considering it casually or skeptically. The sinologist (China expert) Richard Wilhelm, however, held that the trigrams are intended to convey not limited physical phenomena, but "states of change." He connects this notion of change to principles he traces to the *Daode Jing*'s point that events in the physical world are reflections of ideas from the world beyond human perception.

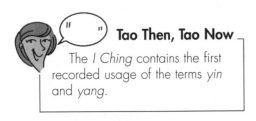

Tao Then, Tao Now

"The *I Ching* encompasses many, many different ways of interacting with the nature of the time to follow the changing Way, which are often mutually exclusive. It is not just a book of wisdom to read, it is an oracle to talk with. Through invoking chance in the act of consulting the oracle, we effectively 'disentangle' ourselves from rationalizations, and allow the underlying reality of the moment—the Tao—in."

—From "The *I Ching* and the Tao" (www.onlineclarity.co.uk, 2001) (Online Clarity is an "*I Ching* consultation service whose mission it is to make the *I Ching*'s help and insight readily and simply available to all who need it.")

Wilhelm goes on to observe that "both of the two branches of Chinese philosophy, Confucianism and Taoism, are rooted in the *I Ching*." He concludes that the oracle "sheds many a new light on many a secret hidden in the often puzzling modes of thought of that mysterious sage, Lao-tse, and of his pupils, as well as many ideas that appear in the Confucian tradition as axioms" (*The I Ching, or Book of Changes*, Princeton University Press, 1967).

The hexagram represents the dynamic, changing yin-yang constitution of a situation *relative to an actor and a practical question*. The book's guiding principle, then, is that the "random" changes in circumstances *for the questioner thinking about this question in this context* correspond to the effects of her casting coins or sorting yarrow stalks here and now (while concentrating on the question). (Often, people explain this as subtle influences from the caster on the coins and the fact that he must personally sort the stalks—you can't cast a question for someone else!) Of this process of correspondence, the psychologist Carl Jung had the following to say:

By No Means Easy

"It is by no means easy to feel one's way into such a remote and mysterious mentality as that underlying the *I Ching*. One cannot easily disregard such great minds as Confucius and Lao-tse, if one is at all able to appreciate the quality of the thoughts they represent; much less can one overlook the fact that the *I Ching* was their main source of inspiration."

—Carl Gustav Jung, in the Foreword to the *I Ching* (Wilhelm/Baynes translation)

Tai Chi

Tai chi is a system of gentle rhythmic movements and breathing postures that is held to improve blood pressure and circulation, digestion, and elimination of wastes by tensing muscles, massaging, and improving the functions of internal organs, directing the flow of qi through the meridians of the body. It is also believed to improve cardiovascular fitness.

The name (rendered *taiji* in the official romanization) means "the great ultimate" and comes from the diagram we discussed earlier with the trigrams surrounding a yin-yang symbol. Scholars regard tai chi as the ancestor of all the Chinese boxing skills, notably kung fu (or gong fu) and its neighbors, karate and tai kuan dou (or tae kwan do). However, in this company, tai chi is the ultimate "soft" martial arts form (probably even softer than judo—the so-called "weak" way).

All actions in tai chi are based on circular (oval) movements and are designed to absorb energy and turn it to the practitioner's purpose. This makes it ideal for older practitioners and explains why every morning you can find crowds of practitioners in the streets and parks all over Greater China (a term referring to China, Taiwan, Hong Kong, and Singapore).

The tai chi actions require slow, smooth movement, shifting of weight, flexibility, and extremely good balance. These elements, too, help make tai chi the exercise of choice of the elderly.

Recent medical studies estimate that activities such as tai chi, which improve strength, balance, flexibility, and coordination, reduce the risk of falls among both healthy and frail people. Studies demonstrate that a 40 to 60 percent reduction in hip fracture risk is associated with such activity, and tai chi is the most commonly recommended form.

Tai chi, which requires the coordination of breath and movement, seems to provide a viable alternative to high-impact aerobics, which have been found sometimes to lead to a variety of unintended ailments. Tai chi offers a fitness program that will improve the health of virtually

 Tao Then, Tao Now

The popular martial arts disciplines kung fu and tai chi are each derived from early practice within religious Taoism.

anyone, no matter his or her age or state of health. While those at advanced levels of practice may find tai chi to be a useful tool in self-defense, the average person may find its greatest value in its internal improvements. Its main value in self-defense lies in the promotion of calm self-control that prevents panic and desperation in tense situations.

Acupuncture and Herbal Medicine

Acupuncture is the most famous ancient Chinese medical practice, although it is one of a cluster of traditional physical techniques still practiced in China.

Acupuncture has had the greatest impact on Western medical theory in the last 30 years, a period during which Western experimentation with and observation of acupuncture have intensified. Like other traditional practices, acupuncture is based on the theory of qi, or life-energy, and the meridians, or pathways, it uses to travel through the body. There are traditional body-maps showing these meridians and the various acupuncture points.

The most studied effect of acupuncture is its ability to block pain, nausea, and other nerve-related conditions. Some use it to stop addiction to smoking and other drugs. The most widely accepted theory of the analgesic effect of acupuncture is that it stimulates the natural production of opiates found in neurons throughout the body. Some link this explanation to the so-called "gate theory"—the notion that pain messages have to pass through a neural gate to get to the brain. Overloading this gate prevents the pain message from reaching the brain. Other theories link the effect with the phantom pain phenomenon (for instance, pain in an amputated limb) and the tender trigger points in muscles.

Traditionally, stimulation of acupuncture points involved slender needles inserted shallowly (or perhaps not so shallowly!) in the skin. More recently, both in China and in Western adaptations, electricity has been used either in conjunction with needles or alone.

Traditional Chinese medicine also includes a wide array of herbal substances prescribed for all manner of disease. The basis for this medical practice is not so clearly linked to any Taoist cosmic theory. There are clusters of theories about a number of these herbs, but the most common explanation has to do with traditional concepts of folk magic, specifically, the idea that "like cures like." This explains the long-standing demand in the East for snake products and tiger penis as virility medicines. (The development of Viagra is the best news the endangered Siberian Tiger population has heard for a long time!)

Western interest in herbal medicine focuses mainly on its role in holistic treatment and preventive health maintenance. Individual herbal treatments are occasionally discovered to involve an agent known to Western medical science or discovered to have a clear therapeutic effect. Some of these are now familiar over-the-counter products to Westerners, notably ginkgo biloba and ginseng.

There is little systematic information about which traditional preparations are effective and which are not. Before trying any of these remedies, you should consult your doctor. To learn more about all of these disciplines, see Chapter 17, "The Tao and Health," or Appendix E, "Taoist-Related Health Resources."

Feng Shui

The Chinese tradition of feng shui (wind-water) has been popular in Southern China for centuries. It seems less widely followed in Northern China, but has spread there since the decline of Maoism. It is hard to determine the true age of feng shui, since it is mainly transmitted from master to disciple. Still, its underlying theory resonates undeniably with Taoist philosophy.

The key ideas are harmony with nature, an emphasis on harmonious relationships with things around us, and the maintenance of effective flow of yin and yang qi. Feng shui presents a view of the world in which balance is achieved between these two omnipresent qi, allowing a desirable circulation of qi through physical space. Appropriate placement of color, pictures, plants, crystals, and furniture are believed to enhance the energy within the space, thereby energizing those who occupy the space.

Some principles of feng shui are easy to learn and understand (for instance, one should avoid setting up a room so that an open window faces a sharp angle of some kind); others are so contextual that the intuitions of the practitioner explain more than any abstract principles. (In this respect, feng shui is not unlike divination by means of the *I Ching*.) Some feng shui practices are combined with Cantonese number puns; for instance, the word for eight rhymes with "get rich," the word for four sounds like "death," and so on.

Feng shui has experienced a remarkable wave of popularity in the West in recent years. However, unlike acupuncture and tai chi, little scientific work has been done to explore its validity. It is, however, great fun, and many, even while skeptical, have dabbled in it.

Move Forward with the Flow of Life

The mysterious world of feng shui began in China thousands of years ago as a study of nature and survival; [the discipline was] used to find the best location to grow successful crops. Feng shui is considered one of the eight branches of the Tao Healing Arts, which include meditation, tai chi, acupuncture, herbology, nutrition, and the *I Ching*. Today we can use feng shui knowledge to ensure that our personal energy is balanced with the energy of our homes. Feng shui works at the subconscious level with our inner chi to free up our energy so we are able to move forward with the flow of life.

—Gina Dolinsky, "Feng Shui in the Home" (www.intouchmag.com, 2001)

To find out about feng shui resources near you, see Appendix C, "Feng Shui Resources."

The Tao and Sexology

Taoism and Buddhism are often confused, but two confusions are easily dispelled. First, Taoists are not necessarily vegetarians. In being "natural," a Taoist takes our nature as omnivores as nothing to be condemned—excepting, perhaps, qualms arising from requirements of balance and from the granting of equal concern for animals. (So modern Taoists might be vegetarians on political grounds, as a result, say, of opposition to turkey farms where the animals are never allowed to walk.)

The second—and more exciting—confusion has to do with sex. Buddhists, like Christians, are often accused of having a suspicion of the body and of bodily pleasures. For Taoists, on the other hand, bodily pleasure and the paradigm of "natural" (as opposed to social) desire constitute perfect examples of wu-wei. The entire yin-yang cosmology uses a sexual reproduction metaphor as the root explanation: All things come from the interpenetration of yin and yang—the ultimate generative force in the universe.

In Taoism, the sex organs represent yin and yang energies and are the source of life; they are referred to as "the stove"! Without a hot stove, the "food" of life cannot be cooked or eaten. It should not be surprising, then, to learn that many religious Taoists view human sexuality as a means of supporting mental and physical well-being.

At some point in its development, religious Taoism incorporated many frankly erotic elements, and the result was a host of elaborate rules regarding the proper physical postures for lovemaking. Practices bordered on the pornographic, with Taoist monks moving from nun to nun inducing the yin-energy contribution to long life that results from female orgasm, while "holding in" their yang-energy ejaculation or "forcing it up to the brain" to revitalize the practitioner.

Tao Then, Tao Now

"The valley-energy never dies. This is called 'fathomless female.' The channel of the fathomless female:
This is called the basis of the cosmos.
Silken! It's as if it abides.
Handle it gently!"

—*Daode Jing*, chapter 6 (Hansen translation)

The perpetuation of life energy by means of sexual intercourse is, for many Taoists, a perfect expression of the harmonious interaction of yin and yang. The nature and aims of that expression may, at first, come as a bit of a shock to non-Taoists, or at any rate to those of the yang persuasion. While the female orgasm is celebrated evocatively as "high tide," ejaculation by the male is equated with "throwing oneself away"—or even, in the case of the man who reaches orgasm before his partner does, with "being killed" by the woman.

Here's the bottom line, guys: The ancient (and for that matter, modern) Taoist sexual ideal is one in which the male routinely practices— shall we say—rigorous personal discipline during lovemaking. The idea here is to conserve and replenish life energies rather than disperse them heedlessly. And yes, that means exactly what you think it means.

The ideals of longevity and restraint, it turns out, can be approached from any number of vantage points in the Taoist tradition.

There's something to think about. And maybe, just maybe, talk over with the woman in your life.

> **Tao Then, Tao Now**
>
> "By patterning their sexual relations on the models of heaven and earth, and conforming to the nature of yin and yang, men may derive life-giving benefits from the sexual forces, rather than being forever at their mercy."
>
> —From "Tao Sexual Yoga" (www.hps-online.com/tsy1.htm)

Qigong

The word *qigong* draws on the ancient notion of qi (matter-energy) and the medieval notion of spiritually cultivated practice. It translates roughly as "daily effort with regard to life energy." It is controversial how far back in history qigong practice actually goes. It emerged to the Western traveler's attention after the decline of Maoism in China.

Practitioners understand qigong not merely as part of a healing process but as a manner of living your life. Just as you learn to drive a stick-shift before driving race cars competitively, swim with the dog paddle before winning a gold medal in the 100-meter breast stroke, or boot up a computer before becoming a senior programmer, you learn to develop effective use of your qi a little bit at a time. With practice, you develop expertise.

Qigong practice uses physical exercises and postures to help build internal energy and overcome mental and physical tension. Breathing and visualization are also important parts of this practice.

Western medicine has begun to take seriously the possibility of psychological states having impact on physiological or medical states. Exactly how these work is still controversial. The study continues under Greek-derived name of *psychoneuroimmunology*.

> **Spoken and Unspoken**
>
> **Psychoneuroimmunology** is a comparatively new scientific discipline focusing on bi-directional influences among the human nervous system, hormone system, and immune system. The discipline also takes into account a patient's stress level and psychological state, as well as the role of humor in elevating personal health.

Meditation and Qigong

"Though most meditative techniques are taught in sitting postures, the recent influx into the West from China of qigong standing practices have opened the door to a powerful new ... approach to self-study and self-transformation. Authentic qigong standing practices ... are designed to help conserve, balance, and transform our inner energies as well as help open us to the energies of the earth, of nature, and of the heavens."

—From "The Transformative Power of Conscious Standing" (www.breath.org)

The practice of qigong is meant to help practitioners develop, store, and circulate qi more effectively.

The Least You Need to Know

- The complex of practices described by the umbrella term "religious Taoism" reflect an ancient and diverse tradition.

- Religious Taoism has a pantheon of deities and an emphasis on the practices of alchemy, astrology, divination, and the medical arts.

- The *I Ching* is an ancient book of divination that focuses on the interpretation of 64 hexagrams, each composed of two trigrams, or three-line combinations.

- Tai chi is the most popular Chinese exercise and a highly beneficial one—with medical proof.

- The emergence of qigong ("daily effort with regard to life energy") is difficult to date precisely, although its theory taps ancient ideas.

- Acupuncture has some medical evidence behind it; herbal medicine and feng shui are more fun than scientifically sound. So is Taoist sex!

Part 2

Landmarks on the Path

In this part, you learn about the history and development of Taoism in the East. You'll get an overview of the history of the tradition, learn how it influenced the emerging tradition of Zen Buddhism, and find out about the repression—and survival—of religious Taoism in the modern period.

Chapter 9

Fifteen Epochs

In This Chapter

- ◆ The historical backdrop
- ◆ Chaos and unity in China
- ◆ Taoism's cultural interplay with Confucianism, Buddhism, and traditional Chinese religious practice

Taoism has been called the oldest continuously functioning religion in human history. Whether that's true or not, the philosophical and religious movements we now assemble under the single term Taoism evolved over an immense stretch of time in Chinese history.

Dating the beginning of Taoism is about as simple as dating the beginning of Hinduism. Both traditions appear, somewhat surrealistically, to predate their own assumed origins, arising from influential traditions that extend from times long preceding any formal naming. Although the rise of Taoist philosophy, which preceded the Taoist religion, is generally traced to the composition of the *Daode Jing* (perhaps in the sixth or fifth century B.C.), Taoist-like influences in Chinese thought are detectable long before that.

In this chapter, you'll get a brief overview of the Taoist timeline in China over more than 15 distinct historical periods—and you'll get a sense of how the religious and cultural impact of Taoism played out in China over that period.

The Shang Dynasty

(Generally dated from circa 1600 to circa 1050 B.C.)

The Shang dynasty is the first Chinese dynasty for which reliable historical evidence is available. (A semilegendary dynasty known as the Hsia dynasty preceded it.) Oracle bones dated to this period refer to a god, known as Shang-ti, who held supreme power over all other entities, whether human or supernatural. This deity was an important precursor to the notion of heaven, a concept that would, in time, contribute to the notion of the all-encompassing Tao.

The Shang divination practice is our main source of knowledge of this ancient civilization. People in the Shang period divined using bones or turtle shells. The form of divination probably resembled that of the *I Ching*, or *Book of Changes*, in starting with a practical question, then writing several what-to-do answers on the shell and heating it. The practitioners then "read" the cracks caused by the heat. These oracles were then stored in underground libraries for preserving tao. They could be consulted for guidance in other situations. (This Shang practice may have been the initial impetus for the development of writing in China.)

Tao Then, Tao Now

The oldest text that would come to be associated with Taoist religious and philosophical thought predates the Shang period considerably. Scholars believe that oral composition of the earliest strata of the *I Ching*, or *Book of Changes*, dates to roughly 4000 B.C., or approximately 2,400 years before the Shang dynasty. For more on the *I Ching*, refer to Chapter 8, "Branches of the Tao."

The Shang period preceded the classical era associated with Laozi; it is the high point of the Bronze Age in China. Historical and archaeological research associates the period with a well-developed agricultural tradition, a clearly established social hierarchy, and an emerging governmental apparatus. Writing and divination had long since emerged by this point in Chinese history. Artifacts of the period include exquisite bronze vessels and tools made from jade. The first Chinese calendar system is also attributed to the Shang dynasty.

Zhou Dynasty

(ca. 1050 B.C.–256 B.C.)

Composition of the *Daode Jing*, the central text of Taoism, took place during the Zhou dynasty, beginning perhaps around 600 to 500 B.C. The *Zhuangzi*, a collection of virtuoso and less politically oriented essays attributed to a hermit of the same name, is assigned to the same dynastic period and is thought to have been composed in the fourth century B.C. (see Chapters 2, "Laozi and Zhuangzi," and 4, "The Other Book: The *Zhuangzi*").

Two towering figures of Chinese culture are strongly associated with the Zhou dynasty. The first is Laozi, who is, at least in the traditional view, thought to have lived in the sixth century B.C. The other is Confucius, who was born circa 550 B.C. For a detailed discussion of the various historical and philosophical issues associated with these two massively influential personages, see Chapter 2.

Also associated with this period is Taoism's great "second voice," Zhuangzi, about whom you can learn more in Chapter 4. Zhaungzi lived from circa 369 B.C. to circa 286 B.C.

Other important figures of the Zhou period include Mozi, the first important philosopher who wrote after Confucius (around 400 B.C.) and Mencius (also known as Mengzi), who lived from circa 371 to circa 288 B.C.

> **Taoist Tip-Off**
>
> The dating and method of composition of the *Daode Jing* is a matter of heated scholarly debate; don't assume that any one date or theory is accurate or widely embraced. We have seen dates as early as 650 B.C. and as late as 200 B.C. proposed. It is possible that the text, whatever its origin, was in flux over an extended period of time during the Zhou dynasty.

Mozi is important in the history of Taoism. (He is listed in the *Zhuangzi*'s history of thought—neither Confucius nor Mencius are.) Mozi represented the first emergence of a philosophy of impartiality and equality. He challenged Confucians to defend their commitment to traditional ritual as the norm of human behavior. He proposed instead to follow the natural norm of utility. The correct tao was the tao that led to the greatest benefit and least harm to everyone in the world. This led him to be the first Chinese to advocate universal love, in contrast to Confucianism's partial concern for family members—the nepotism from which China still suffers.

Mencius defended Confucian philosophy from the Mohist challenge. He held that human nature was inherently good, so following natural impulses was morally correct. He then argued that Confucian rituals were not arbitrary historical practices but had evolved from natural feelings. He theorized that this innate goodness had to be cultivated properly in order to reach full expression. Environmental effects, Mencius felt, could deprive and stunt the growth of the inborn moral capacity. Mencius implied that the sound guide to moral judgment was the direct intuition of the cultivated heart-mind—the heart-mind of the sage. This mind could respond to the qi throughout the world and adjust all things to a perfect harmony. Mencius searched in vain for a leader who could implement his political ideals. He had little impact on classical Chinese thought, but his ideas became the orthodox form of Confucianism in the Song dynasty and dominate Chinese thought to this day. His teachings are contained in *The Book of Mengzi*.

Spoken and Unspoken

The **Zhou dynasty** was a long period (ca. 1050 B.C.–256 B.C.) now closely identified with the classical age in China. The era was marked by both political instability and literary as well as philosophical genius; the development of the core Taoist texts took place during this period.

Cultural landmarks during the *Zhou dynasty* include the development of a written legal system and an economy based on currency. Other high points during this period included the use of iron and improved methods of cultivation, notably plows drawn by farm animals.

The Zhou dynasty endured for the longest period of any dynasty in Chinese history. Near its end, it collapsed into chaos during a period known as the Warring States period, 403 B.C. to 221 B.C.

Almost Every Lord

"Powerful regional states which had grown into major territorial powers were the main focus of interest in [the Warring States] stage of Chinese history. The goal among the rules was to acquire military power and wealth; war was perpetuated because tradition already demanded that all Chinese be unified, and because almost every lord aspired to become the great unifier."

—From "The Warring States: A Timeline" (www.omart.org/itoc/time/warringstates.html)

Qin Dynasty

(221 B.C.–206 B.C.)

This period saw the construction of a large portion of one of the marvels of human ingenuity and design, the Great Wall of China.

Spoken and Unspoken

The **Qin dynasty** was a brief period (221 B.C.–206 B.C.) notable for both cultural consolidation (such as the regulation of the Chinese writing system) and the official suppression of Taoist and Confucian ideas. The word *China* is derived from the Qin dynasty.

It was also during the *Qin dynasty* that the reunification of the country under the uncompromising authority of the emperor Qin Shi Huang Di took place. Among the chief events of his reign were the suppression and burning of various Taoist and other classic Chinese texts and the vigorous implementation of a centralized political authority. This initiated a philosophical "dark age" in China that, in timing and effect, eerily mirrors the similar period in the West.

Qin Shi Huang Di's fixation on the idea of immortality expressed itself in the now-famous army of terra-cotta soldiers apparently intended to guard his tomb. There were in excess of 7,000 of them; they were not unearthed until the latter portion of the twentieth century.

Han Dynasty

(206 B.C.–220 C.E.)

During this period of consolidation of power and cultural expansion, many key ideas found in religious Taoism—such as the quest for immortality and various meditations on the infinity of the universe—began to be consolidated. It was also during this period that Laozi himself was deified (elevated to the status of a god). Popular culture and a number of rulers were attracted to the cult of Huang-Lao (The Yellow Emperor and Laozi).

Rebellions brought about by Taoist teachings helped bring about this dynasty's downfall in the third century A.D. Following the fall of the Han, Buddhism began to play an important role in Chinese life. Buddhism's transmission to China was aided and abetted by the reemergence of Taoism (in a movement known as Neo-Taoism) during the period of disorder following the Han.

> **Tao Then, Tao Now**
>
> During the Han dynasty, the Taoist search for immortality gave rise to the development of countless potions. This development has been cited as the origin of Chinese science, and, thus, as the starting point for a staggering series of medical and technical advances in China.

> **On the Path**
>
> The decline of the Han Empire coincided with the rise of Taoism as an organized religion. As the Sinophilia website (www.geocities.com/chinesevenice/infotao.htm) reports in "A Brief History of Taoism":
>
> "At the end of the Han empire, revolutionary and messianic sects emerge; among them, Zhang Daoling's Way of the Five Measures of Rice (*Wudow mi dao*), also known as Orthodox One (*Zhengyi*). In 215 his nephew Zhang Lu changes the name of the school to Celestial Masters (*Tianshi*), and makes of it the first hierarchically organized Taoist 'church,' concerned with the limitation of popular cults and the establishment of social ideals through moral precepts and public liturgical ceremonies. The school becomes the highest authority on ritual orthodoxy."

The Three Kingdoms Period

(220–265)

As the name suggests, China was, during this period, divided into three nations. These were Wei, Shu, and Wu, with Wei developing a steady advance in influence over time.

During this period, Confucianism fell into a period of decline, and Buddhism took on greater importance as a religious movement, while the religious expression of Taoism (sometimes called Neo-Taoism to distinguish it from philosophical Taoism) continued its rise in influence.

The Mysterious Learning

"Neo-Taoism, which was called 'the mysterious learning' in early China, had grown during the waning years of the Later Han …. [It] had both a scholarly and a popular form. The scholarly form concentrated on discussing the Taoist classics …. It was the popular form, however, that spread like wildfire and changed Chinese History. The folk Neo-Taoism was a pantheistic, moral, and salvation religion; all human acts, both good and evil, would be punished or rewarded in an afterlife."

—Richard Hooker (www.wsu.edu:8000/~dee/chempire/sui.htm)

Jin Dynasty

(265–420)

During this period, a succession of barbarian leaders reigned in Northern China as the Wei nation expanded. Buddhism continued to grow in influence.

It was during the Jin dynasty that two distinctive elements of Taoist religious practice emerged as theological directions linking it with Mahayana Buddhism: a mystical emphasis on union with the infinite and belief in the possibility of the salvation of all beings.

The Northern and Southern Dynasties

(386–589)

It was during this period that Taoism, which began as a philosophical movement, was proclaimed the official religion of the Northern Wei court (fifth century). Veneration of Laozi as a deity was increasingly common among the people.

The period of the Northern and Southern dynasties overlaps with that of the Jin dynasty; the shared time period reflects the political instability that followed the collapse of the Han dynasty. Fragmentation and conflicts were, not infrequently, the order of the day.

CAUTION

Taoist Tip-Off

Beware of confusing historical labels. The era of the Northern and Southern dynasties is sometimes also known as the Six dynasties.

The Sui Dynasty

(581–618)

This is the period that saw the reunion of the country and the reestablishment of a strong, central governmental authority. This restoration of unity was important for the subsequent Tang dynasty.

During this period, both Taoism and Buddhism gained further recognition and approval. In addition, the Great Wall was strengthened, and a series of extraordinary canals was developed, allowing transport of foodstuffs during times of famine.

The Sui period was also marked by an increased emphasis on the development of a coherent foreign policy. The Sui dynasty was comparatively brief, but it was quite important in terms of the consolidation of power and authority.

Tang Dynasty

(618–906)

This period in Chinese history was marked by territorial and political preeminence in Asia; Chinese influence made itself felt in many foreign lands. Cultural life was unusually rich even by Chinese standards, a situation attributable to the cross-fertilization of ideas from all over the world fostered by Taoist openness and creativity. It is also the period when indirect contacts with the European West first began.

Buddhism exerted a powerful influence until the final years of this dynasty, at which point it encountered a period of imperial persecution. Taoism, on the other hand, did not suffer from the "foreign" label, and its "similarity" to Buddhism made it more acceptable to imperial authorities. It therefore gained a influence and respect. Nonetheless, as usual, Taoist-influenced rebellious movements contributed to the fall of the leadership. Anarchistic Taoism, unlike orderly Confucianism, has seldom been a reliable friend for political rulers.

Despite the decline of Buddhism in China that began in the final years of the *Tang dynasty*, the nation's dominant traditions—Taoism, Buddhism, Confucianism, and traditional

Chinese religious practice—had by then established a complex series of interrelationships. Buddhism and Taoism in particular exerted strong influences upon each other's development. As the Taoism and the Taoist Arts website (www.geocities.com/Athens/Delphi/2883/general.html#tex) explains:

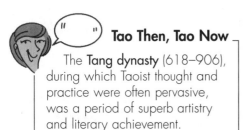

Tao Then, Tao Now

The **Tang dynasty** (618–906), during which Taoist thought and practice were often pervasive, was a period of superb artistry and literary achievement.

"Buddhism arrived from India bringing with it a host of gods, and as Confucianism began to emerge complex rituals were added to the mix. These strands were constantly intermingling as China developed, and even today they are all followed to a greater or lesser extent. And all the while the more enlightened Chinese were training themselves with meditation and physical exercise such as martial arts, all of which looked to, and in turn influenced, the emerging philosophy that we now know as Taoism."

The Five Dynasties and Ten Kingdoms

(907–960)

A difficult period marked by armed conflict, political instability, corruption in high places, and economic decline, this era was notable for cultural and technological advances. Printing came into prominence, and the circulation of paper money was first noted.

This period also was known for a brief phase of violence and militarism that served primarily to illustrate the failure of any of the nation's religious or philosophical traditions to forestall chaos and bloodshed in the political arena.

The Song Dynasty

(960–1279)

This era saw a renewed period of unity after the chaotic Five dynasties phase. De-emphasizing military strength, the new leaders of China chose instead to improve merchant relationships and expand ocean trade routes. Printing and publishing became powerful cultural forces, and the development of industries and transport technologies reached remarkably high levels.

A new variation on Confucianism that incorporated both Buddhist and Taoist ideas, known as Neo-Confucianism, became prominent. It targeted both Taoism and Buddhism as "empty" or "amoral" systems, though most Neo-Confucian thinkers went through a Taoist or Buddhist phase in their intellectual development. They constructed a Confucianism that they argued was consistent with Taoism. Within religious Taoism, folk deities were assimilated with the earlier expressions of the faith, and the practice of inner alchemy (visualized meditation designed to manipulate the body's yin and yang energy in order to refine an internal "elixir of immortality") became popular.

The emperors of the Song period were lavish supporters of the arts. It was the high point of Chinese painting. It was during this period that gunpowder was first given its military application.

The Yuan Dynasty

(1279–1368)

During this period, China was occupied by the tribes of Mongolia. The dynasty was founded by Kublai Khan, grandson of *Genghis Khan*.

Educated members of Chinese society encountered opposition and prejudice from their foreign overlords and evoked the triumphs and achievements of the past by placing renewed emphasis and energy in artistic and cultural pursuits.

One of these was the theater, which was strongly affected by the Taoist tradition. (The Yuan dynasty is revered today as a period of exceptional achievement in Chinese drama.) Other cultural institutions and practices that thrived under the influence of Taoist ideas were painting and poetry.

The Ming Dynasty

(1368–1644)

This era saw the reestablishment of native political rule and the expulsion of the Mongols.

Confucianism was once again an important force. At the same time, however, Ming rulers were energetic supporters of initiatives intended to renovate Taoist temples and related sites, and they also encouraged Taoist practice in new forms.

On the Path

Genghis Khan (ca. 1167–1267) was a Mongol warrior and political leader whose spectacular success on the battlefield led to political control of a vast area extending from the Black Sea to the Yellow Sea. He is generally acknowledged as history's supreme conqueror.

Tao Then, Tao Now

Kublai Kahn, grandson of Genghis Khan, was emperor of China from 1259 to 1294; he completed Genghis Khan's capture of Northern China in 1240 and assumed imperial power in 1259 upon the death of his brother.

Tao Then, Tao Now

During the Ming dynasty, the Taoist deity Zhenwu became an important national guardian.

Another recipient of political and financial support from the Ming rulers was, famously, the porcelain industry, which produced work that was (and is) highly prized. Contacts with Europeans began in the sixteenth century, when a Portuguese expedition found its way to China. Catholic missionaries followed in the seventeenth century, and soon trading relations with European nations were underway. Literature and theater thrived.

The Qing Dynasty (a.k.a. the Manchu Dynasty)

(1644–1911)

The foreign Manchu regime overtook an impotent Ming empire in the mid-seventeenth century. The result was that the Manchus eventually executed a successful occupation of the entire country.

The territorial size of the empire grew, but its influence in the region slowly declined, as did the notion of centralized political power. Trading with the Europeans rose in importance. Foreign nations divided the country into sections and exercised dominance within those sections.

For the most part, emperors and political authorities under the Qing dynasty were supporters of Taoist practice and observance, even though they themselves followed Tibetan Buddhism.

And Then Things Got *Really* Interesting

So much for the background summary. For a discussion of the tumultuous history of Taoism in China in the twentieth and twenty-first centuries, see Chapter 11, "The Long Run: Religious Taoism Endures."

The Least You Need to Know

- ◆ The philosophical and religious movements we now assemble under the single term Taoism evolved over an immense stretch of time in Chinese history.
- ◆ The Zhou dynasty was a long period marked by both political instability and literary as well as philosophical genius; the development of the core Taoist texts took place during this period.
- ◆ The Qin dynasty was notable for both cultural consolidation (such as the regulation of the Chinese writing system) and the official suppression of Taoist and Confucian ideas.

- The decline of the Han Empire coincided with the rise of Taoism as an organized religion and with rebellious political movements deeply influenced by Taoist thought.

- The Tang dynasty, during which Taoist thought and practice were often pervasive, was a period of superb artistry and literary achievement.

The Tao and Zen

In This Chapter

- ◆ More about Buddhism
- ◆ The lowdown on Zen
- ◆ The Taoist influence

In this chapter, you will learn about Buddhism and about Taoism's influence on Zen, one of the most influential and best-known Buddhist traditions.

Mingling with the Tao

Sometime around the first century A.D., Taoist thought encountered Buddhism in China. When this happened, a remarkable new tradition, which we know today as *Zen*, began to emerge.

Buddhists were able to enter into Taoist metaphysical debates and, thus, could integrate and spread their new ideas. Taoism, at the same time, encountered the monastic and religious hierarchical organization of the Buddhists. The blending of these two great religions produced *Zen*—a remarkable and, initially, distinctively Chinese Buddhist sect—and Taoism became a full-fledged religion.

Spoken and Unspoken

Zen is the most common descriptive term associated with the popular school of Buddhism that emerged in China under the influence of Taoism. The word *Zen* is actually the Japanese form of the Chinese word *Ch'an,* which is derived from the Sanskrit word *dhyana,* or "meditation." Eventually, Buddhism was repressed in China; its evolution continued in Japan, Korea, and Vietnam.

On the Path

Zen Buddhism traces its lineage through the daunting and historically ambiguous figure known as Bodhidharma, who is said to have shown up in China from India near the end of the fifth century A.D. He is regarded as a patriarch in the line of succession extending from the Buddha's disciple Mahakashyapa.

This new tradition synthesized Taoist attitudes and Buddhist concepts—Taoism in Buddhist guise, as it were. The Taoist elements included the anti-theory emphasis on practice, the rejection of any fixed doctrine, egalitarianism, and the denial of a distinction between samsara (ordinary life) and nirvana (release). Buddhism contributed the language of enlightenment (satori), meditation (zazen), and illusion.

The spontaneity of Taoism, its respect for full presence and attention in everyday affairs, and its openness to natural beauty combined with Buddhism's philosophical framework. The most advanced versions of that theory, for example, the theories of Nargarjuna, recognized the Taoist conclusions as the logical implications of Buddhist theory and paradox. (It's also worth noting that a split within Buddhism produced a universalist version of the religion that was acceptable in egalitarian China.)

The resulting strand of Buddhism, a distinctive blend of Indian and Chinese approaches to spirituality, has endured for centuries and has now captured the imagination of thoughtful people in both the East and the West.

If you're new to Zen in particular, or to Buddhism as a whole, you may be curious about the origins of that tradition. Here's a condensed introduction.

Buddhism 101

In the sixth century B.C. (or thereabouts), Siddhartha Gautama was born. He was a prince, the son of the wealthy and powerful ruler of a small kingdom located near present-day Nepal. Legend holds that his conception was "divine" (an elephant pierced his mother's side in a dream) and that, at his birth, a sage predicted that the infant prince would "succeed"—a prediction that could be read as foretelling political or religious success.

The boy's father, eager to secure the latter destiny for his son, sought to shield Prince Gautama from all suffering. He kept his son cooped up in the palace and never denied him any desire or whim—including hundreds of "dancing girls" for his companionship when he was 16.

Gautama married and had a son. Then a mysterious "charioteer" took him on three trips out of the palace. On these journeys into the real world, Gautama was confronted by sickness, old age, and death … the three realities that formed the core of the "first noble truth"—life is suffering!

The experience left the prince profoundly shaken. He left his son and wife, abandoned his political responsibilities, and embarked on a search for the ultimate release from suffering. He tried a range of traditional Indian practices, including asceticism. Eventually he combined these with meditation in what Buddhism calls "the middle way." He sat under a Bodhi ("enlightenment") tree, and when he finished meditating, he was Buddha.

Taoist Tip-Off

The Mahayana and Theravada (or Hinayana) schools of Buddhism use the term Buddha differently. Theravadins use it to refer to Siddhartha Gautama. Mahayana use "historical Buddha" to designate the person; "Buddha" becomes a metaphysical state. All who reach enlightenment or nirvana have this "Buddha-nature" and are Buddha. Another term for this metaphysical state is Tathagata ("thus come!").

Other deities visited the new Buddha and persuaded him to put off his entry into nirvana (a term we'll discuss a little later in this chapter) to teach his way to others. Buddha was reluctant—contemptuous of the "filth" of the world. Persuaded that there might be a few "lotus blossoms in the muck," he agreed and founded a new tradition that was to become one of the world's great religions.

A Bowl of Milk

"Giving up the ascetic's life, Siddhartha accepted a bowl of milk from a young girl named Sujata. Strengthened, he sought the shade of a fig tree, sat down, and resolved to remain in that position until he had achieved enlightenment …. With his enlightenment, he became, for his followers, the Buddha."

—From "Bodhgaya" ("The Site of the Bodhi Tree"; www.padamsambhava.org/pbc/pilgrimage/bodhgaya/bodhgaya.asp)

Some Core Elements of Buddhist Practice

What follows is a shamefully abrupt condensation of some of the major principles of Buddhism. For a more complete accounting of the faith, see *The Complete Idiot's Guide to World Religions, Second Edition* (Alpha Books, 2002), or visit www.dharmanet.org.

The Importance of Awakening from Delusion

The Buddha accepted the principle of reincarnation and the essential framework of Indian thought. Note, however, that Buddhism rejects the authority of the Vedic hymns and denies the existence of a soul or self. Buddhism does start, however, with the Indian conception of living beings trapped in samsara—a cycle of birth, death, and rebirth.

Tao Then, Tao Now

Indian thought and religion largely shared with Western religion a conception of humans as having a rational soul or mind. It also shared the Western distinction of the mind and heart—a highly valued cognitive, rational faculty and an emotional, disruptive, physically controlled faculty. The mind was valued over the body as the true locus of personal identity; "lower" desires (such as sex) were seen as distractions from reason's search for knowledge of ultimate truth. Indian thought also shared the Western analysis of experience as an inner "appearance" of a purported outer "reality."

Indian thought was distinguished by its notion of the law of *karma*—moral cause and effect. The idea was that a rebirth was karmic "payment" for the way you lived your last life: punishment by rebirth at a lower level or reward by rebirth at a higher point on the spiritual ladder. Some kind of mystic release was held to lie at the end of this progress—in the release of the man in the highest caste (the Brahaman) and profession (religious guru).

Buddhism, however, taught that the release came from an intellectual insight into the fact that the individual soul, the self or ego, was actually an illusion. This insight's full realization (in the sense of "making real") resulted in a dissolution of individuality that was the mystical (and puzzling) state of nirvana (more on nirvana in a moment).

Spoken and Unspoken

The principle of **karma**, a doctrine of both Hinduism and Buddhism, holds that there is an impartial principle of moral cause and effect. Under this principle, actions have unavoidable implications and even affect one's future incarnations. In Hinduism and Buddhism, only those who escape the cycle of birth and death are held to move beyond the law of karma.

Buddha's teaching mission was to enable disciples to attain this difficult understanding so that the "illusion" of life and suffering would cease—and the cycle of rebirth and suffering would end. One could finally die and stay dead!

Nirvana

Nirvana is perhaps best defined as a final desireless state reached at the culmination of a journey of many lifetimes. Though similar in some respects to the Christian concept of heaven, it is nevertheless different, because Christianity has historically emphasized the retention of one's individual body and identity for eternity. Traditional Christianity also emphasizes the desirability of eternal life in a way that is quite unlike Buddhism. Buddhists take eternal life as a given—the problem, not the solution.

Nirvana, accordingly, is a far more negative idea (signaled in Sanskrit as in other Indo-European languages by the initial *N* sound). It is shared in traditional Hinduism and Buddhism. In the *Surangama*, Buddha describes nirvana as the place "where it is recognized that there is nothing but what is seen of the mind itself; where, recognizing the nature of the self-mind, one no longer cherishes the dualisms of discrimination; where there is no more thirst nor grasping; where there is no more attachment to external things."

A common example illustrating nirvana is the blowing out of a candle. Where does the flame go?

The Four Noble Truths

The Buddha taught that …

- ◆ Life is suffering. The very nature of human existence is inherently painful because it involves desire. Because of the wheel of death and rebirth (samsara), death does not bring an end to suffering.
- ◆ Suffering has a cause: desire, craving, or attachment.
- ◆ Eliminating desire is the way to end suffering.
- ◆ The way to end desire is the Eightfold Path:
    Right understanding
    Right purpose
    Right speech
    Right conduct
    Right livelihood
    Right effort
    Right alertness
    Right concentration

And Then There Was Zen

After becoming an official religion in India, Buddhism developed a theoretical schism between the Mahayana and Theravada interpretations. The Mahayana ("great vehicle") school taught that all could be enlightened; the Theravada school (which Mahayana Buddhists call Hinayana or "lesser vehicle" or "small vehicle") did not.

The Mahayana school developed the theory that there have been many Buddhas and that they are all still in "this world" (and are called Boddhisatvas). The Theravada school, on the other hand, held to the traditional idea that when someone reaches nirvana, the person disappears from "this world." The Theravada counterpart of the Boddhisatva is the Arhat who achieves nirvana and disappears.

Mahayana's doctrine grew out of a famous paradox at the heart of Buddhism. It encourages us to eliminate our desires, first for inessentials like wealth and status, then for sex, then for food, and eventually even for breath. When these desires are extinguished, one is nearly ready for nirvana, but one desire remains. It's the desire that motivated the entire exercise—the desire to enter nirvana.

Taoist Tip-Off

Hinayana is a Mahayana word (meaning "lesser vehicle") that Theravada followers consider an insult. It is, therefore, impolite to ask, "Are you Hinayana Buddhist?"

The budding Boddhisatva must, therefore, lose all desire for nirvana before entering. If this undertaking is successful, the Boddhisatva decides voluntarily to return to life in order to help others. For the Mahayana Buddhist (and Zen is part of the Mahayana school), all enlightenment and release takes place at once. No one enters nirvana until we are all ready to enter together!

It's easy to see the path to Zen from here. Why make the desire to get to nirvana the *last* desire you extinguish? Make it the first!

It's also easy to see the Taoist contribution from this viewpoint. How do you extinguish the desire for nirvana? Simple. Abandon the distinction between nirvana and samsara, accept that we all have the Buddha nature (are all already Buddha), and return to living everyday life!

Meet Bodhidharma

It is said that Zen was brought to China from India by a figure known as Bodhidharma, of the Mahayana school of Buddhism. (The name translates roughly as "Enlightened Tradition.")

Tao Then, Tao Now

Bodhidharma is said to have described Zen as "a special transmission outside the scriptures, [with] no need for dependence on words and letters; direct pointing to the real person; seeing into one's nature, identical with all reality."

The earliest development of Bodhidharma's school in China is hard to trace. We know that he is said to have meditated for nine straight years and that he is regarded as having attained direct insight into his own (and, indeed, everyone's) Buddha-nature. In addition, he—or someone—appears to have incorporated a number of distinctively Taoist elements within the Buddhist model.

A Disarming Pupil, a Dust-Free Poem

Eventually, we are told, Bodhidharma refused disciples until Hui Ke, the second patriarch, after being turned down repeatedly, sat in the path of Bodhidarma's gaze and calmly hacked off his right arm to prove his dedication. Bodhidarma accepted him as a disciple and said nothing. The wordless transmission of Zen in China had begun. The most important step in the line of transmission was the sixth patriarch, Hui Neng. His story is recorded in the *Platform Sutra of the 6th Patriarch*, which is the major source of Zen theory. The heart of the story is a competition launched by the fifth patriarch for the "robe of transmission." The scholarly Shen Xiu wrote this poem:

> The body is a Bodhi tree,
> The mind a bright mirror stand.
> Time and again wipe it clean,
> And let no dust alight.

Hui Neng had the poem read to him and dictated his own verse:

> Originally Bodhi has no tree,
> Nor the mirror any stand.
> Basically nothing can be;
> Where can dust land?

The two poems represent the orientation of the Gradual Enlightenment (Northern) School and the Sudden Enlightenment (Southern) School of Zen. Starting with Hui Neng and his highly successful disciple Shen Hui, Sudden Enlightenment spread from the south to become the dominant school of Buddhism during the Tang dynasty, when contacts with Japan transplanted the ideas to the Samurai class.

Although Buddhism was ultimately suppressed in China and Zen eventually declined there, it assumed a vigorous new life in Japan, where it was widely practiced among members of the military class.

On the Path

Profoundly influenced by Taoism, Zen sees all of one's interactions with the world as part of a seamless whole in which "self" and "world" are actually one. The Zen tradition also views words and explanations with deep suspicion. Rinzai, a famous Zen master, echoed Laozi and Zhuangzi when he said, "Rather than attaching yourself to my words, it is better to calm down and seek nothing further. Do not cling to the past or long for the future. This is better than a pilgrimage of 10 years' duration."

Some Fascinating Overlaps

Here are some of the most interesting outlooks Zen Buddhism shares with Taoist thought and practice.

Beyond Words

As we have seen, any formulation of the defect of language shares the defect. The Zen version of "A tao that is a tao is not a constant tao" is "The highest truth is inexpressible."

A famous maxim holds that descriptions of Zen are to Zen as a finger pointing to the moon is to the moon. If the finger actually gets you to look at the moon, that's wonderful. If you stare at someone's finger for 15 or 20 years, however, both you and the finger-pointer should consider the possibility that you have been missing something.

This profound mistrust of words and phrases is almost certainly inherited from Taoism. (Consider Zhuangzi's hilarious question "Where can I find a man who has forgotten words so I can have a word with him?")

Naturalness and Spontaneity

Sudden enlightenment is sudden because there is no process to a goal. It is the realization that we are already at the goal. We find enlightenment in everyday activities and practices. Zen emphasizes an openness to the moment and a total focus on the lived life. Distraction by questions of ultimate meaning, purpose, truth, or metaphysics are signals that true realization has been overlooked.

The Zen tradition, like the Taoist tradition, celebrates the everyday enlightenment of everyone—and all things. There is nothing but Buddha-nature.

This focus on simplicity of direct action shows up in Zen art. If you've ever seen one of those Zen paintings of a virtually perfect circle, clearly brought into existence by a single swift stroke of the brush (or any graceful figure executed by a single flowing stroke), you've seen a visual representation of this spontaneity in artistic action. This conception of action shares much with Zhuangzi's beloved butcher, who carves oxen with the grace of a ballet dancer.

The intensity of focus on everyday activities is "it." Press a Taoist or a Zen student for an answer regarding what, precisely, "it" is, and you're likely to get a smile and a tactful change of subject. (If you were to ask a writer, on the other hand, you'd be likely to get this explanation: In Taoism, "it" is the Tao; in Buddhism, "it" is one's own Buddha-nature. Of course, "it" is also the act of typing this sentence on a personal computer.)

The notion that one might undertake any course of action without conscious intent is, from one point of view, logically absurd. From another point of view, however—and one fully in keeping with the Taoist reverence for skill (see the following section)—we perform actions like these all the time. Do we always think consciously about each individual action we take when we dial a familiar phone number, type a letter, or ride a bicycle?

Buddhist Paradox

Buddhist history is filled with attempts to fix the paradox that lies at its deepest core. Zen recommends ceasing the search and the attempt to render it coherent. One old saying simply pronounces that "there is nothing much in Buddhist teaching." A famous Zen story describes the sacred sutras as "useful only for wiping puss from your boils."

The notion that logical analysis will not, on its own, reveal the Buddha is as pronounced within Zen Buddhism as is the Taoist notion that the Tao that can be elucidated or explained is not the actual Tao.

If a disciple walked into a Zen master's chamber and asked "What is Buddha?" or "What is truth?" (or any similarly metaphysical question) the master would be likely to laugh, spit in the student's face, or even deliver a beating before throwing the questioner out the window! These shocking techniques were designed to remind the student to keep his focus on everyday life. The essential Zen message is "wake up."

These teaching methods, though famous, did break a few bones, and the Japanese perfected an alternative—the *koan*. The koan is designed to achieve the same goal—keeping focused on everyday life—by presenting the student with some question without a rational answer. The koan's purpose is to get us to stop looking for such answers and get on with life.

Practical Applications in Everyday Living

Where Taoism, and Zhuangzi in particular, elevates the experience of practical skill to nearly mystical status, Zen takes a very similar approach. It demands full and aware participation in all activities (not simply meditation).

The famous images of Zen monks sitting in meditation are balanced by a famous story of a master who encounters a disciple sitting in classic posture. The master asks the student, "What are you doing?"

"I'm trying to become Buddha" the disciple answers.

Spoken and Unspoken

A Zen **koan** is a riddle transcending logic that forces the student to abandon the search for enlightenment ... so that he can become enlightened. "What is the sound of one hand clapping?" is a classic beginner's koan. There is no "correct" answer to a koan ... other than the realization that one is looking in the wrong place for what was always already there.

The master sits next to him and starts rubbing a brick on the stone floor.

"What are you doing?" the disciple asks.

"I'm making a mirror," the master replies.

"You can't make a mirror by grinding stones!" the disciple observes.

"You can't make a Buddha by sitting in meditation," the master retorts.

Real meditation, the total absorption in what you're doing, is also enlightenment (satori). Its underlying explanation is the same one we noticed in our discussion of Zhuangzi's ideas of skill.

The sixth patriarch (the one who composed that "correct" poem) was illiterate. He lived by gathering wood. When he went to the temple, he never studied scripture but worked in the kitchen pounding rice. When he had left the temple, he returned to his life, gathering wood where he had already been enlightened. A famous Zen slogan tells us, "In the end, nothing is gained." Another advises: "In carrying water and chopping wood, therein lies the wonderful tao."

Every-Minute Zen

Here's a famous Zen story about attentiveness in everyday life.

A student went anxiously to visit his master, who was deep in meditation and thought. When he entered the room, the master asked if he had been practicing his every-minute Zen. The student replied, "Yes, master."

Then the master asked, "Did you place your umbrella on the left or the right of your shoes?" The student realized he had lapsed in not noticing this detail, and withdrew.

Such rapt attention to total detail are important parts of Japanese arts long associated with Zen (for instance, the tea ceremony, flower arranging, and martial arts). Every detail of a movement is subject to scrutiny and correction by one's master, and the focus and concentration required from the student are extreme.

Zen stories frequently incorporate shocking irreverence for proper language and even Buddhist symbolism. Another famous story tells of someone who asked the Zen master Joshu for the secret of enlightenment and received the following answer: "I have to go take a pee now. It's silly, isn't it? Such a little thing. And yet one must do it in person."

On the Path

As important as Zen's emphasis is on the present moment, it's important to bear in mind that the actual practice of Zen typically involves both meditation and the pursuit of a particular skill. One of the most illuminating examinations of this aspect of Zen Buddhism, which matches up closely with Taoism's emphasis on skill, is Eugen Herrigel's *Zen in the Art of Archery* (Random House, 1953).

Urinating … noticing where one puts ones shoes … A modern Zen master might ask about the color of the car one parked behind. Zen's emphasis on direct experience and openness to the situation has shown its influence in any number of seemingly trivial activities as well as in disciplines and crafts one can envision Zhuangzi rhapsodizing about (art, music, archery, flower arranging, pottery, literature, and so forth). In both instances, however, the idea is to put the conscious, grasping mind aside and let appropriate activity arise spontaneously.

Within the Zen tradition, a certain inspired irreverence accompanies this every-minute awareness. The answer to (insert "big question" of your choice here) might well be "Eat, drink, and move your bowels." Zen masters sometimes make their point by burning statues of the Buddha. ("Find me a piece of wood that is not Buddha," one master is quoted as saying, "and I'll burn that instead.") Others recommend killing the Buddha, using sutras as toilet paper, and so on.

Tao Then, Tao Now

Although Zen Buddhism is not the most popular Buddhist denomination, it has certainly been among the most influential, particularly in the West. More than one observer has noted the irony that this tradition, which inherited from Taoism a fundamental distrust of any written or verbal exposition of ultimate truth, has spawned a truly extraordinary number of books, magazine articles, and websites over the years.

Full Presence in the Moment

Committed Zen students, like those who follow the teachings of Laozi and Zhuangzi, emphasize full, even transcendent, presence in the moment. (Think of Zhuangzi's butcher.) They aim to stay completely involved in the present, because that's the only place true realization can be found.

A classic Zen story goes like this: A Zen master was weighing some flax one day when a monk walked up and asked him, "What is Buddha-nature?" Without hesitation, the master responded: "It's three pounds."

After composing his verse, the sixth patriarch was asked some grand question by the master. The student replied, "The rice is nearly ready," and the master gave him his robe.

It's not hard to picture a Taoist sage giving a similarly immediate and honest response to the question, "What is the Tao?"

The Ultimate Zen Story

A ferocious, hungry tiger chased a man over a cliff. Clinging to a vine with the tiger swiping angrily, the man saw the rocks thousands of feet below. The tiger's claws loosened the vine, and it started to tear away. The man noticed a ripe strawberry nearby, reached out, and plucked it as the vine broke. *It tasted so good!*

And One Big Difference

We've explored some (but certainly not all) of the parallels between Zen Buddhism and the Taoist tradition. It may (or may not) be relevant to note here that the Taoist sage Zhuangzi was skeptical of the ability of masters to pass along their own experience and insights to their students. This kind of master-to-disciple transmission is, however, central to Zen practice.

Learning More About Zen

If you're interested in learning more about Zen Buddhism, here are some websites you may wish to check out.

Zen and Tao on the Internet

Here are eight interesting websites that we've bookmarked. Our question for you: Are they the same as, or different from, the Tao?

Daily Zen
www.dailyzen.com/

One cool quote a day, plus an archive that allows you to look up past quotes. If you're into the whole words thing, that is.

Zen Meditation
www.do-not-zzz.com/

This site offers an electronic tutorial in the art of meditation. It's a good place to start, and not as hokey as one might expect.

Zen Stories to Tell Your Neighbors

www.rider.edu/users/suler/zenstory/zenstory.html

From the site: "A collection of stories from the Orient, mostly Zen and Taoist tales. Why am I suggesting that you tell these stories to your neighbors? Is it because these are among the oldest stories in human history and have withstood the test of time? Is it because Zen and Taoism are ancient religions offering profound insights into human nature, the cosmos, and spirituality? … Maybe. Or maybe it's just because they are fun to tell."

Zen, Women, and Buddhism

www.geocities.com/zennun12_8/

Offers insights on "Zen, the Tao, enlightenment, and Buddhism from the woman's perspective."

Zen Buddhism WWW Virtual Library

www.ciolek.com/WWWVL-Zen.html

Provides "Zen-related links to 196 information facilities world-wide."

The Zen Studies Society

www.zenstudies.org/

From the site: "The Zen Studies Society was established in 1956 to assist the Buddhist scholar D. T. Suzuki in his efforts to introduce Zen to the West. In 1965 it came under the leadership of a Japanese Zen monk, Eido Tai Shimano, who shifted the emphasis toward zazen (Zen meditation) practice. With his dedicated energy, and the help of many Dharma friends and supporters, two centers for Zen practice came into being: New York Zendo Shobo-ji, on the upper east side of Manhattan, and Dai Bosatsu Zendo Kongo-ji, deep in the Catskill Mountains of upstate New York."

Zen@Metalab

www.ibiblio.org/zen/

Koan practice. Not for the faint of heart or those addicted to logic. From the site: "If you've wandered here wanting to know what Zen is, then more than likely you will come away disappointed. This is a question that is easily asked but not easily answered. A Hindu story tells of a fish who asked of another fish: 'I have always heard about the sea, but what is it? Where is it?' The other fish replied: 'You live, move and have your being in the sea. The sea is within you and without you, and you are made of sea, and you will end in sea. The sea surrounds you as your own being.' The only true answer is the one that you find for yourself."

Database of World Zen Centers

www.iijnet.or.jp/iriz/zen_centers/country_list_e.html

Don't just stare at the computer. Do something! Or nothing. As the case may be.

The Least You Need to Know

♦ Many centuries ago, Taoist thought encountered Buddhism in China. When this happened, a remarkable new tradition, which we know today as Zen, began to emerge.

♦ Zen was deeply influenced by Taoist thought and practice.

♦ Zen shares with Taoism an approach to life that is skeptical of words and explanations, emphasizes openness and spontaneity, has practical applications in everyday life, and requires full presence in the moment (like Zhuangzi's butcher).

The Long Run: Religious Taoism Endures

In This Chapter

◆ Taoism under assault

◆ Taoism in today's China

◆ Taoism elsewhere in the East

◆ Restoring an ancient heritage

From roughly the second century A.D., religious Taoism—complete with the miracle workers, soothsayers, alchemists, and seekers of immortality that distinguish it from philosophical Taoism—had been a central element of Chinese popular society. Untold millions of people, particularly in the peasant classes, had made some form of religious expression an important complement to their Confucian and Legalist lives, and had, over centuries, confirmed Taoism's position as a foundation stone of Chinese culture.

Then the twentieth century came along.

Taoism Under Assault

Imperial support for religious Taoism concluded with the downfall of the Qing dynasty in 1911. A complex and chaotic period ensued in China.

The Communist victory in 1949 brought with it severe religious restrictions and outright persecution of practitioners of all religions including religious Taoism. The constraints included arrest, but authorities stepped back from their initial campaign of placing an outright ban on Taoism.

> " " **Tao Then, Tao Now**
>
> The Chinese Communist campaign to stamp out all religion caused many Taoist religious leaders to relocate to Taiwan in the years following the revolution.

The government did, however, confiscate the holdings and temples of the nation's estimated five million monks and enacted legislation severely limiting their activities. The picture was clear: The old traditions were not part of the new China.

A little over a decade after the revolution, the five million monks had been reduced to approximately 50,000. Laws imposing official limitations on Taoist activity were targeted with extraordinary specificity under the government of Mao Zedong. A statute passed in 1950 that helped to initiate the era of religious persecution spelled out the new social category of "superstitious practitioners" to be subject to arrest. It read …

> "All those who for three years immediately prior to liberation derived the main part of their income from such religions and superstitious professions as those of clergymen, priests, monks, Taoists, lay Taoists, geomancers, fortune tellers, and diviners, are to be classified as superstitious practitioners."

The law paved the way for the wholesale confiscation of property, the forced denunciation of beliefs, and the dismantling of monasteries and other religious facilities.

> " " **Tao Then, Tao Now**
>
> The Chinese Taoist Association (CTA), founded in 1957, is an umbrella group representing China's many Taoist communities of religious practitioners. Today its activities include preservation efforts for sacred sites in China.

The Chinese Communists viewed themselves as the agents of modernity and saw the expression of any religion, and particularly any expression of Taoism, as evidence of an antiquated, irrational outlook on life. Thus was one of the world's oldest and most diverse faith traditions officially discouraged under the single ominously broad heading of "superstition."

Then, oddly, the pendulum swung back toward the center. In 1957, the Communists organized the Chinese Taoist Association (CTA) in Beijing and permitted gatherings of monks and nuns from all over the country. Perhaps the leadership had finally come to terms with the ancient roots and the enduring power of traditional Chinese religious practice. Mao himself acknowledged that Taoism had understood the "logic" of dialectic (the Marxist process of change arising from the conflict of opposing elements). Tolerance, it seemed, might carry the day after all.

The Pendulum Swings Again

The so-called *Cultural Revolution* of (dated variously, but 1966 to 1976 is a common timeframe) brought new troubles to all traditional beliefs including, again, all religious Taoists in China.

Mao launched the struggle against his own bureaucratic structure, the Communist Party, because he felt their "attitudes" undermined his commands. Mao's war against his own bureaucrats required that he make an appeal that went over their heads—directly to the angry and egalitarian instincts of the people. "Rebellion," the slogan of the day went, "is justified!"

He found his most receptive target in the inflamed passions and hero-worship of the country's youth. He did this by means of two startlingly effective public relations campaigns: one against intellectuals and another against China's own culture and history. The result was an ecstatic tornado of popular rage and intolerance that swirled its way through all ancient faiths— indeed, through anything that didn't smell sufficiently orthodox to energetic Mao-worshipping youngsters.

In the decade following 1949, monks had very nearly been legislated out of existence, but then they had been granted a measure of official acceptance. During the Cultural Revolution, the administrative subtleties of that bygone era were set aside, Taoism was officially prohibited, and Mao's earnest young disciples took matters into

Spoken and Unspoken

The **Cultural Revolution** of the 1960s and 1970s was a campaign engineered by Mao Zedong that aimed to eradicate the culture of pre-revolutionary China, destabilize existing power centers within the Chinese Communist Party, and punish Mao's political enemies. The mechanism that made this possible was the virtual deification of Mao himself.

Taoist Tip-Off

The persecution experienced by religious Taoists under the Chinese Communists in the second half of the twentieth century applied to *all* religions—to any manifestation of Christianity, Zen Buddhism, or Taoist and popular worship. Just as the Chinese people are comfortable practicing a number of religions simultaneously, the Communists were quite willing to *persecute* several faiths at the same time.

their own hands. Consumed by a fury for anything symbolizing their own nation's ancient traditions, they set about torturing and killing Taoist monks, or, in moments of lesser enthusiasm, consigning them to forced labor camps.

As part of the "Great Helmsman's" unrelenting campaign to "Destroy the Four Olds"— old ideas, old culture, old customs, and old habits—a number of monasteries and other sacred sites, some dating back to the previous millennium, were summarily destroyed. Countless architectural treasures and ancient relics were consigned to the flames.

 Tao Then, Tao Now

Mao Zedong (1893–1976) was head of the Chinese Communist Party and supreme ruler in China from 1949 until his death. He was also a ruthless enemy of his own country's traditional heritage, which he blamed for China's backward state. Religious Taoists suffered intensely under his reign.

If these were the fruits of the "perpetual revolution" that Mao celebrated in his writings, many Taoists may have wondered about the wisdom of planting the seed in the first place.

Miraculously, however, traditional Taoist religious practices were not completely eradicated as a result of the national disaster that was the Cultural Revolution. There was still something to tolerate when Deng Xiaoping saw fit to initiate a measure of official religious tolerance in 1982, six years after Mao's death. That this occurred is a testament to the deep connection the Chinese people have to their ancient traditions and the folly of trying to legislate them, or hound them, out of existence.

A Way of Life So Worthy of Affection and Respect

"Two and a half millennia of intolerance and defamation by Confucian bureaucrats and scholars, culminating in the total dispersal of their communities by the new regime, must have persuaded many a Taoist Immortal that wisdom lies in leaving this world of dust to its own devices. All the same, it is tragic that a way of life so worthy of affection and respect—even if some of its aspects now and then make one want to smile—should have vanished so swiftly and so completely."

—John Blofield, *Secret and Sublime: Taoist Mysteries and Magic* (George Allen and Unwin, 1973)

Taoism in China Today

That Chinese Taoism still exists is inspiring and undeniable. That it has been dealt a serious structural blow by decades of sporadic but ruthless Communist suppression is, alas, also undeniable.

Although estimates on the total number of practicing Taoists in China vary widely, most would agree on two points. First, millions of Chinese still practice some form of Taoism. (There are at least 86 sects.) Second, the persecutions of the twentieth century have combined to present a serious challenge to the traditions and continuity of this ancient, intricate, and many-layered set of faith traditions. Though Taoist practice continues, the maintenance of Taoist continuity and tradition is a matter of ongoing concern.

> ### Tao Then, Tao Now _____
>
> "The state now sanctions Taoism and Buddhism, along with western religion. The latter account for only a small percentage of the population, and official statistics say that 6 percent practice Taoism openly—a figure challenged by many outside observers, who feel the number should be much higher."
>
> —Peter Occhiogrosso, in *The Joy of Sects: A Spirited Guide to the World's Religious Traditions* (Doubleday, 1996)

The CTA still functions as the official representative of the traditional Taoist religious tradition in China. Its work with environmental organizations in maintaining sacred sites has been especially noteworthy (see Chapter 23, "Wired and Wireless").

Religious Taoism Elsewhere in the East

Following are brief summaries of notable communities of religious Taoists outside of China.

Cambodia

Taoism has a strong following among Cambodia's ethnic Chinese; it's estimated that 1 percent of the country identifies religious Taoism as a primary faith tradition. This amounts to a little more than a hundred thousand people.

Hong Kong

The Hong Kong Taoist Association identifies 70 local groups under its jurisdiction. Here, as elsewhere in the East, one can choose from a number of distinctive Taoist groups and practices. Also, Taoism is often practiced simultaneously with one or more other faiths, typically Buddhism and/or Confucianism.

"Buddhist and Taoist deities are present in about 600 Chinese temples in Hong Kong. The most popular deities are those associated with the sea and the weather …. Almost 96 percent of the population (of 6.5 million) is ethnic Chinese."

—From "Hong Kong: Local Life" (www.1uptravel.com/international/asia/hong-kong/locallife.html)

Singapore

In 1989 it was estimated that just over 13 percent of Singapore's population of 2.6 million people described themselves as Taoists. The "Best of Singapore" website (www.marimari.com/content/singapore/best_of/religion/religion.html) notes that the practice overlaps with that of Confucianism and Buddhism and that worship expresses itself in a "versatile mix in Chinese temples."

Practicing at Home

"Many of Singapore's temples formerly had a resident medium, including Kaun Yin's on Waterloo Street, their use indicated by a black flag at the entrance …. [Now they only appear] during festivals, which was when I was lucky enough to see one. Regardless of the long list of temples in the Singapore Yellow Pages, many of them have been demolished, forcing what shamans remain into practicing at home."

—From "The Tao of Singapore" (www.thingsasian.com, 1998)

Taiwan

Estimates of the total number of Taiwanese Taoists vary widely; one conservative, but probably reliable, estimate puts the figure at three million. During the time of the Cultural Revolution, Taiwan became the most visible center for open observance of religious Taoism.

Goddess of the Sea

"Taoism, which has close links with folk religion, entered Taiwan in the mid-seventeenth century and has up to 3,000,000 followers …. It is common to see that Taiwan folk deity Goddess of the Sea (Matsu) and the Buddhist Goddess of Mercy (Kuanyin) are worshipped in the same temple or even home. People often go to the temples to present petitions and solicit divine assistance on some important occasion."

—From "Religions in Taiwan," by C. Y. Li (www.adherents.com, 1996)

Restoring an Ancient Heritage in China

The Taoist Restoration Society (TRS) is a nonprofit organization "dedicated to the rehabilitation and rebirth of China's Taoist tradition."

The organization aims not to proselytize, not to get people to change religions, and not to promote any particular philosophical or religious point of view. Instead, it works to rescue oral traditions and practices that may be lost forever if the current generation of Taoist monks and nuns perishes without passing along what it has learned. TRS is also active in the reclamation of temples, mountains, and other sacred Taoist sites, and it supports the scholarly and monastic work that furthers the religious Taoist tradition in China.

> **Tao Then, Tao Now**
>
> "Important temples need to be rebuilt and repaired ... Works of scripture need to be restored and made available to the Taoist community. Basic scholarship needs to be funded. Thousands of years of mystic devotions must not be wasted! ... [So be] active. See how you can help. Encourage religious freedom. Help repair a Taoist Temple. Balance Yin and Yang. Tell your friends about us. Protect ancient cultural traditions ... Donate your time, energy, and money, before it's too late."
>
> —From the TRS's website (www.taorestore.org)

The blow sustained by China's inherited faith in the last century was extraordinary, and the work to sustain it in this century will need to be extraordinary as well. If you are interested in supporting that work, visit www.taorestore.org and learn more about TRS's distinctive and important mission.

A Trip Like No Other

TRS organizes trips to historically significant Taoist sites within China. Known as "reclusions," these journeys expose Westerners to the reality of traditional Taoist religious practice ... a reality that is likely to be a good deal more meaningful than written assessments of the history and practice of Taoism (of the kind you're reading right now).

As TRS puts it: "Unfortunately, most people do not have direct, personal experience with Taoism. We all know that books can only take us so far, and that Taoism must be experienced in order to be understood. And this is the goal of TRS's reclusions—to find people who want and deserve that experience, and to take them to Taoism's remote holy places. TRS has relationships with monks and monasteries throughout China, and our groups and representatives are always warmly welcomed. The local Taoists know that we are not average tourists, but interested and respectful friends who support their unique culture."

Interested in taking a trip like no other you've ever experienced? Visit TRS's website at www.taorestore.org to learn more.

Up from the Ashes

Here's a heartening example of religious Taoism's vitality and resilience. The following message was posted on a Taoist Internet message board in 1999:

Grand Opening of the Yellow Dragon Taoist Monastery

In April, 1998, the Yellow Dragon Temple was officially opened to the public once again after having been forced to close down in 1949, along with most of the other temples in China. During the Cultural Revolution of the Communist regime, the over 700-year-old temple was leveled. All that remained was a single stone block with the monastery's name carved on it. This monolithic block now guards the main entrance to the temple's new grounds. Grand Master Share K. Lew (now of San Diego, California) is the last known surviving monk of the temple. Last November, he and his wife Juanita brought a group of American students to China to help celebrate the long-awaited reopening of the monastery. Grand Master Lew was one of the first Chinese Masters to teach QiGong and the Taoist Healing Arts openly in America. Grand Master Lew can be contacted in San Diego at this telefax number: 619-295-9855.

Slowly but surely, China appears, at long last, to be taking steps to reclaim and preserve its cultural heritage.

Veneration of Nature and Simplicity

Is there something in the mountains?

Religious Taoism, for all its emphasis on the otherworldly, has an important common element with the philosophical Taoism that is the main focus of this book. Though remarkably (and probably indescribably) diverse, religious Taoism shares with philosophical Taoism an emphasis on "a spiritual veneration of nature and simplicity." Such a veneration is held to sustain the believer in all situations, including times of trouble.

It's tempting to conclude that this complex tradition's endurance in the face of powerful opposition during the twentieth century may well have had something to do with its practitioners' ability to draw support from a direct communion with nature, a communion that transcends even the destruction of a sacred temple.

If that's the case, one may be forgiven for wondering whether the gap between religious and philosophical Taoism is really so vast after all.

The Least You Need to Know

- The Communist victory in 1949 brought with it severe religious restrictions and the outright persecution of practitioners of religious Taoism.
- After a period of tolerance, the repression of Taoism became still fiercer during the disastrous assault on Chinese history known as the Cultural Revolution.
- Religious Taoism is practiced in Cambodia, Taiwan, Singapore, and Hong Kong.
- The Taoist Restoration Society (TRS) is a nonprofit organization "dedicated to the rehabilitation and rebirth of China's Taoist tradition."

Part

The Music of the Tao

What does Taoism have to teach us about nature, about skill, and about life and death? You'll find some of the answers in this part.

Chapter 12

What Taoism Teaches About Nature

In This Chapter

- ◆ What Taoists mean when they say "nature"
- ◆ Openness to natural processes
- ◆ Listening to the sages

This is the first of three chapters exploring specific elements of Taoist thought and practice as they have been expressed through the centuries.

From the many possibilities for topics, we have selected three master ideas as points of entry to the teachings and inspirations of Taoism: nature, skill, and that ultimate pairing of opposites, life and death. Rather than spend a great deal of time exploring the intricacies of religious doctrine as it has evolved over time or the competing points of the various philosophical schools, we have opted to explore each of these three ideas in depth in this part of the book. There is a certain amount of overlap among the ideas, but we feel that is as it should be.

Tao Then, Tao Now

For centuries, the concepts of nature, skill, and life/death have figured prominently in definitions of and discussions of the Tao. The notion of skill and smooth spontaneous execution is a dominant theme in the *Zhuangzi*.

Before we begin, we want to reiterate that any book about Taoism runs a risk of paradox, and any attempt to elucidate specific points of observance should be, by definition, fraught with danger. Taoism is supposed to be indefinable. What follows braves that danger, but with this caveat—these doctrines do not "define" Taoism. They are beliefs that *some* Taoists have. Remember: Taoism is a system of thought that tolerates a wide variety of outlooks and accepts no final authority on which is correct. We certainly are not that authority.

Defining Things? Remember ...

Laozi observed that any tao that could guide was subject to reformulation, interpretation, and exceptions. (That is to say, no tao that does its job is constant.) So let us preface our observations in this part of the book with two suggestions. These suggestions serve not only as a warning, but also as the best summary of what follows. Here they are:

Read This First

Two suggestions regarding tao:

◆ Anything we say about tao will itself presuppose a tao we haven't formulated. Zhuangzi likened the human relation to tao like that of fish to water. Tao is inescapable in human thinking, and we usually do not notice how we depend on it.

◆ Listen for tao carefully and act accordingly. (You actually don't need this advice! You are ... and you will.)

Now that we've gotten that out of the way, you can skip the next three chapters entirely and get on with whatever you were doing—a prospect that includes, of course, the possibility of reading the next three chapters. Be forewarned, though, that these chapters are presented more as music to accompany Taoism than as prose designed to "define" it.

Nature and the Tao

Humanity follows the earth.
Earth follows nature.
Nature follows tao.
Tao follows what is so.

—*Daode Jing*, chapter 25 (Hansen translation)

Three ancient Chinese terms are translated as "nature." The Taoist's main interest is in two that occur in this passage.

One is the concept of nature symbolized by sky (complementing the earth and together forming the compound for cosmos). This is the notion of natural constancy—the motions of the heavens and (for Confucians and Mohists) the ultimate moral authority.

The other term refers to "the way it is" or "what is so." We could explain it as "the given." Why is (whatever it is) given? The best answer we can offer is: "Simply because we're here now and not over there back then."

Discussions of tao usually incorporate nature imagery or find some way to focus on openness to the processes of the natural world. In *Tao: The Watercourse Way* (Pantheon, 1975), Alan Watts defined Taoism as "the way of man's cooperation with the course or trend of the natural world." This is not fatalism, because the Taoist attitude to the way things are and naturally work is one of awe and respect—tinged with an inclination to go along.

 Tao Then, Tao Now _____

Alan Watts (1915–1973) was for many years the West's preeminent interpreter of Eastern philosophy and religion and of Taoist and Zen thought in particular. An Englishman who eventually settled in California, Watts developed an influential body of writings and teachings that included the books *Tao: The Watercourse Way, The Tao of Philosophy,* and *The Book on the Taboo Against Knowing Who You Are,* as well as the television program *Eastern Wisdom and Modern Life.* For more information on Watts's work and his legacy, visit www.alanwatts.com.

Again and again, when we approach the Tao and the idea of nature, we are guided gently back to the notion of remaining open to the influence of something vast that is already unfolding of its own accord.

Pervasiveness

Tao unfolds naturally in all situations and to all beings—including us—whether we notice it or not. For nonhuman contexts, tao seems a substitute for our notion of a natural law.

Consider a force like gravity, which operates on every object we encounter during the day. The apple's tendency to move toward the center of the earth is natural tao. It gets more complicated to see natural law as continuous with our moral codes, prescriptions for dress, dating behavior, and so on, but that is the Taoist view. The intermediate steps would include other social animals that coordinate their behavior by signaling behavior (think of bees and their food location dances); these steps would also include plants that respond to changing situations (think of sunflowers turning).

Human beings happen to be parts of nature who are *naturally* guided in situations by certain noises and certain marks. But we also have a way (tao) of using the noises and marks that is not itself noises and marks. Something that is simply *there*.

On the Path _____

The Tao (with a capital "T") may be understood as the expression of any of the myriad natural processes (streams rushing, fish swimming, people being born) and the vast complex of principles that can be depended upon to guide those processes. The idea is to acknowledge our continuity with our environment in nature's process. This idea is often resisted in Confucian and Western thought. We want to contrast natural and human norms.

The continuity in the Taoist view deserves deep respect. An old Zen story tells of a master who was preparing to take a bath. Finding the water too hot, he instructed a student to bring a bucket of cold water with which to cool the bath water. The student obeyed; when the water reached a temperature the master approved of, the student carelessly threw the remaining water to the ground and prepared to leave.

The master, however, stopped him in his tracks. "What a fool you are!" he exclaimed. "Instead of throwing the water away, you might have watered the plants with it. What on earth led you to believe you could squander even a drop of water in my temple?"

At that moment, the student became enlightened.

Water as a Redemptive Force

Although the previous story comes from the later Zen tradition, the water imagery, as well as the emphasis on effortless natural efficiency, is strongly Taoist. Water is frequently used as a symbol of how we simultaneously follow and make tao: It finds and follows a path allowing it to flow down and creates a channel or path for itself in doing so. When it meets resistance, it conforms to the obstacle and gradually, patiently, erodes and incorporates it into its path. Waterways are indeed ways.

Chinese cosmology lists water as one of the five processes. Because the list is familiar, we too easily confuse these with the Western notion of fundamental elements. The Chinese term is actually five-*xing*, five "walkings." Walking is what we do with a tao. Water stands not for the stuff, but for the pattern of behavior symbolized by water's natural action. The other natural processes are wood (spontaneous growing, seeking means of surviving), fire (natural processes of destroying—the law of entropy), metal (processes of cutting through), and earth (processes of nurturing and sustaining). Each expresses itself in cycles and patterns, and each corresponds to many things: time of day, directions, colors, rituals, seasons, and so on.

Spoken and Unspoken _____

Water is an important teaching symbol in the Taoist tradition. Its yin character, coolness, passivity, life-nurturing quality, ability to overcome obstacles with patience and conformity, and inherent capacity to seek its own path have placed it at the center of many Taoist maxims and stories. The *Daode Jing* observes that "In all the world, there is nothing more submissive and weak than water. Yet for attacking that which is hard and strong, nothing can surpass it." Zhuangzi said, "The sound of the water says what I think."

Pathways

Pathways and roads are everywhere in nature, and those that are human-made are no exception. Think of a mountain pass or a valley. Each can be seen as a pathway to creating a pathway.

One might say that the goal in Taoism is simply to learn how to appreciate and value natural signs and to find ways to journey through life, just as one might journey through a forest, a valley, or along a riverbank. Note that this journey does not start at birth, because our birth is part of a larger journey—a journey of which our path from birth to death is a component.

Trust in Nature as an Organic Pattern

The Chinese yin-yang conception of nature is an organic reproduction pattern of nature and the cosmos. Nature exists outside of and beyond human control. Taoists regard this human embedding in larger universal processes with wonder, awe, and deep appreciation.

In nature, there is an ordering—dizzying and exquisite in its variety—that exists endlessly. (Think of the infinitely proportioned, kaleidoscopic images of fractal geometry, and you'll begin to get a sense of the intricacy, beauty, and endless "scalability" of natural patterns in the Taoist view.)

This order, this series of resonances, is both indescribably vast and intricately interdependent. It is an order that includes other "makers" of order—like bees and humans. The associated notion from the poem "Desiderata"—that we are all children of the universe, on a par with the planets and the stars, and that the universe unfolds in the proper way whether or not we recognize it as doing so—comes close to providing a parallel with the Taoist reverence of nature and its patterns.

Action in Accordance with the Flow

The expression "go with the flow," if stripped of its stereotyped layer of aimless (or even valueless) passivity, offers an interesting parallel with the Taoist ideal of inspired use of the guiding forces of nature.

> **Tao Then, Tao Now** _____
>
> The concept of wu-wei, discussed in Chapter 5, "In the Flow: Key Concepts," is difficult to appreciate fully without some recourse to the larger concept of nature. As Mel Thompson writes in *Eastern Philosophy*:
>
> "The key term for a Taoist approach to the evaluation of action is wu-wei. This means 'non-action,' but it does not mean total inactivity. Rather, it is action that is undertaken on two principles: no effort is to be wasted, and nothing should be done that is against nature ... It is action that is based on reality, not on fantasy."

A general attitude of respect for and conformity with nature can help our own tao of discovery and construction. When we follow a natural pathway between two mountains, we reach our destination easily. When we set our sails to take full advantage of the prevailing winds, we cross the lake quickly. When we reach the point where we know that our work for the day is complete, we go to bed. By remaining open to the natural "next thing to do," we don't struggle to *follow* the way. We unite with it.

Economy of Action

If you've ever looked closely at the passageways of an ant colony, the interior structure of a seashell, or the geometric arrangement of seeds in a mature sunflower, you've probably realized, with amazement, that nature is fantastically efficient. Taoism urges us to follow its example in our everyday life.

If we mirror the Tao, we will put everything in its right place, allow nothing to go to waste (compare the preceding Zen story), flaunt no excess, and countenance no anxious hoarding for the future. In Chapter 15, "The Tao and the Judeo-Christian Tradition," you'll learn about one of the most intriguing Gospel parallels with the *Daode Jing*: Jesus' instruction to his followers to ponder—and presumably follow the example of—the lilies of the field. As Jesus noted, flowers that grow wild, without wearying themselves, spinning out cloth, or fretting endlessly, somehow manage to capture an effortless beauty that eludes the garments of kings.

Spontaneity

There is nothing forced, hasty, or panicked in the Taoist conception of nature, or in the example of the human who successfully opens himself or herself to natural processes. Regardless of what we may imagine to be taking place at any given moment, the right things arrive of their own accord on the correct timeline. The "right response" to each and every situation is waiting to rise to the surface—without our forcing it to battle to victory over a "wrong response." Such is the Taoist view.

A Taoist-influenced proverb in the Zen Buddhist tradition reminds students: "Spring comes; the grass grows by itself." A meadow that has to be coerced, badgered, or bribed into blossoming every spring would be a strange meadow indeed. Similarly, the best human responses, from the Taoist viewpoint, are authentic, unplanned, and utterly without embellishment or hidden agenda.

Union with Nature

Taoists regard the myriad manifestations of the Tao as integral parts of a single grand design. Any perceived separation from natural processes is seen as illusory. It is in order to overcome such illusions that many Taoists decided to spend time in direct communion with rivers, trees, oceans, or meadows—and away from cities filled with intricate, self-obsessed, distracting, and frequently awkward "conveniences" that do not always seem to support instinctive openness to the Way. But Taoism does not require separation from society. Properly understood, Taoism helps us find our way in society, too.

The apparent divisions arise, a Taoist might argue, because we choose to see society, culture, and conventions as something separate from nature. Some Christian thinkers, for instance, have a tendency to view "humanity" in contrast with "the world." Many in the West take umbrage when Darwin suggests that human beings are a fully natural animal. Often, we reject this conception: "We are made in the image of the supernatural—not in the image of this world!" Or "Our moral codes give us a special status and right in nature." Or "Human cities destroy nature." (Aren't they actually part of nature—wouldn't space creatures regard cities as they do anthills?)

It's as though all we believe to be nature had somehow been placed as a stage on which we enact something utterly different and separate from nature. We treat nature as an object, a gift to exploit or repackage.

Taoism regards human society itself as a component of the great unfolding ... and tends to view with skepticism any system of thought (notably Confucianism) that ignores the status and ways of life of other animals or entities.

Listening

Listening, as in the other three master ideas discussed in this section of the book, is absolutely essential. It reminds us that the metaphor of a tao is, for us, something we normally hear. We must learn to "hear" natural constancies (natural laws) and learn, too, to hear the given (the way things are).

A Taoist would argue that we must listen, for instance, to any situation as it exists, before acting, in order to correct our conception of the ways open to us. When we make a point of listening attentively for the guidance of natural processes, we often find a way by an obstacle, as water does.

There is an old Chinese story about an aggressive horse. The horse was secured outside a shop and had a nasty habit of kicking any passerby who tried to move past him on the extremely narrow street where the shop was located. A number of villagers gathered and debated the question of how to restrain the animal but reached no conclusions. Then someone reported that the village sage was on his way into town at that very moment. Surely, the villagers reasoned among themselves, the oldest and wisest man in the village would know how to deal with the horse.

All eyes were set on the end of the street in anticipation of the master's arrival. When he finally appeared, he took one look at the horse, turned on his heel, and chose another street that would lead him safely to his destination.

A water-inspired response!

Melody and Harmony: Nature and the Tao

Following are some "notes" in the ongoing symphony of human teaching and observation composed over the centuries regarding the Tao as it is expressed in nature.

Please note that our point here is not that Taoism per se was consciously accepted as a guiding school of thought by each and every one of the people quoted in the following section. Rather, we mean to suggest that the core tenets of Taoism in general, and its attitude toward nature, are reflected in many philosophical and religious traditions.

Nature and Identity

Are we the same as, or different from, the natural world that surrounds us? What is our true identity?

> **Student:** "Who am I?"
>
> **Master:** "There is nothing to be found in the entire universe that is not you."
>
> —Traditional Taoist teaching of our interconnectedness and continuity with nature

No Principle That Forces

Does the natural universe unfold by means of compulsion and control or by something more effortless?

> "Tao means the course of nature ... [Laozi] said the principle of the Tao is spontaneity, and that 'the great Tao flows everywhere, both to the left and to the right. It loves and nourishes all things and does not lord it over them.' Of course, there is a very great difference between the Chinese idea of Tao, as the informing principle of God, and the Judeo-Christian idea of God as nature's lord and master, because the Tao does not act as a boss. There is no principle that forces things to behave the way they do, and so it is a completely democratic theory of nature."
>
> —Alan Watts, *The Tao of Philosophy*

Presence

> "Does human interaction with the natural world require special theological tools? Or is it a matter of direct experience?
>
> "Spring comes, and I look at the birds;
> Summer comes, and I take a bath in the stream;
> Autumn comes, and I climb to the top of the mountain;
> Winter comes, and I make the most of the sunlight for warmth.
> This is how I savor the passage of the seasons."
>
> —Shih T'ao (seventeenth-century Chinese poet)

Every Moss and Cobweb

> "What makes nature nature and where, exactly, is it? Every thing in nature contains all the powers of nature. Every thing is made of one hidden stuff .... The world globes itself in a drop of dew. The microscope cannot find the animalcule which is less perfect for being little. Eyes, ears, taste, smell, motion, resistance, appetite, and organs of reproduction that take hold on eternity—all find room to consist in the small creature. So do we put our life into every act. The true doctrine of omnipresence is that God reappears with all his parts in every moss and cobweb."
>
> —Ralph Waldo Emerson

"Something True to Say"

"This intuitive truth that nature points us towards—are words sufficient for it?

"Gathering chrysanthemums at the eastern hedgerow,
I look silently at the mountains to the south.
This mountain sunset air is beautiful;
Flocks of birds gather together on their way home.
In and among these things there is certainly something true to say,
Yet when I try to tell someone, I am lost in no-words."

—T'ao Chien

Where Is It?

Is this natural guidance something that's far away from us?

"Heaven is under our feet as well as over our heads."

—Henry David Thoreau

The Identity of All Forms

How does the person who follows the Tao resemble nature itself?

 Tao Then, Tao Now

"The mountains are high and the oceans are wide."

—Zen Master Hsueh-doh, in response to the question "What is the living meaning of Zen?" (Centuries later, the answer still withstands scrutiny.)

"To the man who does not reside in himself, the identity of all forms becomes clear. He passes about like water, shows a reflection as though he were a mirror, and answers as though he were an echo. He is so light as to seem to vanish altogether. He is placid and clear as a calm lake. His interactions with others are utterly harmonious, regardless of whether he gains or loses something. He does not bustle forward in front of people, but rather follows them."

—Zhuangzi

"For Zhuangi, to come back to one's nature is to come home to nature in general ...."

—Kuang-Ming Wu, *Zhuangzi*

"The Guiding Principle"

How can the scientific mind approach the processes of nature?

> "The scientist's religious feeling takes the form of a rapturous amazement at the harmony of natural law, which reveals an intelligence of such superiority that, in comparison with it, the highest intelligence of human beings is an utterly insignificant reflection. This feeling is the guiding principle of his life and work."
>
> —Albert Einstein

Nature and Wu-Wei

How does the principle of wu-wei relate to nature?

> "Taoism encourages working with natural forces, not against them. Taoism teaches the path of wu-wei—the technique of mastering circumstances, not trying to control them. Teachers of the Tao often use examples of the bending reed or grass blowing in the wind to illustrate this important point. A Taoist would encourage an individual to work with obstacles and problems instead of fighting adversity at every turn."
>
> —"Taoism" (Pacific University, Matshushita Center for Electronic Learning; mcel.pacificu.edu/as/students/vb/Taoism, 2001)

Interdependence

Do elements within nature (including human beings) operate separately from one another?

> "When Western science studies and observes an organism in nature, from an atomic particle to a mammal or fish … [scientists have concluded] that the organism cannot be monitored or measured without monitoring or measuring its environment. If a change is made to one, it affects the other. Thus the term 'a unified field of behavior.' If you are studying a yak, you must also study its immediate family, its herd, the terrain it roams, the climate in which it lives, the lakes, streams, and rivers that are present, all the trees, plants, animals, and insects that live in their roaming area, and so forth."
>
> —*Unified Field of Behavior* (yakrider.com, 2001)

> "When starting to teach me about what it meant to be 'ahimsa,' or non-violent, and the effect on the environment around you, [on] the vibrations—when he started to teach me about energy and vibrations, his opening statement was 'Snakes Know

Heart. Yogis in jungle need not fear.' Because if you're pure enough, cool it, don't worry. But you've got to be very pure."

—Ram Dass, *Be Here Now*

Tao Then, Tao Now

"Natural Tao (often translated 'heavenly Tao') is akin to what we would consider the constancies of science. It is the way things reliably happen."

—Chad Hansen, "Taoism" (*Stanford Encyclopedia of Philosophy*, 2001)

Harmony

How should people pursue the goals of attaining inner peace and wisdom?

"Perhaps the best explanation is that Tao is the way of nature, or the way of the heavens. Taoism is concerned with the sublime patterns of nature, [and holds that] a person can achieve peace and enlightenment by harmonizing himself or herself with the course of nature."

—"Tao" (www.vibrationdata.com, 2001)

Longevity and Vigor

How has the Taoist emphasis on nature been reflected in Chinese culture?

"If Taoist ideas and images inspired in the Chinese a love of nature and an occasional retreat to it from the cares of the world to rest and heal, it also inspired an intense affirmation of life: physical life—health, well-being, vitality, longevity, and even immortality. Laozi and Zhuangzi had reinterpreted the ancient nature worship and esoteric arts, but they crept back into the tradition as ways of using knowledge of the Dao to enhance and prolong life."

—Judith A. Berling, "Taoism, or the Way" (*Focus on Asian Studies*, Vol. II, No. 1, 1982)

Different Worlds, Different Viewpoints

Is the human viewpoint the only viewpoint to consider within nature?

"A human being is a part of the whole that we call the universe, a part limited in time and space. He experiences himself, his thoughts and feelings, as something separated from the rest—a kind of optical illusion of his consciousness. This illusion is a prison for us, restricting us to our personal desires and to affection for only the few people nearest us. Our task must be to free ourselves from this prison by widening our circle of compassion to embrace all living beings and all of nature."

—Albert Einstein

And here's another take on the same question:

> "This is where Daoism diverges from Confucianism in its most radical terms. For Daoists, the human world is interwoven with other worlds that are entertained from other perspectives—trees, animals, rocks, and so on—[and] these worlds add up to an ever-expanding composite cosmos."
>
> —William A. Callahan, *Cook Ding's Life on the Whetstone*

A Final Word from Zhuangzi

While we're on the subject of viewpoints and nature, consider the following famous anecdote about Zhuangzi:

> "Zhuangzi and Hui Shi were walking on a bridge over a river. Zhuangzi said, 'Those fish darting about—that's happiness for a fish!' Hui Shi said, 'You're not a fish. How do you know what happiness is to a fish?' Zhuangzi replied, 'You're not me—how do you know I don't know what fish happiness is?'"
>
> —*Zhuangzi*, chapter 17

Who *are* we to say Zhuangzi didn't know what made fish happy?

The Least You Need to Know

- Tao permeates the vast and elegant processes of nature.
- Water is an important teaching symbol in Taoism.
- Pathway imagery is also essential to Taoism.
- Taoists see nature in organic metaphors, in patterns of creation through interaction, and in harmony arising through infinite resonances within our environment.
- Taoists also emphasize action in accordance with the "flow," an economy of action, and spontaneity.
- Union with nature is a given in the Taoist tradition.

What Taoism Teaches About Skill

In This Chapter

- ◆ Eastern and Western notions of skill
- ◆ Lose yourself to find yourself
- ◆ Listening to the sages

Many Westerners are inclined to think of skill in terms of cleverness; of consciously cultivated dexterity; or of the manipulation of carefully hoarded facts, aptitudes, and various tricks of the trade. It is something of a shock, then, when Westerners first encounter the Taoist point of view on skill, which has much more to do with openness to the total context of action and which emphasizes spotting unique clues to the ways in which the present situation is different from all the others one has previously executed the skill in.

You might even say that a unique mindlessness takes over when the skillful person employs his or her skill in accordance with Taoist principles.

Skill and the Tao

Zhuangzi tells a story of a wheelwright named Pian. Pian's now-obscure trade was once vitally important to trade and industry; at the time of the story, a wheelwright was someone whose job it was to chisel wheels from massive blocks of stone.

On the Path

Although the notion of skill is associated strongly with Zhuangzi, Laozi explores it as well. The *Daode Jing* advises us: "Therefore the sage is guided by what he feels, not what he sees."

One day, Pian happened to come across a powerful duke engrossed in study. To the duke's surprise, the humble wheelwright ventured a caustic opinion about the books of wisdom the duke was spending all his time reading. The lowly worker insisted that by reading the words of men who were already dead, the duke was himself focusing on death instead of life. Insulted, the duke demanded an explanation—and threatened to have the wheelwright executed if the clarification of his presumptuous remarks was not a persuasive one.

To save his life, the wheelwright said this:

"For me, my lord, I look at life as though I were looking at my work. Now, let's think of the wheel I chisel. When I go too slow, my chisel jumps away from me and does not do as I wish. If I go too fast, the chisel jams and ruins the wheel, because it does not make the proper motion. However, if I find the point that is neither too slow nor too fast, the chisel connects perfectly with my hand and I connect perfectly from my heart to the chisel.

"Here is the point: One cannot explain this process to another person. I am afraid that the words that can come out of my mouth won't do much in describing what I mean to someone who must use a chisel, but I, nevertheless, mean something. This 'something' I cannot expect to teach my son, and my son cannot expect to pick it up from me.

"In any event, I am now 70 years old, and getting older, simply making wheels with my chisel. These ancient men whose words you are reading, I believe, are just the same: When they died, they held something that could not be transmitted by anything other than experience. And so I believe that what you are reading is their dregs."

The wheelwright lived.

> **Nothing That It Cannot Do**
>
> "The Tao never acts with force,
> Yet there is nothing that it cannot do.
> If rulers could follow the way of the Tao,
> Then all of creation would willingly follow their example.
> If selfish desires were to arise after their transformation,
> I would erase them with the power of the uncarved block.
> By the power of the uncarved block,
> Future generations would lose their selfish desires.
> By losing selfish desires,
> The world would naturally settle into place."
>
> —*Tao Te Ching*, chapter 37 (McDonald translation)

A similar focus on spontaneity and authenticity can be seen in the true story of Walter Cronkite as he broadcast the first manned mission to the moon. (Note: What follows is not meant to suggest that Walter Cronkite is or was a Taoist, though of course, like everyone who has never thought about the matter, he was. However, we merely want to highlight the way virtuosity in anything can illustrate the Taoist insights into skill.)

Cronkite's companion at the anchor desk asked him at one point what he planned to say to the world at the fateful moment when Neil Armstrong first set foot on the moon. To the commentator's surprise, Cronkite insisted that he would rather not try to prepare any specific remark, but would prefer simply to respond as the events unfolded. Not exactly what one would expect from the most admired news professional in the country! But Cronkite clearly saw the importance of responding authentically, without attempting to develop an unnatural or scripted response. He seems to have felt that by attempting to develop such a response in advance he would have only delivered a stale and artificial moment to the world (and to himself).

In the event, when Armstrong finally took his first footstep onto the moon, Cronkite was in fact left completely speechless! He pulled off his glasses, rubbed his eyes, and shook his head back and forth, and yet, speechless as he was, his response was authentic, totally appropriate to the situation, and in keeping with what the Taoists call wu-wei. (You remember about wu-wei from Chapter 5, "In the Flow: Key Concepts," right?) Armstrong's own rehearsed "speech," by contrast, might strike some people as shallow, pretentious, or even silly.

Although Cronkite's "performance" didn't live up to the predetermined expectations of his broadcasting companion, it did serve as the perfect emotional benchmark for America and the world. It also served to provide an example of "skill-less skill" that a Taoist could embrace easily.

Here's the point: Something you already know how to do well—like chiseling a wheel or reacting to a major news event on camera—shouldn't be practiced or nailed down too definitively beforehand. Appropriate preparation, when it's necessary (and it frequently is), should be spontaneous and should somehow take the form of a listening exercise.

Again and again, when we approach the Tao and the idea of skill, we are guided gently back to the notion of remaining open to the influence of something vast that is already unfolding of its own accord.

Pervasiveness

Every situation, in the Taoist view, provides an opportunity for some kind of harmonious interaction with the Tao. When one has mastered the ultimate skill—the skill of living itself—there is no fretting or stumbling about whether or not one has the "proper" skill. One simply responds authentically at all times. But this is the skill of the sage!

For one who follows the Tao, skill expresses itself effortlessly and appropriately. Baseball star Mickey Rivers captured something of this open, trusting attitude toward all experience when he said, "Ain't no use worrying about things you control, because if you've got control over them, ain't no use worrying. And ain't no use worrying about things you *can't* control, because if you can't control them, ain't no use worrying."

When you think about it, you realize that each and every situation we face in life, at each and every moment, asks for some kind of response from us—even if that response is, like Walter Cronkite's, an admission that we *have* no formal response at the moment, only ourselves.

The real question is not whether we have "mastered" all possible contingencies in advance, but whether we are wasting time and energy worrying about whether we have control over a given moment. A better course, a Taoist would argue, would be simply to do what we are naturally inspired to do, time and time and time and time again. From this kind of daily commitment, sages may emerge.

Openness

Zhuangzi advocates a kind of youthful clarity and flexibility that informs and supports the practical experience of age—without using that experience as an excuse to "shut down" mentally or spiritually. This openness to the Tao is an important part of both the philosophical and religious traditions, one that is reflected in the concept of *ming* (clarity), which encompasses an openness to experience that transcends even language.

Spoken and Unspoken

Zhuangzi generally avoided contrasting our limited perspectives to any cosmic or total perspective. He contrasted them mainly with each other, distrusted "sages" who projected their perspectives on nature, and called his own perspective on the relativity of language to perspective **ming** (clarity). The term suggests that Zhuangzi's approach to the cultivation of skill in everyday life involves an open appreciation to the variety of tao in a way that avoids the trap of the anti-language paradox.

Unity of Actor and Action

Zhuangzi usually looks with great favor on the kind of specialization that allows someone to "lose self" utterly (or is it "find self" utterly?) in some focused action or pursuit. In this, he is consistent with Aristotle, who observed that human life offers no more fulfilling activity than the exercise of some acquired skill. Highly honed expertise invites paradoxical, almost mystical, description from Zhuangzi—and from many others who, wittingly or otherwise, embrace the Taoist outlook on skill.

In "walking a tao" (performing it), we seem to experience a unity of actor and action; this "practice" is a way of losing ourselves, much as one might in meditation, in contemplation, or even in a trance. The accuracy and efficiency of our own actions sometimes mystifies us. We do not understand how we did it, and we certainly cannot explain it to others.

The person who may think the notion of "following the Tao" alien and distant is likely to be quite comfortable with the feeling of purposeful union that arises from an action such as painting, delivering a presentation, setting up a spreadsheet, or playing the saxophone. When we "lose ourselves" in such a moment, have we found what the sages have been talking about for all these centuries? Is there something from this near-universal experience of "doing the job well" that we can expand into other areas of our lives?

Here is Zhuangzi's most famous account of the kind of skill that unites actor and action:

A Tao That Advances My Skill

Cook Ting was slicing up an oxen for Lord Wenhui. At every push of his hand, every angle of his shoulder, every step with his foot, every bend of his knee—zip! zoop!—he slithered the knife along with a zing, and all was in perfect rhythm, as though he were dancing to Mulberry Grove or keeping time, as in Qingshou music.

"Ah, this is marvelous," said Lord Wenhui. "Imagine skill reaching such heights!"

Cook Ting laid down his knife and replied, "What I care about is a Tao that advances my skill. When first I began cutting up oxen, I could see nothing that was not ox. After three years, I never saw a whole ox. And now—now I go at it by spirit and do not look with my eyes. Controlling knowledge has stopped, and my spirit wills the performance. I depend on the natural makeup, cut through the creases, guide through the fissures. I depend on things as they are. So I never touch the smallest ligament or tendon, much less bone.

"A good cook changes his knife once a year because he cuts. A mediocre cook changes his knife once a month because he hacks. I have had this knife of mine for nineteen years and I've cut up thousands of oxen with it. Yet the blade is as good as if it had just come from the grindstone."

Cook Ting can be aware that others may have different ways of dissecting an ox; he simply cannot exercise his skill while he is trying to choose among them.

 **On the Path** _____

The *Ting* in Zhuangzi's famous Cook Ting story may be trying to tell us something about humility. Ting may not be the cook's name at all, but rather a sign of coming third. (A Ting would be a C as a class grade.) The choice of a butcher for the parable is similarly instructive, as butchering is rarely held to be a noble or exalted profession in Asia. Zhuangzi's point is that this attitude can be taken by anyone in any activity.

In realizing the way of some activity in us, we make it real in us. The internalized way becomes our de—our virtuosity, our character, our acquired second nature.

Listening

The Taoist view of skill does not demand that you master all possible responses to an unfamiliar situation, only that you be willing to notice tao in what is given in all situations of action.

Consider the words of Cook Ting as he continues his discourse to Lord Wenhui, this time explaining how he handles "the end of what one is used to":

> "I regularly come to the end of what I am used to. I see its being hard to carry on. I become alert; my gaze comes to rest. I slow down my performance and move the blade with delicacy. Then—zhrup!—it cuts through and falls to the ground. I stand

with the knife erect, look all around, deem it wonderfully fulfilling, strop the knife, and put it away."

To master a skill fully, we must be able to execute it in real time. This requires taking the distinctions (concepts) used in our instructions and "mapping" them on nature as it appears in *this* situation. In the event, though, we don't have time to read a map; we simply begin to see ourselves as reading the *world*. Once we do so, we discover it has become second nature to see our way through (what are always) unique situations.

Mastering any skill (which might be expressed as a tao with a lowercase "t") thus can yield this sense of harmony with the world and its vast complex of guiding processes (that is, Tao, with an uppercase "T"). It is as if the world, not the instructions, guides us.

Melody and Harmony: Skill and the Tao

Following are some "notes" in the ongoing symphony of human teaching and observation composed over the centuries regarding the Tao as it is expressed in the notion of skill.

Please note that, as before, our point here is not that the people quoted in the following section would have identified themselves as Taoists. Rather, we suggest only that insights of Taoism into skill are insights learned spontaneously by those who truly become skilled virtuosi.

On the Path

A Taoist would contend that one's spontaneous, unforced skill in, for instance, making a perfect wheel, should also serve as the pattern for living one's life as it is meant to be lived.

A Playful Mode of Action

Is the Taoist conception of skill rooted in simple complacency and passivity, or is it more childlike?

> "Wu-wei is not so much a principle of utter passivity or 'non-action' but the idea of a 'natural,' 'purposeless,' 'playful' or 'disinterested' mode of action, set in distinction to the willful and socially structured 'face work' emphasized within the Confucian tradition."
>
> —N. J. Girardot, *Myth and Meaning in Early Taoism*

Tao Then, Tao Now

"I listen to the audience, and the audience tells me where the laughs are supposed to be."

—Bert Lahr, vaudevillian (and *The Wizard of Oz* star), explaining a performance that featured many laughs from the audience at unexpected places in the script

Or consider this ancient insight:

> "Man is most nearly himself when he achieves the seriousness of a child at play."
>
> —Heraclitus

And this:

> "Growth in life is growth in the perception of unsuspected connections, which often shock common sense. Such shocks are expressed in ironies. He who can connect ironically is a mature man."
>
> —Kuang-Ming Wu, *The Butterfly as Companion*

And while we're on the subject of unexpected connections:

> "Wu-wei ... literally means 'no action,' but not in the sense of sitting all day like a dead tree stump ... rather it means avoiding action that is not spontaneous ... eschewing artfully calculated action and every activity stemming from a profit motive."
>
> —John Blofield, *Taoism*

Complete Openness to the Situation

When we assure ourselves that we "know what we're doing," have we really reached our deepest capacities? Or is there an even more authentic and effective level of action ... one that's rooted in openness to the situation?

> "In the beginner's mind, there are many possibilities; in the expert's mind, there are few."
>
> —Shunryu Suzuki

And consider this mind-opening prospect:

> "It is the receptivity of the Dao that guarantees its inexhaustible possibilities."
>
> —Isabelle Robinet, *The Diverse Interpretation of the* Laozi

And what about the potential for personal liberation to be found in the action we often dismiss as simply "going to work"?

> "Unless you start again, become that trusting, open, surrendered being, the energy can't come in. That is the kingdom of heaven .... Purify enough. Become; immerse. Beauty! Become it. The potter becomes his pot. Embrace the 10,000 beautiful visions. Become one with the universe, and all the energy passes through you. You *are* all the energy .... There is a task to do. You *are* the task."
>
> —Ram Dass, *Be Here Now*

What Is Success?

Is it a level of social status? Or is it something rooted in one's identity and one's ability to contribute?

> "Success is peace of mind, which is a direct result of self-satisfaction in knowing you have done your best to become the best you are capable of becoming."
>
> —John Wooden

Do we find our true selves in our possessions, our relationships, our accomplishments? Or is the answer to the question "Who am I?" to be found in following a path of spontaneous action?

> "The source of all discrimination, it is found, lies in the tendency to split one's identity into many different "I's" by comparing oneself with others and making deliberate choices …. Any conscious ego-identity, according to Zhuangzi, will always be one-sided. It shifts continuously from one 'I' to the next without any constancy …. Having understood this flaw in one's thinking, the fundamental error in one's conception of oneself and the world, one can now proceed to get rid of it. The process that leads to spontaneity is called 'forgetting': first one forgets living beings without, then one forgets mental classifications within. Increasingly one merges one's mind with the Tao, the underlying flow of existence as such …."
>
> —Livia Kohn, *Early Chinese Mysticism*

> **Tao Then, Tao Now**
>
> "[T]he way to success lies in apprehending and giving actuality to the way of the universe [Tao], which, as a law running through end and beginning, brings about all phenomena in time."
>
> —Richard Wilhelm, in the Introduction to the *I Ching*, or *Book of Changes* (Wilhelm and Baynes, trans., Princeton University Press, 1967)

Intuition, Not Belief

When we "have a feeling" about what should happen next in a given task and act on that feeling, have we somehow opened ourselves to a level of functioning that transcends intellectual argument?

> "We develop and trust our intuition as our direct connection to the Tao. We heed the intelligence of our whole body, not only our brain. And we learn through our own environment, which of course includes ourselves. And just as the Tao functions in a manner to promote harmony and balance, our own actions, performed in the spirit of wu-wei, produce the same result …. From a Taoist point of view, it is our cherished beliefs—that we exist as separate beings, that we can exercise a willful control over all situations, and that our role is to conquer our environment—that lead to a state of disharmony and imbalance."
>
> —Ted Kardash, "Taoism—the Wu-Wei Principle" (www.jadedragon.com, 1998)

Consider this insight on how intuition is likely to express itself:

> "One acts only at an irresistible urge. Therefore one experiences no 'inner turmoil' and naturally ceases to meddle with things or with men, going after nothing, welcoming nothing ...."
>
> —Kuang-Ming Wu, *Chuang Tzu*

Tao Then, Tao Now

"The journey is the reward."
—Traditional Taoist maxim

Or this unassailable reasoning from one of Hollywood's great directors:

> "Trust your own instinct. Your mistakes might as well be your own, instead of someone else's."
>
> —Billy Wilder

Detachment

What does Taoism tell us about undertaking a task for its own sake and not for the reward we may be tempted to associate with it?

> "Detachment, forgetfulness of results, and abandonment of all hope of profit."
>
> —Zhuangzi's elements of skill

And here's an interesting restatement of the same principle in a contemporary context:

> "Tao of Steve Rule No. 1: Eliminate your desires. If you're thinking about getting laid, you're finished. A woman can smell an agenda."
>
> —From *The Tao of Steve*, screenplay by Jenniphr Goodman and Greer Goodman (2000)

"Nothing Is Initiated from the Ego-Self"

"When one seeks to regulate something,
He is in fact going contrary to it.
Where he seeks to embellish something,
He is in fact harming it.
Nonaction does not mean being completely inert,
But rather that nothing is initiated from the ego-self."

—From *Huai Nan Tzu* (Roger T. Ames, trans.)

The Last Word

How do you know when you're done? True skill has an economy of action and direction that is instantly (and intuitively) recognizable.

> "Everything should be as simple as possible—but not simpler."
> —Albert Einstein

That's good enough for us.

The Least You Need to Know

- In the Taoist view, true skill embraces values of responsiveness to a situation and authentic acceptance of your connections with nature that are sometimes left out of the equation by Western focus on principles and conscious thinking and reasoning.

- The notion of skill as an expression of the Tao is addressed by Laozi and examined in depth by Zhuangzi.

- Mastery of a limited skill often expresses itself in a sensation of "losing oneself." This attitude toward skill can be expanded to encompass all practice in life. Anyone can use it in any art, discipline, or even ritual activity.

Chapter 14

What Taoism Teaches About Life and Death

In This Chapter

- ◆ Understanding emptiness
- ◆ Coming to terms with the drama of life and death
- ◆ Listening to the sages

Emptiness may seem, to the Westerner, a strange idea around which to address the challenges associated with the cycle of birth and death. All the same, there it is, waiting.

Running on Empty

For all the talk of immortality, youth-preserving potions, and life extension by means of breath control that has captured the imagination and attention of countless Taoists through the centuries, an even deeper idea within the tradition seems to be rooted in an understanding of the cycle of life and death. This understanding holds that all physical transformations—including those associated with human birth and death—are part of the cosmic process we have called the Great Tao.

One analysis of the cosmos (Wang Bi) envisions it as nonbeing at the center, giving rise to and controlling being. The alternative view (Guo Xiang) just has being giving rise to itself in an endless cycle of interdependence. There is no nothing, so nothing at the center.

For a Taoist, the way to realize the emptiness is simply to realize that it is not there. There is only this life—being. Wang Bi's notion of a primal emptiness, *ben wu* or *wu ji* (from the *I Ching*), added a cosmology to Taoism that provided important parallels with Buddhism that facilitated its entrance into China. It resonates as well with other mystical expressions in distant traditions.

 On the Path _____

The *Daode Jing's* use of negative knowledge or reversal leads it frequently to emphasize the value of *wu* (nonbeing) in guiding our choices. Chapter 4 counsels that "[t]he Tao is like an empty container; it can never be emptied and can never be filled. Infinitely deep, it is the source of all things; it dulls the sharp, unties the knotted, shades the lighted, and unites all of creation with dust. It is hidden but always present."

—McDonald translation

Thirty Spokes

As anyone familiar with the *Daode Jing* can attest, there is frequent use of the notion of emptiness. Consider the following:

The Emptiness Inside

"Thirty spokes are joined together in a wheel,
But it is the center hole
That allows the wheel to function.
We mold clay into a pot,
But it is the emptiness inside
That makes the vessel useful.
We fashion wood for a house,
But it is the emptiness inside
That makes it livable.
We work with the substantial,
But the emptiness is what we use."

—*Daode Jing*, chapter 5 (McDonald translation)

The Taoist notion of wu (nonbeing) seemed a natural counterpart of the Buddhist notion of *kong* (emptiness). An intriguing Zen parallel with the previous passage suggests that the evocative initial image of the wheel may be far more than a simple engineering illustration. In *The Gateless Gate* (available at www.ibiblio.org/zen/cgi-bin/koan-index.pl), the Zen master Mu-mon deconstructs the image with a *koan* (teaching riddle) that goes something like this:

> "Once there was a master wheelwright in China who built two wheels, each with fifty spokes. What kind of wheel would result if one were to take away the hub? What kind of wheelwright would that be?"

The idea of a great wheel without a hub may seem logically absurd. And yet Mu-mon (the fool!) goes on to assure us that, when the wheel without a hub rotates, it is so powerful in its course that it is impossible for anyone to stop, so powerful that it rotates above the heavens, under the earth, and in all four directions simultaneously.

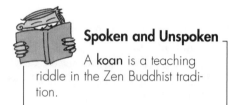

Spoken and Unspoken

A **koan** is a teaching riddle in the Zen Buddhist tradition.

Neo-Taoism and its influence on Zen Buddhism both reflect the Chinese tendency to make nothing something. Only Guo Xiang pointedly resists this urge to incoherence. Later Taoists and Zen express this notion of a "something" that is both vast and unfilled, and both imply or state outright that this "something" (or is it nothing?) resides as the source of all perceived things. We won't try to explain this attraction to oxymoronic paradoxes by analyzing them. Let us instead pose a few questions that may be helpful in reaching a useful understanding of the Taoist view of the cycles of life and death.

- Is emptiness really necessary to there being being?
- Does being "rest on" emptiness?
- Are the galaxy clusters radiating spokes extending from a black hole (or whole) at the center?
- *Is* there an utterly empty center?
- Could the best and most direct response to questions about the "meaning of life and death" simply be "Nothing"? (Is "You must find the meaning of life in life" not the same answer?)

Encountering the Emptiness

A Westerner may decide that a nature religion like Taoism undermines the "meaning of life" because he is used to thinking that questions about life require a transcendental state, realm, or being. For some people, there must be something *outside* this life to give meaning to it—"God's plan," for instance.

Full absorption, participation, and appreciation of this life, Taoists hold, requires accepting that *nothing* lies outside or beyond it—the very nothing on which constrasting existence depends. This insight is intended to guide us back to the present moment and force us to accept here and now as the locus of whatever meaning life has. For a Taoist, that is not taking meaning away, but learning to imbue nature (including your self-nature and ordinary activities) with awesome meaning and value. However we come to grips with the advice to seek meaning "where we are," it helps to accept that life is part of an endless process of transformation of being from form to form. That does not make it less beautiful or valuable, nor does it make life less spiritual or divine. The divinity lies in nature— not viewed as a creation of something with true value, but viewed as just here—from nothing! In chapter 6 of the *Daode Jing* we read, "The spirit of emptiness is immortal; it is called the Great Mother, because it gives birth to Heaven and Earth." Chapter 75 of the *Daode Jing* counsels, "Only those who do not cling to their lives can save it" (both quotes: McDonald translation).

In other words, what are we searching for when we are searching for ourselves? When we find it, isn't it just where we left it?

Acceptance of the Moment

Finding something to say "yes" to in the present moment is a common theme in Taoist thought and Zen's "every-minute" practice. This means focusing on what you are doing— not on eternal or transcendent meaning about the nature of life or the reason for death. A Taoist might counsel, "Don't spend time wondering whether there's a bigger plan you should be trying to fulfill; don't waste energy trying to manipulate, predict, or analyze that bigger plan. Do your thing!"

In chapter 29 of the *Daode Jing* we read that "[t]he Master accepts things as they are, and out of compassion avoids extravagance, excess, and extremes."

Here's a contemporary example of that practice. In his classic spiritual overview, *Be Here Now*, the Western-scholar-turned-Eastern-influenced-mystic Ram Dass (a.k.a. Dr. Richard Alpert) recounts a story involving a man he met in India whose name was Bhagwan Dass. Having been impressed with this young man's spiritual insights, Alpert agreed to follow him through the Himalayas. During the trip, the two men encountered a way of life very different from that which Alpert had left behind in the United States.

Alpert describes Bhagwan Dass as a forbidding figure, someone capable of imparting important lessons through silence and brief reprimands. For instance, Alpert would start speaking of an experience he and one of his colleagues had undertaken and would hear a stony reply: "Don't think about the past—just be here now." A long pause would follow, after which Alpert would ask how long the current phase of the journey was likely to last. Bhagwan Dass would urge him not to be distracted by thoughts of the future. Another pause would descend, and then Alpert would mention that he hadn't been sleeping well, as a result of which he had had pain in his hips. Bhagwan Dass would answer, "Emotions are like waves; watch them disappear in the vast, calm ocean."

Little was left of the rational Western academic's social "ammunition" once stories of the past, insights or worries about the future, and emotional reactions were laid aside. It is that way, of course, for all of us. Do we dare to be silent enough to listen for the sound of emptiness?

Taoism teaches the importance of listening carefully to the moment without distraction and following its directions attentively.

> **On the Path**
>
> Ram Dass (Richard Alpert) is a spiritual writer and lecturer whose spiritual transformation was sparked by a memorable journey to India. His book *Be Here Now* (Crown, 1971) synthesized many elements of Hindu, Zen Buddhist, Sikh, Jewish, and Christian religious practices. The book was hugely influential among countercultural baby boomers in the United States in the early 1970s.

Transcending the Illusion of Selfhood

Zhuangzi's famous parable of the butterfly can be read to embellish this point. While a butterfly, he flew with energy and total absorption, happy and fulfilled. Suddenly he was Zhuangzi ... and as the philosopher he immediately became absorbed in a philosophical problem! ("Is the butterfly actually dreaming the man?")

In the Taoist view, human beings are particularly complex manifestations of the interplay of yin and yang. They are not separate from the processes that generate, sustain, and reabsorb them. In classical Taoist philosophy, it is not hard to detect a certain indifference to those who would drag their heels in an attempt to slow down the seasons, oversentimentalize one's own role in the great drama, or otherwise cling to the transient spectacle of self-expression. One gets the sense that those who would elevate the self (or attempt to preserve it at all costs, or contrast it obsessively with the rest of creation) are regarded by the great Taoist sages as taking a narrow perspective.

The sage Yan Hsuing, who lived more than three centuries after Zhaungzi died, wrote, "The sky and sun rotate and the weak and strong interact. They return to their original position and thus the beginning and end are determined. Life and death succeed each other and thus the nature and the destiny are made clear. Looking up, we see the form of the heavens. Looking down, we see the condition of the earth. We examine our nature and understand our destiny. We trace our beginning and see our end" (Yang Hsiung, *Tai Hsuan Ching*, Michael Nylan, trans., State University of New York Press, 1993).

Transcending Ritualized Instructions for Living Life

Most Taoists would intuitively reject an emphasis on ritualized behavior and etiquette, preferring instead to emphasize spontaneity and creative responses to situations. This approach, which has historically distinguished Taoism from Confucianism, guides all of one's interactions with the world. Yet it is important to understand that even ritual is natural. The trick is to realize that ritual rests on an endless regression of other taos of interpretation, adaptation, and evaluation.

Listening and Responding

When we follow tao, we listen to instructions using words, rules, or distinctions. What tao do we use to identify the words? To understand the rules? To make the distinctions? Whenever we follow a tao, we are following an infinite chain of taos of interpretation and application. It is tao all the way down! Nothing is standing at the bottom supporting it as a command.

Tao is just here—and as a result, we are guided easily on a path through living and dying.

Any listening evokes responding. When we respond, we rely on ways that guide us spontaneously. Does emptiness lie at the bottom? Zhuangzi said, "A sage embraces things first. The common person, on the other hand, will make distinctions among things, and then make a show for others of all the distinctions they have made. This is why I say: When people make discriminations there is something they don't see."

Melody and Harmony: Life and Death and Tao

Following are a "coda" to the ongoing symphony of human teaching and observation composed over the centuries regarding tao as it relates to the great drama of life and death.

Please note again that the voices that follow are not all advocates of Taoism. They offer ways of thinking about life, death, and meaning that resonate with Taoist themes.

No External Path

Does meaning reside in making a journey … or in arriving at a destination?

"Tao Qian's famous 'Peach Blossom Spring' told the story of a fisherman who discovered by chance an idyllic community of Chinese who centuries earlier had fled a war-torn land and had since lived in perfect simplicity, harmony, and peace, obliviously unaware of the turmoil of history beyond their grove. Although these utopians urged him to stay, the fisherman left to share his discovery with friends and a local official. He could never find his way back. He did not understand that this ideal world was to be found not by following an external path, but a spiritual path; it was a state of mind, and attitude, that comprised the utopia."

—Judith A. Berling, "Taoism, or the Way" (*Focus on Asian Studies*, Vol. II, No. 1, 1982)

Visions

If God is everywhere and everything, does God look back at us from the bathroom mirror?

"The eye with which I see God is the same eye with which God sees me."

—Meister Eckhart

Zhuangzi's Thoughts on Death

Who are we to say that the following extract isn't the most important you'll come across in this book?

"Who am I to say that rejoicing in life is not an illusion? Who am I to say that in despising death we do not resemble children who are lost and have no idea how to get home? Lady Li was born the daughter of a man who worked in Ai as a border guard. When she was taken into captivity by the authorities in Jin, she wept bitterly, and her clothes became drenched. Yet once she made her way to the palace, and enjoyed the favors of the king's bed, and ate sumptuous meals, she repented her weeping. Who am I to say that dead people do not repent all of their graspings to maintain hold of life? Someone who has a dream of getting drunk may well weep in the morning out of regret. Someone who has a dream of weeping may decide to go out hunting the next morning. When we are dreaming, we have no idea that we dream. We may even dream that we interpret a dream! On awakening, we know to treat it as dreaming. Then there may be a Great Awakening and we will know to treat this as a Great Dream; fools will think themselves awake, proudly knowing it and saying 'I am a ruler,' or 'I am a shepherd.' Stubborn! Confucius and you are dreaming and I, who call you dreamers, am also dreaming. This is the saying. And it's called dangerous dangling. After ten thousand generations we may chance on a great sage who knows how to explain this. We see them every morning and evening."

—Zhuangzi

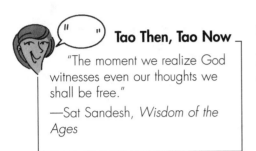

"The moment we realize God witnesses even our thoughts we shall be free."

—Sat Sandesh, *Wisdom of the Ages*

Ch-Ch-Changes

In the following quote, is it the man or the river that changes?

"No man ever steps in the same river twice."

—Heraclitus

Beyond Duality

How definitive are (apparent) opposites, anyway?

"Everything leads us to believe that there exists a certain point of the intelligence at which life and death, the real and the imaginary, the past and the future ... cease to be perceived as opposites."

—André Breton

Beyond Grief

Is the passing of a loved one a reason for agony or celebration?

"The Taoist criticizes those who cause tragic associations to be felt by others at their physical demise, and the primary reason for this is that it is a measure of how well we have passed through life that we avoid interfering with its balanced nature."

—"Life and Death" (www.thetemple.com/TheWesternTaoist, 2001)

"More Nearly 'Us' Than 'I'"

"Underneath the superficial self, which pays attention to this and that, there is another self more really *us* than *I*. And the more you become aware of the unknown self—if you become aware of it—the more you realize that it is inseparably connected with everything that is. You are a function of this total galaxy, bounded by the Milky Way, and this galaxy is a function of all other galaxies. You are that vast thing that you see far, far off with great telescopes. You look and look, and one day you are going to wake up and say, 'Why, that's me!' And in knowing that, you know that you never die."

—Alan Watts, *The Tao of Philosophy*

And Zhuangzi Has the Last Word

What's to conclude a song of life and death? The final note of this piece comes from Taoism's great player:

> "Happiness is the absence of striving for happiness."
>
> —Zhuangzi

The Least You Need to Know

- Nonbeing is a puzzling but pervasive concept within Taoism.
- Tao has no transcendent support—it is just here, and it's tao all the way down. Meaning comes from tao.
- Find meaning in activities where you are.
- Humans are manifestations of the natural interplay of yin and yang. They are not separate from the processes that generate, sustain, and reabsorb them.
- While Taoists are suspicious of ritualized behavior and etiquette, preferring instead to emphasize spontaneity and adherence to natural processes, the deeper message is that rituals are natural and rest on an endless regress of other taos of interpretation, adaptation, and evaluation.

Part 4

Tao Jones: The West Discovers Taoism

Taoism has already touched your life—it just may not have been obvious to you at the time. In this part, you learn about Taoist interconnections with the West's popular culture, science, and environmental movements—and about how Taoism is influencing the ongoing search for meaning and spiritual fulfillment in the West.

Chapter 15

The Tao and the Judeo-Christian Tradition

In This Chapter

◆ Preconceptions and challenges
◆ Deconstructing the Gospels
◆ Intriguing parallels with Taoist thought

Here's the biggie: East meets West on the religious front. Or would it be more accurate to say that both East and West have really been talking about more or less the same thing all along? You be the judge.

The Label Problem

Labels can be tricky things. Experience shows that people can feel quite strongly about them. This is especially true with regard to religious matters, where the names and theological assumptions people associate with an established faith tradition can carry enormous emotional weight—and strong associations, both positive or negative.

Taoist Tip-Off _____

Check your preconceptions at the door when considering parallels between Taoism and Western religious observance.

Because of this tendency toward attachment to the names of things, and especially because of peoples' powerful emotional reactions to the two labels "Tao" and "Jesus," we were tempted to skip writing this chapter of the book altogether.

We knew, for instance, that a good percentage—probably a majority—of the people in the West who were most receptive to and interested in Taoism would be skeptical about exploring possible connections with that tradition and the teachings of Jesus. Indeed, for many people, one of the most powerful appeals of an Eastern religious tradition is its apparent lack of connection with Christianity. "Why," such people might ask, "do I need to look again at something I've already seen?"

By the same token, we knew that many—and again, probably most—Christian believers would be just as skeptical. They might even be offended at the idea of examining ancient Taoist teachings and their possible overlaps with the New Testament or with the Hebrew scriptures that Jesus himself clearly studied reverently. Many would ask, "Aren't our scriptures sufficient on their own? What, exactly, is to be gained by comparing them with another system of thought—one that has evolved with little or no influence from the Judeo-Christian tradition? Doesn't such an exercise actually weaken the _Gospel_ message?"

Spoken and Unspoken _____

The four **Gospels** of Matthew, Mark, Luke, and John are the ancient traditional accounts of Jesus' ministry. Each offers a narrative of his life and death. A fifth Gospel, the Gospel of Thomas, was discovered in 1945 (along with many other early Christian texts) and has attracted interest in recent years. It appears to date from between A.D. 70 and 100, or roughly the same time period as the four traditional Gospels. Thomas is a sayings gospel; it does not place Jesus' teachings within a narrative context.

We also knew that members of both groups were likely to react with even deeper skepticism if we responded to such questions by suggesting that the _Daode Jing_ could actually _illuminate_ core teachings contained within the Gospel, and vice versa.

Finally, we knew that the kind of skepticism we were likely to encounter—the kind that arises when someone is asked to rethink apparent religious certainty—has an unfortunate way of turning into fear and then into the kind of "hard-wired" opposition that leads to closed minds.

And Yet ...

The parallels between Taoism and Christianity are there. They are striking, they demand not to be ignored, and they support and extend one's understanding of both the teachings of Laozi and the teachings of Jesus.

Intriguingly, these parallels cast a light on a side of Christianity that we believe has received less attention than it deserves—namely, the path toward embracing the eternal unity of apparent opposites. This timeless approach is in fact suggested again and again within the challenging, frequently nature-based, and seemingly paradoxical teachings of Jesus of Nazareth. So we decided to go ahead and write about them here, in the hope that doing so might help reveal something new and exciting.

We can only hope that the connections suggested here are as interesting to those on either side of the religious fence as they are to us. And we can hope, too, to capture the interest of those willing to entertain the possibility that the fence itself is illusory.

 Tao Then, Tao Now

Thomas Merton (1915–1968), a brilliant Trappist monk and poet, was perhaps the most prominent modern Christian to explore Taoism. His translation of sections of the *Zhuangzi* (*The Way of Chuang Tzu;* New Directions Publishing Corporation, 1965) was particularly influential.

On the Path

Within the structure of the Christian Gospels, the teaching sayings of Jesus are frequently accompanied by an ancient narrator's "logical" connection of a maxim to a superimposed story or anecdote, or by the ambiguous explanation that Jesus "spoke in parables." These short teaching sayings were transmitted *orally* for 40 to 70 years after Jesus' crucifixion, long before the Gospels were completed. Many of the sayings originally had nothing to do with the longer narratives in which they were later inserted. We believe that, when viewed independently from their (frequently superfluous) story structure and set side-by-side with the teachings of Laozi, the maxims of Jesus contained in the Gospels can take on new and unexpected power.

Challenging Teachings

Like Laozi's lessons, Jesus' teaching sayings challenge us, they suspend apparent "logic" to make a deeper intuitive point, and they confront the listener head-on and leave no room for evasion or complacency. What dogma could encompass such teaching?

In this chapter, we ask you to approach the teachings of two masters who appear, with startling frequency, to be talking about precisely the same things. We offer their parallel

Tao Then, Tao Now

Most of the quotes and stories concerning Jesus that appear in this chapter are derived from the four traditional Gospels. (The exception is one from the Book of Revelation.) For an alternate and equally ancient account of Jesus' sayings, see the Gospel of Thomas in *The Complete Gospels* (Robert J. Miller, ed., Harper San Francisco, 1994).

teachings with no in-depth commentary and with the conviction that these deceptively short adages are not meant to be elucidated briskly within the course of a half-hour sermon or a two-hour college lecture, but rather pondered at length … perhaps for a lifetime.

All the Taoist quotes are attributed to Laozi; all the New Testament quotes are attributed to Jesus or relate exchanges with him. We are not suggesting that Jesus studied Taoism. We are not suggesting that Taoists should become Christians. We are, however, suggesting that looking without preconception at what both Jesus and Laozi actually taught may well open some doors that humanity seems habitually accustomed to bolt shut.

To non-Christians who are inclined to dismiss the teachings of Jesus as the authoritarian pronouncements of a manipulative and paternalistic religious tradition, we ask, "Does what you see in this chapter support that?" And to Christians who have grown accustomed to viewing God as something separate and very distant indeed from themselves, and who see Eastern expressions of spirituality as inherently exotic, intricate, and "out of the mainstream," we ask, "Does what you see in this chapter really support that?"

The Constant and Eternal Name

Both the Bible and Laozi point us toward something constant and enduring.

Taoist Tip-Off

There are many translations of the relevant passages to choose from, and not all the parallels cited in this chapter will show up identically in all translations of the Gospels or of Laozi. Unless otherwise noted, the translations used here are Chad Hansen's translation of the *Daode Jing* and the King James translation of Biblical texts. (See Appendix A, "Recommended Reading," for full details.)

"To guide what can be guided is not constant guiding. To name what can be named is not constant naming. 'Not-exist' names the beginning of the cosmos. 'Exists' names the mother of the ten thousand natural kinds."

—*Daode Jing*, chapter 1

"The tao that can be described
Is not the eternal Tao.
The name that can be spoken
is not the eternal Name.
The nameless is the boundary of Heaven and Earth.
The named is the mother of creation."

—*Daode Jing*, chapter 1 (McDonald translation)

Now compare:

> "And Moses said unto God, Behold, when I come unto the children of Israel, and say unto them, The God of your fathers hath sent me unto you; and they shall say to me, What is his name? what shall I say unto them? And God said unto Moses, I AM THAT I AM: And he said, Thus shalt thou say unto the children of Israel, I AM hath sent me unto you."
>
> —Exodus 3:13–14

> "I appeared to Abraham, to Isaac, and to Jacob as God Almighty, though I did not reveal my name, the LORD, to them."
>
> —Exodus 6:3

> "In the beginning was the Word, and the Word was with God, and the Word was God. The same was in the beginning with God. All things were made by him; and without him was not any thing made that was made."
>
> —John 1:1–3

Beginnings and Endings

Both Jesus and Laozi isolate a kind of transcendent ambiguity about ultimate beginnings and endings.

> "'Exists' and 'not-exists' mutually sprout."
>
> —*Daode Jing*, chapter 2

> "Since the beginning of time, the Tao has always existed.
> It is beyond *existing* and *not existing*."
>
> —*Daode Jing*, chapter 21 (McDonald translation)

Now compare:

> "Verily, verily, I say unto you, Before Abraham was, I am."
>
> —John 8:58

> "I am Alpha and Omega, the beginning and the ending, saith the Lord, which is, and which was, and which is to come, the Almighty."
>
> —Revelation 1:8

Possessions

Both Jesus and Laozi warn against overreliance on material possessions.

> "When gold and jade fill the hall, you can't keep any of it.
> Rich, ennobled, and thus proud bequeaths ruin."
>
> —*Daode Jing*, chapter 9

> "If you overvalue possessions, people will begin to steal.
> Do not display your treasures, or people will become envious.
> The Master leads by emptying people's minds."
>
> —*Daode Jing*, chapter 3 (McDonald translation)

Now compare:

> "The ground of a certain rich man brought forth plentifully. And he thought within himself, saying, 'What shall I do, because I have no room where to bestow my fruits?' And he said, 'This I will do. I will pull down my barns, and build greater, and there will I bestow all my fruits and my goods. And I will say to my soul, "Soul, thou hast much goods laid up for many years; take thine ease, eat, drink, and be merry."' But God said unto him, 'Thou fool, this night thy soul shall be required of thee. Then whose shall those things be, which thou hast provided?' So is he that layeth up treasure for himself, and is not rich toward God."
>
> —Luke 12:16–21

> "Lay not up for yourselves treasures upon earth, where moth and rust doth corrupt, and where thieves break through and steal: But lay up for yourselves treasure in heaven, where neither moth or rust doth corrupt, and where thieves do not break through nor steal."
>
> —Matthew 6:19–20

First and Last

Both Jesus and Laozi warn against struggling for high position.

> "Sages 'later' themselves—and yet they come first!"
>
> —*Daode Jing*, chapter 7

> "The Master puts himself last, and finds himself in the place of authority."
>
> —*Daode Jing*, chapter 7 (adapted from McDonald translation)

"The noble uses the plebeian as its base.
The high uses the low as its foundation."
—*Daode Jing*, chapter 39

"Those who esteem themselves do not become elders."
—*Daode Jing*, chapter 24

"The reason rivers and oceans can act as kings of a hundred valleys
Is that they are good at lowering themselves."
—*Daode Jing*, chapter 66

"That which is low—raise them up!"
—*Daode Jing*, chapter 77

"Taking the non-auspicious state—this is being deemed king of the social world."
—*Daode Jing*, chapter 78

Now compare:

"Many that are first shall be last; and the last shall be first."
—Matthew 19:30

"Therefore when thou doest thine alms, do not sound a trumpet before thee, as the hypocrites do in the synagogues and in the streets, that they may have glory of men. Verily I say unto you, They have their reward."
—Matthew 6:2

"And he sat down, and called the twelve, and saith unto them, If any man desire to be first, the same shall be last of all, and servant of all."
—Mark 9:35

"Blessed are the meek: for they shall inherit the earth."
—Matthew 5:5

"Whosoever therefore shall humble himself as this little child, the same is greatest in the kingdom of heaven."
—Matthew 18:4

Transcending Apparent Division

Both Jesus and Laozi suggest that we should be skeptical of apparent opposites.

> "There is a thing-kind made up of a mix.
> It emerges before the cosmos.
> Solitary! Inchoate!
> Self-grounded and unchanging!
> Permeating all processes without extremity."
>
> —*Daode Jing*, chapter 25

> "The Tao does not choose sides."
>
> —*Daode Jing*, chapter 79 (McDonald translation)

> "The ten thousand natural kinds achieve oneness in life."
>
> —*Daode Jing*, chapter 39

> "When heaven lacks that with which to become clear,
> We're on the point of fearing splitting!"
>
> —*Daode Jing*, chapter 39

Now compare:

> "Every kingdom divided against itself is brought to desolation; and every city or house divided against itself shall not stand."
>
> —Matthew 12:25

> "And one of the company said unto him, Master, speak to my brother, that he divide the inheritance with me. And he said unto him, Man, who made me a judge or a divider …?"
>
> —Luke 12:13–14

> "But I say unto you, Love your enemies, bless them that curse you, do good to them that hate you, and pray for them which despitefully use you, and persecute you; That ye may be the children of your Father which is in heaven: for he maketh his sun to rise on the evil on the good, and sendeth rain on the just and on the unjust."
>
> —Matthew 5:44–45

The Problem with Talking

Both Jesus and Laozi recognize the limits of language.

> "Many words, and numbers unlimited, are not as good as holding the center."
>
> —*Daode Jing*, chapter 5

> "If you try to talk your way into a better life, there will be no end to your trouble."
>
> —*Daode Jing*, chapter 52 (McDonald translation)

> "Those who know to act do not speak.
> Those who speak do not know to act."
>
> —*Daode Jing*, chapter 56

Tao Then, Tao Now

In the version of the "divider" story that appears in the Gospel of Thomas, Jesus concludes the lesson by turning to his disciples and asking, "I'm not a divider, am I?" He sounds, for all the world, like Zhuangzi.

Now compare:

> "Swear not at all; neither by heaven; for it is God's throne: nor by the earth; for it is his footstool: neither by Jerusalem; for it is the city of the great King. Neither shalt thou swear by thy head, because thou canst not make one hair white or black. But let your communication be, Yea, yea; Nay, nay: for whatsoever is more than these cometh of evil."
>
> —Matthew 5:34–37

> "And when thou prayest, thou shalt not be as the hypocrites are: for they love to pray standing in the synagogues and in the corners of the streets, that they may be seen of man. Verily I say unto you, They have their reward. But thou, when thou prayest, enter into thy closet, and when thou has shut thy door, pray to thy Father which is in secret, and thy Father which seeth in secret shall reward thee openly."
>
> —Matthew 6:5–6

> "Use not vain repetitions, as the heathen do: for they think that they shall be heard for their much speaking. Be not ye therefore like unto them: for your Father knoweth what things ye have need of, before ye ask him."
>
> —Matthew 6:7–8

Difficulty in Knowing How

Both Jesus and Laozi claim (often to the consternation of their followers!) that their teachings are simplicity itself.

> "My words are profoundly easy to know,
> Profoundly easy to perform.
> (Yet) In the social world, none are able to know or perform."
>
> —*Daode Jing*, chapter 70

Now compare:

> "Come unto me, all ye that labor and are heavy laden, and I will give you rest. Take my yoke upon you, and learn of me; for I am meek and lowly in heart: and ye shall find rest unto your souls. For my yoke is easy, and my burden is light."
>
> —Matthew 11:28–30

The Silent Guiding Spirit

Both Jesus and Laozi tell us that there is an underlying process that silently and reliably sustains itself.

> "Looking at it, it is not visible.
> Listening to it, it is not audible."
>
> —*Daode Jing*, chapter 35

> "Administer a 'no-words' teaching. The ten thousand natural kinds work by it and don't make phrases. They sprout—but don't 'exist.' They deem, they act, yet they don't rely on anything. They accomplish their work and don't dwell in it."
>
> —*Daode Jing*, chapter 2

Now compare:

> "So is the kingdom of God, as if a man should cast seed into the ground; And should sleep, and rise day and night, and the seed should spring and grow up, he knoweth not how."
>
> —Mark 4:26–27

> "Whereunto shall I liken the kingdom of God? It is like leaven, which a woman took and hid in three measures of meal, till the whole was leavened."
>
> —Luke 13:20–21

"The wind bloweth where it listeth, and thou hearest the sound thereof, but canst not tell whence it cometh, and whither it goeth: so is every one that is born of the Spirit."

—John 3:8

Be as Children

Both Jesus and Laozi suggest that there is something unexpected and important to be learned from children—even infants.

"In specializing in breath and consummating weakness, can you be a child?"

—*Daode Jing*, chapter 10

"The thickness of implicit virtuosity:
Compare it to a robust infant.
Bees, scorpions, and snakes do not sting him.
Ferocious animals do not seize him.
Birds of prey do not take him.
His bones are weak, his muscles soft, yet he has a firm grasp.
He does not yet know to join male and female, yet he is completely ready.
This is the instinct's having arrived."

—*Daode Jing*, chapter 55

Now compare:

"Marvel not that I said unto thee, Ye must be born again."

—John 3:7

"I thank thee, O Father, Lord of heaven and earth, because thou hast hid these things from the wise and prudent, and hast revealed them unto babes."

—Matthew 11:25

"And Jesus called a little child unto him, and set him in the midst of them, and said, Verily I say unto you, except ye be converted, and become as little children, ye shall not enter the kingdom of heaven."

—Matthew 18:2–3

Clarity and Full Commitment to the Moment

Both Jesus and Laozi emphasize attentive presence and clarity in every moment.

> "Who can, while muddy, using calmness gradually become clear?"
>
> —*Daode Jing*, chapter 15

> "Go to the limits of emptiness;
> Take on quiet dependability."
>
> —*Daode Jing*, chapter 16

> "The people, in pursuing social affairs, take the phase of 'nearly completed' as constant—and then they wreck it."
>
> —*Daode Jing*, chapter 64

Now compare:

> "Now it came to pass, as they went, that he entered into a certain village, and a certain woman named Martha received him into her house. And she had a sister called Mary, which also sat at Jesus' feet, and heard his word. But Martha was cumbered about much serving, and came to him, and said, Lord, dost thou not care that my sister hath left me to serve alone? Bid her therefore that she help me. And Jesus answered her and said, Martha, Martha, thou art careful and troubled about many things: But one thing is needful; And Mary hath chosen that good part, which shall not be taken from her."
>
> —Luke 10:38–42

> "Either what woman having ten pieces of silver, if she lose one piece, doth not light a candle, and sweep the house, and seek diligently till she find it?"
>
> —Luke 15:8

> "No man, having put his hand to the plough, and looking back, is fit for the kingdom of God."
>
> —Luke 9:62

> "I know thy works, that thou art neither cold nor hot: I would thou wert cold or hot. So then because thou art lukewarm, and neither cold nor hot, I will spue thee out of my mouth."
>
> —Revelation 3:15–16

Beyond the Self

Both Jesus and Laozi point intriguingly toward a true self that transcends limitations.

> "[The sages can] 'outside' themselves—and yet they abide!"
>
> —*Daode Jing*, chapter 7

> "Deeming that I have a self is what makes it possible for me to have trouble. And if I had no self, what trouble could I have?"
>
> —*Daode Jing*, chapter 13

> "If you want to become whole,
> first let your self become broken."
>
> —*Daode Jing*, chapter 22 (McDonald translation)

Now compare:

> "If any man will come after me, let him deny himself, and take up his cross, and follow me."
>
> —Matthew 16:24

> "No man can enter into a strong man's house, and spoil his goods, except he will first bind the strong man; and then he will spoil his house."
>
> —Mark 3:27

> "Follow me; and let the dead bury their dead."
>
> —Matthew 8:22

On Nonattachment

Both Jesus and Laozi emphasize nonattachment.

> "Other people have more than they need;
> I alone seem to possess nothing.
> I am lost and drift about with no place to go."
>
> —*Daode Jing*, chapter 20 (McDonald translation)

> "In losing, much is gained,
> and in gaining, much is lost."
>
> —*Daode Jing*, chapter 42 (McDonald translation)

"Your self or your commodities—which counts more?"

—*Daode Jing*, chapter 44

Now compare:

"Foxes have holes, and the birds of the air have nests; but the Son of Man hath not where to lay his head."

—Luke 9:58

"For what is a man advantaged, if he gain the whole world, and lose himself, or be cast away?"

—Luke 9:25

The Great Guide That Sustains All

Both Jesus and Laozi point us toward a great and sustaining guide.

"The great guide is everywhere!
Thus it can 'left' the 'right.'
The ten thousand natural kinds depend on it and thus live."

—*Daode Jing*, chapter 34

Now compare:

"Therefore I say unto you, take no thought for your life, what ye shall eat, or what ye shall drink; nor yet for your body, what ye shall put on. Is not the life more than meat, and the body than raiment? Behold the fowls of the air: for they sow not, neither do they reap, nor gather into barns; yet your heavenly Father feedeth them."

—Matthew 6:25–26

"He that received seed into the good ground is he that heareth the word, and understandeth it; which also beareth fruit, and bringeth forth, some an hundredfold, some sixty, some thirty."

—Matthew 13:23

And Finally ...

Consider these two remarkable parallels:

"Only those who do not cling to their life can save it."

—*Daode Jing*, chapter 75 (McDonald translation)

"He that loveth his life shall lose it; and he that hateth his life in this world shall keep it unto life eternal."

—John 12:25

The parallels are remarkable. So we close with a question: Is there something important to learn from the way these two great teaching traditions reflect one another?

The Least You Need to Know

◆ Some people are skeptical about the possibility of overlaps between Taoist teachings and the Judeo-Christian tradition. But there they are, waiting to be explored.

◆ It seems likely that teachers in both traditions were talking about more or less the same thing.

The Tao and the Search for Meaning

In This Chapter

- ◆ The search for the best way to live
- ◆ Encountering some complex Taoist wisdom with a Western twist
- ◆ The best advice on meditation strategies for Westerners new to Taoism
- ◆ Other resources

Over the last three decades or so, a small (or perhaps not-so-small) industry has emerged in the West in response to the question "What do ancient Taoist principles tell us about the way to live?" Or even, to use the classic appeal, "What would Taoism tell me about the meaning of life?"

This last question may be asked with a distinctively Western assumption—that for life to have meaning, it must lie in some transcendent purpose, outside of nature.

The Tao of (Fill in the Blank)

Responsively, books have appeared endeavoring to explain to us how to find the way to live; in Taoist principles as applied to surfing, sexuality, physical exercise, sales, motorcycle maintenance, psychotherapy, and (no joke here) dog training—to name just a few of the dozens of published topics.

All of these approaches to Taoism have merit. That's exactly the kind of thing taos are—guides to skill in any area. However, the question is often looking for something less specific—something like a moral guide. There Taoism does not seem as clear-headed and practical.

We think there is a sound explanation. Taoism is not a single moral theory: It's what philosophers call a *meta-theory* (meta-ethics). Its answers are mildly skeptical about any particular moral theory and strongly pluralist about the justifications for moral theories. Admittedly, these are rather abstract positions that could take us quickly out of the area of a book for beginners. Fortunately, we are talking about Taoism, and most of the points can be made, as Zhuangzi does, by means of engaging dialog and funny stories. So we've tried to stick to his examples. We'll do that here, too, and recommend a good story for you to read.

Spoken and Unspoken

A **meta-theory** is a theory at the second level; that is, a theory about theories. Meta-ethics is a theory about whether moral truths are objective or subjective, absolute or relative, rational or emotional, knowable or merely matters of opinion. Meta-ethics usually includes an account of the nature of morality and the meaning of moral terms. Taoism is, thus, a cluster of views about whether tao can be formulated, transmitted, known, or followed reliably, and what taos presuppose.

Although Taoism is mainly about "meta" issues in morality, its views do have practical moral and political conclusions. Essentially these emphasize the importance of open-mindedness, tolerance, curiosity, and awe and respect for nature, all motivated by an appropriate modesty about our ability to know the absolute right way to live. Because we know there are many well-justified ways (at least from their own perspective), the way of wisdom is to find a system that allows people to coexist and communicate with each other.

Since we never will probe to the bottom of the taos that guide us, we are best advised to sustain an appreciation of the complex harmony of nature that underpins all of our moral and rational activity.

We proceed here on the assumption that a beginner may be interested in a summary of a few of the most rewarding popular resources of philosophy, speculation, and practice that incorporate Taoist principles.

Zen and Motorcycles

"The cycle you're working on is a cycle called 'yourself.'"

So runs the tagline from the classic 1970s self-discovery novel *Zen and the Art of Motorcycle Maintenance* (Bantam Books, 1974). Robert Pirsig's dense and rewarding journey through America, philosophical quandary, and the realms of the human psyche will stick with you for years after you read it. It recalls, in an invigorating contemporary setting, key points from Zen practice and Taoist philosophy, and particularly Zhuangzi's observations on skill.

This philosophical exploration takes the form of a father-and-son road trip across the continent. During the journey, author Pirsig uses the protagonist's task of motorcycle upkeep to address questions of technology, virtue, and balance. He delightfully illustrates an important point absent from most popular presentations of Taoism: Taoism is not anti-technology, anti-logical, or anti-science. The skill-thrill Cook Ting finds in butchering can be sought in any activity, including mathematics, logic, and motorcycle repair. Pirsig explores a notion suggested by both Taoism and Zen practice, namely that meaning, growth, and virtue are to be found in nothing more (or less) than in unifying utterly with an activity and letting go.

Tackling the Big Questions

The book presents itself as a "study of the art of rationality itself," and sets out an intriguing but ultimately ambiguous philosophical principle (*Quality*) as the point of resolution for many of life's most baffling questions.

This important work, Pirsig's first novel, is, apparently, largely autobiographical. It explores personal—and usually engrossing—encounters with some of the most important questions of twentieth-century philosophy: How has technology affected the way we experience the world in which we live? What is the nature of identity in a changing universe? Can that which is good be defined rationally? If not, how is one to choose the best course of action?

Spoken and Unspoken

"Quality is a characteristic of thought and statement that is recognized by a nonthinking process. Because definitions are a product of rigid, formal thinking, quality cannot be defined."

—*Zen and the Art of Motorcycle Maintenance*

These are, of course, big issues, and a lesser talent would have had fatal difficulties incorporating them as the foundation of a workable novel. Add in the author's desire to meld Eastern concepts of intuitive mindfulness with Western rationalism, and you've got a book that should not, by any reasonable standard of expectation, work. Yet somehow the story hangs together and leaves you feeling energized and aware in a way that few novels do, inspired to follow "the flow" of life attentively and authentically.

Read this book, not for answers, but for an example of intriguing and exhilarating new ways of posing questions to yourself about life. The questions may, in the long run, prove more helpful than any cut-and-dried ideology.

Pirsig's ideal of living a life of "Quality" is a good deal deeper than it may at first sound and has profound resonances with Taoism. It will probably stay with you for quite a while.

Complex Wisdom

One complaint against Pirsig's book has been its intellectualism. It's an informed story in the rational Greek heritage. Those Taoists who think Taoism can only be about poetry and music may find a tension between a sensitive discussion of Western philosophy and the ideas of absorbed engagement that this book exalts. *Zen and the Art of Motorcycle Maintenance* is, to be sure, not an easy book, and it may be tough sledding for some readers. But this work's intellectual rigor is its greatest strength, and it's hard to imagine it in a "boiled-down" version.

Nearly a quarter century after its first publication, Pirsig's book still deserves to be celebrated. We believe that those with a healthy curiosity, a little intellectual stamina, and an attraction to deep philosophical questions are certainly entitled to an introduction to Taoist thought and practice in everyday life. Pirsig's is among the liveliest and most eye-opening.

Check It Out

Check out Robert Pirsig's *Zen and the Art of Motorcycle Maintenance*. For more on Pirsig, visit members.aol.com/fhornig/pirsig.html.

On the Path

Author Benjamin Hoff observed in *The Tao of Pooh* that the simple openness and clarity of Winnie the Pooh offers overlaps with the *Daode Jing*. That this should be so is actually quite appropriate, as the endlessly evocative tone of the ancient Chinese text of Laozi's work has frequently been compared to a nursery rhyme.

The Tao of Pooh

Who is the prototypical Taoist? In *The Tao of Pooh* (Viking Press, 1991), author Benjamin Hoff says it's Winnie the Pooh, A. A. Milne's "bear of very little brain."

If you haven't read Hoff's book, you're in for a treat—and, in all likelihood, a pleasant surprise. The idea that one of the most popular heroes from a classic children's book might actually be a Taoist sage sounds like one of those publishing conceits that almost works, but doesn't quite. Recently, a book comparing Glinda the Good

Witch (from *The Wizard of Oz*) to a Zen master came out; it seemed more than a little forced. After a couple of bad experiences with these "Tao of This" and "Zen of That" packages, one may come to view all such enterprises with skepticism.

With this book, however, you may rest assured that you are in responsible hands.

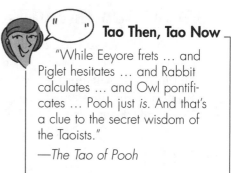

Tao Then, Tao Now

"While Eeyore frets ... and Piglet hesitates ... and Rabbit calculates ... and Owl pontificates ... Pooh just *is*. And that's a clue to the secret wisdom of the Taoists."

—*The Tao of Pooh*

Hoff's gentle tour through the Hundred Acre Wood does, as advertised, offer some astonishing overlaps with the core ideas of Taoism. (It came out in 1983 and has since given rise to a number of similarly packaged but far less eloquent works.) In fact, if you have even the least familiarity with the Pooh stories, there's a good chance that this book will send you scurrying to reconsult the originals to confirm that the passages Hoff quotes really do exist.

Finding that they do, you will then be forced to conclude that, whether he did so accidentally or by design, A. A. Milne created not only a great children's book, but an enduring fable for adults based on timeless spiritual advice.

After you read Hoff, you'll never read the Pooh stories to the kids—or to yourself—in quite the same way again.

Hoff's ideal of simple presence and spontaneity will, in all likelihood, remind you of the importance of approaching life's big questions and challenges with childlike innocence and openness. (Think of Pooh's observant, instinctive use of the large pole needed to fish baby Roo out of the river. It later turned out to be the North Pole!)

Simple Wisdom

As clear and simple as *Zen and the Art of Motorcycle Maintenance* is intricate and occasionally convoluted, *The Tao of Pooh* forms an appropriate complement to Pirsig's complex take on philosophy, technology, alienation, and meaning. Read them both, and you'll have two compelling (and in our view, perfectly balanced) contemporary Western embodiments of Taoist principles for sound living.

Check It Out

Check out Hoff's *The Tao of Pooh*. For more on the book and Hoff, visit www.just-pooh. com/tao.html.

From the Sublime to ...

If you're still not satisfied, then consider this: Taoism is one of the few complex philosophies to have a full-fledged cartoon treatment. Take a look at Tsai Chih Chung's delightful cartoon presentations of Laozi, Zhuangzi, and Zen Buddhism. (He also has books on Confucians, but they're not nearly as fun or funny!) The comics are translated by Brian Bruya and contain a large selection of Taoist and Zen stories, illustrations, and principles.

Check It Out

Check out Tsai Chih Chung's books (Brian Bruya, trans.):

- *Zhuangzi Speaks: The Music of Nature* (Princeton Paperbacks, 1992)
- *The Tao Speaks: Lao-Tzu's Whispers of Wisdom* (Anchor Books, 1995)
- *The Dao of Zhuangzi: The Harmony of Nature* (Anchor Books, 1997)
- *Zen Speaks: Shouts of Nothingness* (Anchor Books, 1994)
- *Zen Masters Wisdom: The Quest for Enlightenment* (Anchor Books, 1998)

From the Ridiculous to ...

If you are or plan to become a philosopher or a serious student of philosophy and want a detailed and analytic account of the conceptual structure of Chinese thought, we humbly recommend you take a look at Chad Hansen's *A Daoist Theory of Chinese Thought* (Oxford University Press, 1992). It takes the (unconventional) view that the "great divide" in world philosophy systems is not between East and West, but between Indo-European and Chinese systems of thought. The book draws on contemporary theories of language both to justify this interpretation and to provide insight into the deep philosophical character of Chinese thought.

This book differs from other accounts by sinologists in that it takes Taoism rather than Confucianism to have the most defensible position in the ancient Chinese philosophical debate. (Standard accounts tend to declare Confucianism the winner and often oversimplify Taoism, consigning it to the role of making silly, confusing, or mystical wise-cracks.)

On the Path

In *A Daoist History of Chinese Thought*, Chad Hansen argues that Chinese thinkers drew mainly on pragmatic insights into language and worked mainly with pragmatic concepts in their arguments. They focused on words rather than on sententials. Their epistemic contexts (i.e., know, believe) were also nonsentential. If you understand this paragraph, you will definitely like the book.

Check It Out

Look for Chad Hansen's *A Daoist Theory of Chinese Thought*. For more on Hansen, visit www.hku.hk/philodep/ch/.

What's Next?

At this point, you may well decide that it's time for a little direct experience. Consider putting philosophically charged analyses and classic children's literature aside for a moment and turn to …

The Tao of Meditation

The Tao of Meditation (Charles E. Tuttle Co., 1991) is a simple, practical introduction to Taoist meditation and is the definitive work on the subject.

Previously, no one had ever attempted to write an accessible textbook for Westerners on tai chi/ Taoist meditation. In this groundbreaking 1991 work, the authors interpret all the essential factors of Taoist meditation—and introduce Westerners with no academic practice to this important topic. Central to the book's message is the necessity of approaching the brief and deceptively simple-sounding question "Who am I?"

Taoist Tip-Off

Don't approach *The Tao of Meditation*'s techniques if you're put off by paradox. The book describes its method as "Using no way as way, having no limitation as limitation." (Having made it this far in the book, though, you should be used to paradox by now.)

This brief work contains just enough theory and philosophy to satisfy the experienced reader, but it is built for beginners. *The Tao of Meditation* is an invaluable resource for anyone interested in Taoist meditative practice.

What Is Man-Made?

"From studying and thinking about the creative process as it is actualized by man, we can next begin to study and think about the creative process as it occurs naturally in the cosmos. What is most important in these two areas of study is that we begin to learn to distinguish between what is man-made and what is natural in ourselves."

—*The Tao of Meditation*, by Tsung Hwa Jou and Hwa Jou Tsug

Check It Out

Check out *The Tao of Meditation* by Tsung Hwa Jou and Hwa Jou Tsug or visit www. tuttlepublishing.com.

And One More Resource ...

You can, of course, turn to the World Wide Web for concise Taoist answers to some of the big questions about life, death, and the Meaning of It All. One good introductory site is www.thetemple.com/alt.philosophy.taoism/taofaq.htm, the frequently asked questions page maintained by the newsgroup alt.philosophy.taoism, which addresses questions like ...

◆ What about God?

◆ Where to Taoists go when they die?

◆ What is a Taoist?

... and so on. Log on and check it out—and then consider joining the newsgroup, which is excellent (see also Chapter 23, "Wired and Wireless").

In addition, the *Stanford Encyclopedia of Philosophy* has extensive sections on Chinese philosophy, including Taoism. You can access it at plato.stanford.edu.

Total Absorption

"Taoism is non-dualistic. Where western religions postulate a supernatural explanation of the wonders of natural existence, Taoism rests in awe of natural existence itself. It takes its guidance from the ways or paths of nature—the Tao .... Sublime religiosity in Taoism is an attitude of focus and absorption we bring to anything we do. A large part of that attitude is an ironic sense that while acting we do not suppose there is any cosmic plan or purpose that justifies what we do .... Taoism's implicit nature-worship may be regarded as pantheism, and its emphasis on total absorption in one's activities is sometimes confused with Western 'mystical experiences.' However, Taoists seldom cite the resulting higher state of awareness as proof of any religious doctrine or being."

—From the alt.philosophy.taoism FAQ page

Notice Any Connections?

Pirsig finds meaning in unifying utterly with an activity and then letting go.

In Hoff's analysis, the attentive Pooh intuitively picks up a nearby stick and, without a trace of self-consciousness or a moment's planning, quickly fishes Roo from the river.

The system outlined in *The Tao of Meditation* emphasizes distinguishing between what is natural and artificial in oneself.

The authors of the alt.philosophy.taoism FAQ page promote a "total absorption in one's activities" that results in a "higher state of awareness."

To the degree that a book like this can point contemporary readers toward an answer to the question "What is the best way to live one's life?" one answer could combine all four of these outlooks.

A Westerner (or anyone else, for that matter) who successfully embraces the Taoist way of life would, therefore, be …

- ◆ Spontaneous
- ◆ Attentive
- ◆ Authentic
- ◆ Absorbed in his or her activities

Laozi and Zhuangzi, we think, would have little problem with the notion that cultivating such characteristics is a good response to the "search for meaning."

So check out the resources in this chapter. Then find something to do well … and do it with full attention!

The Least You Need to Know

- ◆ In *Zen and the Art of Motorcycle Maintenance*, Robert Pirsig explores a notion suggested by both Taoism and Zen practice, namely that meaning, growth, and virtue are to be found in nothing more (or less) than in unifying utterly with the right activity and letting go.
- ◆ In *The Tao of Pooh*, Benjamin Hoff identifies some astonishing overlaps between the Pooh stories and the core ideas of Taoism.
- ◆ *The Tao of Meditation* is a simple, practical, and definitive introduction to Taoist meditation practices.
- ◆ Spontaneousness, attentiveness, authenticity, and absorption in the right activity are likely Taoist responses to the "search for meaning."

Chapter 17

The Tao and Health

In This Chapter

- ◆ Taoist-influenced medicine
- ◆ All about acupuncture and acupressure
- ◆ Benefits of tai chi
- ◆ Learning about herbal medicine
- ◆ Breathing lessons

Did you catch the martial-arts blockbuster *Crouching Tiger, Hidden Dragon* at the local multiplex, on video, or on DVD? If so, you probably remember the sequence near the end of the film in which the hero, played by Chow Yun-Fat, has been infected with a lethal poison by the villain. Someone observes darkly that the poison in question has no antidote.

At this point, the heroine, Michelle Yeoh, vigorously rejects this dour assessment with the words, "*Everything* has an antithesis!"

Now *that's* an action movie built around yin and yang!

Hard as it is to imagine Yeoh's line issuing from the mouth of an American macho icon like Sylvester Stallone or John Wayne, her outburst is perfectly in line with the Taoist spirit of the movie, which, as you may recall, cleaned up at the box office (see Chapter 21, "The Tao and Pop Culture").

As it happens, the jarring (but oddly appropriate) "antithesis" line was also in line with the Taoist spirit of traditional Chinese medicine, which has been the subject of increasing interest in the West since the 1980s. An ancient Taoist saying holds that "For every lock, there is a key; there is also a master key that opens all locks." If that saying didn't inspire the scribe who penned Yeoh's anguished cry, it should have.

In case you were wondering, there was in fact an antidote to the deadly poison Chow-Yun Fat endured in *Crouching Tiger, Hidden Dragon*. (Philosophically speaking, it would seem that there would have to be!) The question was: Would it reach our hero in time?

Body Tao

As *Crouching Tiger, Hidden Dragon* suggests, balance, antithesis, and the willingness to look at the human body as an integrated system (rather than a collection of disparate parts) are characteristics of Taoist-influenced medical practices.

On the Path _____

The ancient Chinese physician Shen Nung, author of *The Yellow Emperor's Classic of Internal Medicine* (the first text on acupuncture), set down important theories regarding blood circulation and the heart 4,000 years before the advent of these ideas in Western medicine.

Thesis and antithesis … toxin and antidote … disease and ease … imbalance and balance … yin and yang. These are concepts that some (though certainly not all) Western physicians have been considering closely, and with something resembling an open mind, in recent years.

That having been said, honesty requires the observation that most Western medical practitioners still appear to regard Taoist-influenced Asian medicine—which has a pedigree of nearly 5,000 years—as an untested, fundamentally experimental movement. The wisdom of that assessment is, of course, open to debate.

Taoist Tip-Off _____

Before embarking on any form of medical treatment, consult with a reliable health professional.

Three Disciplines

It's time to look briefly at Asian medicine as a whole, and at three of the most popular expressions of ancient Taoist ideas to reach the West in the realm of health: tai chi, acupuncture/acupressure, and traditional herbal therapies.

What follows is a brief overview of some rich subject matter. For "where do I go from here" information on these topics, you may also want to see Appendixes B, "Tai Chi Resources," and E, "Taoist-Related Health Resources."

On the Path

A significant amount of overlap exists among various Taoist disciplines; the dividing lines between medical and nonmedical pursuits are not always crystal clear. In this chapter, we examine three traditions with obvious medical applications. Other traditions (such as feng shui) are also regarded as carrying health implications. For a full discussion of the varied interpretations and attributes of Taoist practice, refer to Chapter 8, "Branches of the Tao."

Asian Medicine: An Overview

In his 2001 article "Western and Eastern Medicine Compared" (available at www. acupuncture.com/Acup/Comparison.htm), Al Stone offers the following summary of the divergent approaches of the Western and Asian worlds to the medical arts:

> "Diagnosing the same patient with tremors in her hands, the Western doctor might perform tests to determine [whether] there is a problem in the brain ... [or] the spinal column ... [or perhaps a] lesion .... However, a practitioner of Chinese medicine would quickly [conclude] that that the problem [involved] 'wind' blowing around in the acupuncture channels ... [and] would seek to determine the cause ... which could be deficiency of blood, body fluids, qi energy, or perhaps a high fever. The practitioner of Chinese medicine would look to the color and shape of the tongue to determine what is deficient that is giving rise to the wind, [and] would feel the pulse on the wrist to determine a specific pulse quality that might lead one to a specific diagnosis that includes both the manifestations and the cause. Same symptoms, same signs, same patient, but very different ways of organizing the information."

Tao Then, Tao Now

In the United States, practitioners of Taoist-influenced medical arts face a confusing array of regulations. In some states only M.D.s are permitted to practice acupuncture, and levels of mastery within the discipline achieved by traditional Western doctors may vary widely. (Note, however, that many traditionally trained Western doctors are, in fact, accomplished acupuncture practitioners.) For a listing of traditional Taoist health resources, see Appendix E.

Stone goes on to note that both traditions have their advantages (and their passionate adherents), and acknowledges that Western medicine probably has an edge when it comes to trauma and acute physical problems. He takes the traditional Western treatment

On the Path _____

Centuries-old traditions teach that the flow of qi is essential for the regulation of natural health, and that people whose qi is allowed to flow naturally are healthier than people whose qi is blocked or out of balance.

approach to task, however, for focusing too narrowly on *effects* and overlooking systemic *causes* of everyday ailments. He's not alone. Many contemporary proponents of Asian medicine incorporating Taoist notions of balance, qi, and harmony fault traditional Western medicine for neglecting the interests of the patient as a whole.

Put more simply (and perhaps a little too bluntly), Western medicine is, all too often, predisposed to view patients as petri dishes exhibiting a collection of individualized symptoms. The Taoist-influenced medical tradition, by contrast, focuses on what some Westerners might be inclined to view as "intangibles"—things that cannot be seen, touched, or measured. Taoist-influenced medical practices are more inclined to focus on the patient as a whole rather than focusing exclusively on one or more localized symptoms.

On the Path _____

Where Western medicine is likely to isolate a specific symptom or malady, the ancient Chinese healing arts (which have been profoundly influenced by Taoist thought) are more likely to focus on the patient as a whole and to emphasize the full utilization of the body's natural capacity to heal itself. In the last 10 years, there has been a greater willingness to accept this emphasis in medical practice in certain circles in the West. Seventeen U.S. universities now offer courses on Asian medicine, and acupuncture has been accepted—in a limited capacity—by many within the medical establishment. The National Institutes of Health, for instance, formally acknowledged the acupuncture needle as a medical device during the Clinton administration.

Acupuncture and Acupressure

Acupuncture is the insertion of tiny needles on the surface of the body to positively affect physiological functions. Practitioners of this ancient medical art operate on the assumption that the human body is animated by an energy force (or qi, as mentioned previously) that runs through it, and that blockages of this energy are disruptive to health. Acupuncture aims to restore balance, proper flow, and continuity to the flow of qi by means of the manipulation of *meridians* in the body.

Acupressure aims to manipulate meridians by means of touch, rather than by the insertion of needles. Typically, the practitioner uses the fingers or a special tool. Other variations on standard acupuncture involve the use of the following:

Spoken and Unspoken

In acupuncture, the term **meridian** refers to the pathways of qi energy in the human body. Acupuncture practitioners assume that there are 14 pairs of meridians that run vertically along the surface of the body, as well as two unpaired "main meridians." The connections between these meridians (also known as channels) ensure an even flow of qi.

- Low-level electric impulses
- Wood, metal, or glass jars that form a temporary vacuum over the affected area
- Auriculotherapy (the stimulation of points on the ear believed to correspond with other areas of the body)
- Sound waves
- Lasers
- Heat

The notion of polarity, as one might expect, carries great weight in the field of acupuncture. Meridians or body zones are identified that have to do with some blockage or disruption of qi and their complementary or opposite zones are identified. These opposite zones are the ones that are treated.

Taoist Channel Theory

"The body can be imagined as a unified five segment holographic image or "acugram" composed of …

A spine with a head and torso

A right arm

A left arm

A right leg

A left leg

This energetic body map of meridian symmetry provides us with a way of simply following some of the [Taoist] treatment principles. Acupuncture can be applied to either the arms and/or legs to treat conditions in the spine based on this method. We could also treat a condition in the arm through the leg or a condition in the leg through the arm. The treatment is according to Taoist Channel Theory, which is somewhat different, which … relates to directional functionality and the number of channels and their locations."

—*Trigrams—Meridians and the Kni Chia—Chi Kung Connections: Peals of Wisdom from the Eight Branches Style of Chinese Medicine*, by Jeff Nagle, MA, Lac (www.members.aol.com/bagua64/page2.html)

Does Acupuncture Hurt?

To answer that question: no. A sensation known as *deqi* (*dah-chee*), which is not painful, is, however, often associated with acupuncture treatments. That's probably the most commonly asked question about acupuncture. The second most common is probably "Does it really work?"

Broadly speaking, the answer is yes—at least to the degree that any form of medical therapy "works" (not always, and not in all situations, but more or less reliably).

At the very least, a general acceptance of acupuncture's effectiveness as a strategy for combating pain is now fairly widespread in the Western medical community. Consider the following:

> "A series of doctors … conducted seven surgeries at both Northville State Hospital and at Albert Einstein Medical Center. They used both standard acupuncture and electro-acupuncture techniques. They found that in all cases of surgery (six invasive and one dental), these acupuncture treatments were successful in stopping the pain of surgery without additional anesthetics. In only one case (a repair of inguinal hernia) did the patient complain of 'discomfort,' and only in one additional case did a patient (the same one) complain of post-operative pain."
>
> —"Acupuncture, a Brief Introduction," by Jeffrey A. Singer (www.acupuncture.com, 2001)

Proponents of acupuncture offer similar success stories for patients with arthritis, back problems, muscle spasms, anxiety disorders, depression, migraine headaches, nicotine addiction, and many other ailments. Many traditional Western physicians have been unreceptive to these success stories.

It has taken the Western medical establishment approximately a decade to make a formal acknowledgment of acupuncture's effectiveness in combating pain. Before too many more years pass, it is likely that Western medicine will embrace acupuncture in other ways.

For more information on acupuncture, visit www.acupuncture.com.

Tai Chi

Health benefits are also associated with the user-friendly stretching and extension exercise known as tai chi. The following are some of the many benefits of tai chi:

- ◆ The ability to channel and direct the flow of qi through the meridians of the human body

♦ A long tradition of application for such maladies as hypertension, circulation problems, arthritis, and body pains

♦ Adaptability to people of all ages or physical conditions

The gentle movements of tai chi are meant to overcome the obstacle that Eastern medicine has claimed for centuries is the cause of most physical illness: inactivity. (If that's not something for a nation of couch potatoes to think about seriously, nothing is.) Tai chi's adherents often criticize the most popular Western exercise regimens for failing to incorporate activities that stimulate easy passages of qi through the meridians of the body.

Tai chi is also seen by many as holding advantages over running or similar aerobic activities, which are, as a practical matter, limited to those who already have relatively good health. (Many tai chi enthusiasts are deeply skeptical of the long-term beneficial effects of disruptive high-impact exercise routines such as aerobics.)

Taoist Tip-Off

A reminder: To practitioners, there is no obvious and immediate distinction between the "medical" benefits of the ancient martial art known as tai chi and its "exercise" benefits. The movements associated with tai chi are simply held to promote a functional and healthy flow of qi energy in daily life.

On the Path

A parallel exists between the idea of an adversary when tai chi is applied as a martial art and the notion of illness or disease when the discipline's principles are applied to the healing arts.

Tai Chi and Cardiovascular Activity

"In 1978 noted tai chi instructor Lawrence Galante and an associate conducted an experiment to determine whether tai chi is effective in stimulating cardiovascular development. They used 25 tai chi students ranging in age from 20 to 60 years old as their models. The students had been studying yang-style tai chi short form for a period of one to seven years. Galante and his assistants monitored the pulse rate, blood pressure, and heart rate of all the students before and after they practiced the form. In all cases, the researchers found that if the form was practiced in a low stance, great cardiovascular stimulation occurred—between 60 and 80 percent of the maximum heart rate established by the American Heart Association."

—From "Is Tai Chi the Ultimate Exercise?" by Frank Tetrillo Jr. (www.utah.edu/stc/tai-chi/articles.html)

(Note: The article goes on to note that individuals who suffer from hypertension or are in recovery from heart surgery or other heart problems are advised to perform the movements in what is known as a "high stance." The bottom line is that tai chi's adherents claim that practice of their discipline three times a day can meet circulatory standards established by the AHA.)

In addition to being a form of exercise, tai chi is, of course, also a respected martial arts form (see Chapter 9, "Fifteen Epochs"). Its enthusiasts tend to emphasize its fitness, healing, and meditative qualities over its self-defense applications, however.

For more information on tai chi, visit the Taoist Tai Chi Society at www.taoist.org.

Herbal Medicine

Herbal remedies based on traditional Chinese medicine have grown in popularity in the United States in recent years. Among the most successful (at least in the commercial sense) has been ginseng, and its energy-imparting qualities are undeniable enough to have launched a small industry of "herbal energizer" products. Many other formulations are currently available as well. (A plant known as hai tong pi, for instance, is reputed to be helpful to arthritis sufferers.)

Unfortunately, most Chinese herbal remedies are still categorized as "untested" by Western science. As of this writing, the National Institutes of Health, the Food and Drug Administration, and the Office of Alternative Medicine are still establishing guidelines for the availability and marketing of many Chinese herbal formulations.

We're not doctors, so we're not going to attempt to tell you which herbal preparation to take when. Before you talk to your health professional, however, you may want to do a little research of your own. With that in mind, we offer the following:

- ◆ A detailed listing of herbal resources appears in Appendix E.
- ◆ The subject of Taoist/Chinese herbal medicine is addressed in depth at www. acupuncture.com.
- ◆ A respected guidebook to the subject is *Chinese Herbal Medicine: Materia Medicine*, by Dan Bensky and Andrew Gamble (Eastland Press, Inc., 1999).

And Don't Forget to Breathe

Although it doesn't rank as a separate discipline, the notion that proper breathing plays an essential role in the maintenance of good health is pervasive in Taoism. The following extract (from an ancient inscription on Chinese jade pieces) will illustrate the importance of this principle.

The Vital Breath

"In moving the vital breath [through the body, hold it deep and] thereby accumulate it. Having accumulated it, let it extend. When it extends, it goes downward. After it goes downward, it settles. Once it is settled, it becomes firm. Having become firm, it sprouts. After it sprouts, it grows. Once grown, then it withdraws. Having withdrawn, it becomes celestial. The celestial potency presses upward, the terrestrial potency presses downward. [He who] follows along [with the vital breath] lives; [he who] goes against it dies."

—From "Ku-tai Wen—Tzu Chih Pien Cheng Te Fa-Chan" in *K'ao-Ku* (*Archaeology*) magazine 3 (1972:2–13); quoted in *Tao Te Ching: The Classic Book of Integrity and the Way*, Lao Tzu, translated by Victor H. Mair (Bantam, 1990)

The previous passage is interesting not only because it emphasizes the importance of proper breathing to a healthy life, but also because it has unmistakable parallels with Indian scripture dating between 900 and 200 B.C. Scholars have also noted a number of parallels between ancient Indian texts and certain passages in the *Daode Jing*.

The Tao and the Doctor's Office

A growing number of Western physicians are investing the significant amounts of time and energy necessary to become effective practitioners of the ancient Chinese medical arts. These physicians are combining current Western medical thought with ancient Taoist concepts for treatment.

To learn more about the latest developments in this area, see the *Journal of Alternative and Complementary Medicine*, available at www.liebertpub.com/acm.

The Least You Need to Know

- Balance, antithesis, and the willingness to look at the human body as an integrated system (rather than a collection of disparate parts) are characteristics of Taoist-influenced medical practices.

- Centuries-old traditions teach that the flow of qi is essential for the regulation of natural health and that people whose qi is allowed to flow naturally are healthier than people whose qi is blocked or out of balance.

- Acupuncture aims to restore balance, proper flow, and continuity to the flow of qi by means of the manipulation of meridians in the body.

- The movements associated with tai chi are believed to promote a functional and healthy flow of qi energy in daily life.

- Herbal remedies based on traditional Chinese medicine have grown in popularity in the United States in recent years.

- The notion that proper breathing plays an essential role in the maintenance of good health is pervasive in Taoism.

Chapter 18

Einstein, Meet Laozi

In This Chapter

- ◆ More than you ever wanted to know about waves
- ◆ Even more than that about particles
- ◆ How it all adds up to unity

In this chapter, we examine a truly radical system of thought. This system challenges our most instinctive assumptions about the physical world; defies our own conceptions of the position we hold within that world; rejects the very idea of a separate, abiding self; and makes us think twice about what, exactly, we mean when we use the verb "to be."

It's not Taoism, Buddhism, or any other mystical tradition. It's modern science. In this chapter, you learn how Western science, in pursuing the secrets hidden away in the tiniest compartments of reality, has come face to face with what must certainly have been the last thing it expected to find: the precepts of Taoism.

Who Knew?

It's a good bet that few if any of the scientists who brought about the twentieth century's revolution in physics imagined that they would eventually find

On the Path

In 1916 Albert Einstein expanded his special theory of relativity (which transcended Isaac Newton's reliance on space and time as constant frames of reference) and formulated a general theory of relativity that took into account the effect of gravitation on the shape of space and the progression of time. The general theory of relativity suggests that matter causes space to curve.

Tao Then, Tao Now

Fritjof Capra is a physicist and systems theorist and founder of the Center for Ecoliteracy (www.ecoliteracy.org). He is the author of a number of international best-sellers, including the groundbreaking *The Tao of Physics: An Exploration of the Parallels Between Modern Physics and Eastern Mysticism, Fourth Edition* (Shambhala Publications, 1998).

themselves retracing the steps of ancient Chinese sages. Yet to all appearances, that is what happened.

Here comes the disclaimer: Neither of us are physicists. We are simply reporting on coincidences some physicists report to have found between modern physics and ancient Taoism.

Caution: We are not suggesting that Laozi and Zhuangzi understood particle physics or had anything like the conception of the universe that Einstein had. They reached their conclusions based on their theory of language and human action. Taoism's inherited conceptual structure is different from the classical Western metaphysics (which has to do with enduring particulars with fixed properties). The classic Western view of reality does struggle with quantum reality and relativity in ways that a Taoist view does not ... but this does not show a scientific motivation for Taoist theory.

What follows is a brief summary of what others have observed about these overlaps. (There is a mild joke involved in the use of that word "observed," a joke that will become more obvious as you make your way through this chapter.) For more on the extraordinary subject covered in this chapter, begin with the writings of the physicist Fritjof Capra.

Here's the whole thing in a nutshell. Ready? The discipline of physics—which searches for rules that reliably explain all observed phenomena—started hiccuping unexpectedly in the first half of the twentieth century. Newtonian physics, though still quite adequate for analyzing familiar midrange events, had proved inadequate to the challenges of predicting the outcomes of extremely fast and extremely small events. For very fast events, the work of Einstein brought forward the notion of relativity and a space-time continuum. For very small events, the work of Planck, de Broglie, Schrodinger, Heisenberg, and Dirac brought forth the quantum theory, which holds, among other things, that light can behave as particles (rather than the waves one would expect), and matter can behave as waves (rather than the particles one would expect). These hiccups offered a kind of pattern, and that pattern provided unexpected—for physicists—resonances with Taoist thought.

What This Has to Do with Taoism

To explain, we'll take you on a 25-cent tour of *quantum theory* and Heisenberg's principle of uncertainty. (Relax. It's not as intimidating as it sounds.)

Neither a Wave Nor a Particle

"In 1905, Einstein proposed that light could exist in the form of a particle, a small piece of something known as a particle. This stood in stark contrast to 200 years of experimentation that demonstrated existence of light as a wave. Einstein's proposal showed that light had two distinct and seemingly opposing natures: a wave-like aspect and a particle-like aspect. Niels Bohr, continuing in this field of study, synthesized these opposing aspects of light in his theory of complementarity in 1926, showing that light was neither a wave nor a particle, but was both a wave *and* a particle. A description of light as either one without the other was scientifically inaccurate."

—"The Quantum Universe: An Information Systems Perspective," by William L. Duncan (critical-path.itgo.com/Articlesandcover.html)

The Twenty-Five-Cent Tour

(With apologies to David Letterman.)

10. **Take that, Isaac Newton!** Taken together with the theory of relativity, quantum theory effectively disproved some of the most cherished assumptions of Newtonian physics, for example, the assumptions that time and space do not change, that phenomena can always be analyzed in terms of demonstrable cause and effect, or that these causes and effects can always be observed by an outsider who has no effect on the events being studied. (Distracting side note: Consider also, for comparison's sake, *chaos theory*, a field of mathematics that attempts to "explain the fact that complex and unpredictable results can and will occur in systems that are sensitive to their initial conditions." Source: www.yahoo.com/ask/20010907.html.)

Spoken and Unspoken

Quantum mechanics is the science that studies matter and radiation at the sub-atomic level. **Quantum theory** is a complex theory about the movement and location of sub-atomic particles, the interaction of matter and radiation; it involves the exchange of energy for mass. Particles dissolve into mathematical probabilities of occurrence that our commonsense concepts of objects make unintelligible.

Spoken and Unspoken _____

Equally intriguing brushes with ancient Taoist notions of emptiness, infinity, paradox, self-perpetuation, and the sustaining power of the universe are to be found in the realms of **chaos theory,** which has led to equations—and "fractal" computer images—that repeat themselves infinitely and with great beauty. Some theorize that the principles of chaos theory may illuminate the reproductive processes of nature itself. For more on this endlessly fascinating subject, see *Turbulent Mirror: An Illustrated Guide to Chaos Theory and the Science of Wholeness* (Harper and Row, 1989).

9. **And a one-ah, and a two-ah …** Quantum theory suggests that there is an essential duality, and simultaneously an essential unity, to the universe. (Where have we heard that before?) For instance, light, which one would expect to behave as waves, can also behave as particles; matter, which one would expect to behave as particles, can also behave as waves. Some scientists have theorized that supporting all this is a "flowing wholeness" that transcends any (artificially imposed) division into categories.

8. **Pair off!** Scientists have identified "classical pairs" at the subatomic level. For instance, the position and the momentum of an electron are one such pair. (Wave and particle are another.)

Taoist Tip-Off _____

Don't assume that the theory of relativity and quantum mechanics rendered classical physics useless! It's better to think of Newtonian physics as accurate in the middle range of experience. However, when classical physics encounters extreme phenomena (things that are extremely large, small, fast, or far away), its weaknesses are exposed, and scientists need other tools. So Newton is (Tao alert!) simultaneously essential and insufficient when it comes to assessing the physical world.

7. **Accuracy check!** In measuring events relating to classical pairs, quantum theory holds that there are limits to the degree of accuracy we can expect to impose. These kinds of limitations have nothing to do with the tools we choose to use, as one might be tempted to assume, but rather with that which we're trying to measure.

6. **Ya pays yer money, ya takes yer choice.** These limitations on accuracy are *inverse*. In other words, the *more* we know about one of the elements we're measuring in a classical pair, the *less* we can know about the other. So if we want to know about both the position and the momentum of the electron, we can know *vaguely* about

both of those things. If we want to get more accurate, we have to focus on trying to establish measurements for one of the elements—say, the position. But this information will come at the price of having a correspondingly *lesser* degree of certainty about the electron's momentum.

5. **Whew!** There is no #5. It's just here to give you an opportunity to catch your breath, or to read #6 again if you wish.

4. **Ain't no guarantees at the subatomic level, buddy.** We just learned that we could measure the electron's position "with some certainty"—if we choose to give up a corresponding chunk of certainty about the electron's position. But here's the catch: We can never predict the electron's position *definitively*. In the end, we can only state a level of statistical likelihood that it will show up at some position. Again, this has nothing to do with the methods or tools we employ in measuring the electron.

3. **Huh?** The "no guarantees" idea in #4 raises all kinds of interesting questions about "where the electron really is." The truth is, it isn't anywhere until it's observed somewhere. In other words, quantum mechanics suggests that we have to get out of the habit of thinking of subatomic particles as "really being" anything or anywhere. While we're at it, we might as well come to terms with our own role in the process of "objective" measurement, which brings us to …

2. **You're in the picture whether you like it or not.** The act of *choosing what you want to measure* will inevitably *affect what kind of result you get.* There is no final, objective answer to the question "What exactly is the electron doing?" The observer posing that question ultimately plays a role in the answer. As physicist John Wheeler has put it, scientists in the modern era must begin to consider themselves as participants, rather than as observers.

1. **It all comes down to not mistaking the fish for the fish-trap.** In pondering the implications of items 10 through 2, consider the shrewd assessment on the limits of language attributed to Zhuangzi in chapter 26 of the book that bears his name: "There's a fish-trap for fish; if one catches the fish, one may forget all about the trap. There's a rabbit-snare for rabbits; if one catches the rabbit, one may forget all about the snare." Mathematics now constructs our reality, and the stable objects of common sense have dissolved into probabilities. Zhuangzi's advice illustrates the importance of not assuming that our conceptual scheme "carves reality at the joints."

Conclusion: The goal of quantum mechanics was to learn what subatomic particles were really like—and what was learned was that the tools and preconceptions of quantum mechanics determined the answers one got. Scientists also encountered the inescapable fact that they themselves were part of an inconceivably subtle, self-supporting whole.

We don't know what to call that whole, and the scientists don't seem to, either. For the sake of convenience, let's call it the Tao.

On the Path _____

The theory of the very big and very small come together in the theory of black holes. They begin as stars so large that when they finally run out of fuel and start to collapse, their own gravity accelerates the outer surface to greater than the speed of light, at which point the star … Where *does* all that mass go? Is it Nothing? Pure singularity? (We might as well ask "What is the Tao? Buddha-nature? Nirvana?") The atoms have long since dissolved into the probabilistic mush of quantum mechanics, but does it make any sense to talk of their speed, location, or even time? Black holes are bottomless pits in space-time geometry—the shape of reality.

And Now, a Word from Our Sponsor

The extracts that follow in the rest of this chapter will help to illustrate some of the ways in which Laozi and Zhuangzi astonishingly prefigured conclusions in modern physics. We say astonishingly, but that word can really only be used to describe the reactions of non-Taoists. To those familiar with the *Daode Jing* and the *Zhuangzi*, the notion of a "flowing unity" that pervades apparent opposites, and the discovery that human standards are ultimately relative, are not news.

Taoist Tip-Off _____

Lin Yutang, esteemed translator of Zhuangzi, warns against regarding any human standard or evaluation method as absolute: "Any branch of human knowledge, even the study of the rocks of the earth and the cosmic rays of heaven, strikes mysticism when it reaches any depth at all, and it seems Chinese Taoism skipped the scientific study of nature to reach the same intuitive conclusion by insight alone. Therefore it is not surprising that Albert Einstein and Zhuangzi agree, as agree they must, on the relativity of standards."

The scientific validation of such notions is, however, quite exciting—especially for those who are used to associating the Western intellectual tradition with a narrow kind of on/off, right/wrong, (and, yes, wave/particle) dualism. Is there no way that "on" brings about "off"? Is there no "right" to be found in "wrong"? Is there no "wave" that "particles"?

In the end, Western science may have achieved the greatest of its many triumphs by pursuing the ultimate questions of matter to their furthest lengths … without getting a single right answer. What it got instead—a glimpse of infinity (or emptiness, if you prefer) in a mirror—was much more interesting.

Listen in as the Ph.D.s paraphrase the Tao. (Or is it the other way around?)

Determined by Observation

"[L]ight sometimes seems to be made up of particles, and sometimes of waves, depending on how it is examined. Now, to us, these are fundamentally different things, and it is very tempting to say that light must ultimately be *either* like hail, composed of lots of little objects—photons—*or* like sound ... or ripples on a pond, a vibration in some medium—the hypothetical 'ether'—and not both. But according to all the experimental evidence, descriptions of light as vibration and as particles, are equally valid. And all other sub-atomic particles, including the electron, may also appear as a wave .... In fact, position and momentum, and wave/particle nature, like other characteristics, seem determined by observation."

—From "Physics" (www.ii01.org/qp.html, 2001)

Flowing Ever Onward

Something is carrying us forward. What is it?

> "Another way of thinking of the curvature of space-time was elegantly described by Hans von Baeyer. In a prize-winning essay ('Gravity') he conceives of space-time as an invisible stream flowing ever onward, bending in response to objects in its path, carrying everything in the universe along its twists and turns."
>
> —From "General Relativity" (*Center for Supercomputing Applications,* archive.ncsa.uius.edu/cyberia/numrel/genrelativity.html)

And here's Laozi's take on the matter:

> "All things end in the Tao,
> Just as the small streams and the largest
>   rivers
> Flow through valleys to the sea."
>
> —*Daode Jing*, chapter 32 (McDonald trans-lation)

Spoken and Unspoken

"All things carry yin, yet embrace yang.
They blend their life-breaths
In order to produce harmony."

—*Daode Jing*, chapter 42 (McDonald translation)

Beyond Telling

And here's a little joke based on a familiar passage from the *Daode Jing:*

> "The electron that can be told is not the true electron."
>
> —David Harrison, *Complementarity and the Copenhagen Interpretation of Quantum Mechanics* (www.upscale.utoronto.ca/generalinterest/harrison, 2000)

And for further reflection …

"(1) Complete description of observed behavior of microscopic particles *requires* mutually exclusive concepts and properties. (2) Mutually exclusive properties are not simultaneously observable."

—Niels Bohr's principle of complementarity

"True sayings seem contradictory."

—*Daode Jing*, chapter 78 (McDonald translation)

"Look for it, it can't be seen;
Listen for it, it can't be heard;
Grasp for it, it can't be caught.
These three cannot be further described,
So we treat them as the One."

—*Daode Jing*, chapter 14 (McDonald translation)

Not Exist

Even seemingly fundamental notions of existence, as we have seen, have come into question in the modern scientific era.

"In fact, the electron *does not exist* at any particular position at a given time, unless observed there—it merely has a higher probability of appearing at some positions than others."

—Danah Zohar, *The Quantum Self* (Bloomsbury, 1990)

Now compare:

"We value the being, but the non-being is what we use."

—*Daode Jing*, chapter 11 (Hansen translation)

Flowing Wholeness

Is the universe divisible? Modern scientists have begun to wonder.

"[T]hese paradoxes and others eventually had the effect of driving a number of scientists like David Bohm to theorize that the universe must be fundamentally indivisible, a 'flowing wholeness' as Bohm calls it, in which the observer cannot be essentially separated from the observed …. Bohm theorizes, for example, that 'parts' such as 'particles' or 'waves' are forms of abstraction from the flowing wholeness. In the sense that parts seem autonomous, they are only 'relatively autonomous.' They are like a music lover's favorite passage in a Beethoven symphony. Take the passage out of the piece, and it's possible to analyze the notes. But in the long run, the passage is meaningless without the symphony as a whole."

—John Briggs and F. David Peat, *Turbulent Mirror* (Harper and Row, 1989)

Long before those words were written, of course, Laozi had set out a model of "eternal beginning" with similar overtones:

"Know the white, yet keep to the black:
Be a model for the world.
If you are a model for the world,
The Tao inside you will strengthen,
And you will return whole to your eternal beginning."

—*Daode Jing*, chapter 28 (McDonald translation)

And Finally ...

Consider this telling passage.

"[In 1961] I had occasion to discuss [Niels] Bohr's ideas with the great Japanese physicist [Yukawa] ... I asked Yukawa whether the Japanese physicists had the same difficulty as their western colleagues in assimilating the idea of complementarity ... He answered, 'No, Bohr's argumentation has always appeared quite evident to us; ... you see, we in Japan have not been corrupted by Aristotle.'"

—L. Rosenfeld, article in *Physics Today* (October, 1963)

Perhaps this chapter should really have been titled "Aristotle, Meet Laozi." Einstein, after all, didn't really seem to have any problem with yin and yang.

The Least You Need to Know

♦ Physics searches for standards and principles that reliably explain all observed phenomena; the discipline started hiccuping unexpectedly in the first half of the twentieth century.

♦ The hiccups presented a kind of pattern, and that pattern provided unexpected—for physicists—resonances with Taoist thought.

♦ Paradox alert: At the subatomic level, particles may behave like waves, and vice versa, depending on observation.

♦ To those familiar with the *Daode Jing* and the *Zhuangzi*, the idea of a "flowing unity" that pervades apparent opposites, and the discovery that human standards are ultimately relative, are not news.

Chapter 19

The Tao and Politics

In This Chapter

- ◆ The *Daode Jing*'s political advice
- ◆ Achieving freedom
- ◆ Two modern schools of political thought with Taoist influences

When people think of Taoism, they often think of complete seclusion and detachment from social matters. Perhaps they picture a placid monk meditating in a monastery or someone contemplating a waterfall—or perhaps they don't even think of people at all.

It comes as a surprise to some who are new to Taoism to learn that the *Daode Jing* offers a great deal of practical political advice. It may be even more of a surprise to learn that this ancient philosophy's minimalist approach to government, which emphasizes personal freedom and authenticity, has profoundly influenced Chinese politics.

After Mao

Of particular interest in modern China is the debate between Confucians and Taoists about which best represents Chinese culture as a twenty-first-century replacement for Maoism. Confucianism, in this debate, represents authority, Asian values, and suspicion of human rights and democracy. Taoism represents

Tao Then, Tao Now

Sun Tzu's *The Art of War,* an ancient Chinese classic of military strategy, emphasizes "winning without doing battle." The book's military advice has for centuries been employed in other contexts; in recent years, it has served as a starting point for those planning both business and political campaigns. References to and discussions of the Tao are common in Sun Tzu's analysis of military issues.

egalitarian and almost libertarian conceptions of the importance of freedom. Taoism, however, is not individualistic in the way Western liberalism is. It is, however, pluralistic and envisions a peaceful world in which people, groups, or institutions experiment with ways of life and choose them in openness and toleration.

Let's start by examining the ancient Taoist political outlook that informs both of these schools.

The Taoist Political Heritage

The ancient Taoists, as we have seen, rejected the Confucian emphasis on social hierarchies and rituals, which they saw as an unjustified attempt to manipulate and control relationships. They emphasized instead the importance of the good life. In the context of Ancient Chinese thought, where the entire role of government was to impose a single tao on people (whether a Confucian, a Mohist, or a Legalist one) Taoism effectively opposed government—it was anarchist. Taoist thinkers did not work out a conception of limited government under the rule of law. Some related thinkers toyed unsuccessfully with the idea, but the dominant conception in China continued for millennia to be a conception of *everyone* sharing the same value system.

This emphasis on variety, pluralism, and allowing different perspectives to coexist carries with it two powerful political ideas:

◆ A society can survive with many different points of view represented in it. Repression, enforcement, and war are unnecessary.

◆ Punishment is bad. It should be avoided. Government does best when it follows wu-wei—doing nothing other than facilitating people's natural ways of life.

Spoken and Unspoken

In ancient China, some in the **Legalist** school thought the officials and making punishment were predictable and avoidable. The most widely published and followed laws, however, argued only from the point of the ruler. (Officials constrained by law can't build cliques and overturn the king!) This strict penal code, however, lacked a conception of rational interpretation, and the rigid, operational application led to widespread injustice. The system collapsed in just one generation and sullied the name of rule of law in traditional Confucian eyes.

No single guiding tao can be constantly right, so striving for uniformity of moral outlook was shallow and unwise. A more restrained approach to government, one that stressed a passive rather than a paternal approach, would, Taoists felt, be far more likely to avoid strife. Taoists noticed that wars were usually fought for what each side thought was morally important, seldom for self-interest. What makes people willing to kill or die trying is an extreme confidence in their own moral point of view.

This controversial Taoist political ideal formed the basis of a number of extremely popular political movements in ancient China.

Resistance to Imperial State Ambitions

"The Legalism of Chin Shih Wang Ti, the first great emperor who unified China more than two millennia ago, has much in common with Mao's conception of Marxism and Western ideas of Positive Law … The statism of the Legalist tradition has always been tempered by Taoist individualism and the Confucian emphasis on the family. Together, Taoism and Confucianism [have formed] a strong cultural resistance to imperial state ambitions."

—"Capitalism and the Tao," by William Marina (www.index-china.com, 2001)

The *Daode Jing* and the Ideal Ruler

Many modern readers overlook the *Daode Jing*'s pragmatic advice to political and social leaders, choosing instead to emphasize the book's philosophical and religious dimensions. The political advice, even if only designed to exhibit reversal of dominant Confucian attitudes, is interesting. Take a look now at some of the *Daode Jing*'s most important lessons on the subjects of leadership, political theory, and social harmony.

Lesson One: Trying to Control Society Doesn't Work

Encouraging sophistication or knowledge of a single scheme of norms promotes ambition; competition for status; ostentation; and ultimately competition, strife, violence, and war. To the contrary, Taoist advice is not to value learning, but to remain "stupid," "dull," and easy to satisfy. People's desires should be few and simple, and their lives governed mainly by natural simplicity. (Laozi didn't have much of a vision of the advantages of technology.)

Leaders are warned to de-emphasize divisive initiatives, head off rivalries before they begin, shun material wealth and other gaudy trappings of power, and cultivate simplicity in the population as a whole by means of personal example.

"If you over-esteem talented persons,
people will become overcompetitive.
If you overvalue possessions,
people will begin to steal.
Do not display your treasures,
or people will be come envious.
The Master leads
by emptying people's minds of coveting,
filling their bellies,
weakening their ambitions,
and making them become strong.
If the people are simple and have no desires,
Those without virtue dare not act against them.
Because the Master practices not-doing,
everything will fall into place."

—*Daode Jing*, chapter 3 (McDonald translation)

The bottom line: A good leader knows that drawing people away from their natural roots invites ever more complicated and messy political situations. The process of competition, once started, is usually likely to get out of hand.

Lesson Two: Kindness Counts Less Than Results

Impartiality is a key value in Taoist politics. This kind of political leader doesn't get flustered, focuses on what works, and remains utterly undistracted by troublemakers. The sage knows that extremes of rhetoric are ultimately less important than maintaining one's composure in pursuit of the common good. Political factions, the *Daode Jing* suggests, should be dealt with according to their accomplishments, not their promises or their theories.

Given its historical emphasis on healing and longevity, Taoism has come to be associated, in some people's minds, with the notion that nature never does damage to anything. Anyone who has seen a typhoon in action, however, or watched an inspired leader immobilize a pretentious band of agitators, will not be surprised to learn that the Tao can take down as well as put up.

"The cosmos is not kind. It treats the ten thousand natural kinds as straw dogs.
Sages are not kind. They treat the hundred surname-groups as straw dogs.
Is the space between heaven and earth not like bellows and flutes?
Empty and not warped.
As long as you move them, they produce.
Many words, and numbers unlimited, are not as good as holding the center."

—*Daode Jing*, chapter 5

The bottom line: A good leader stays close to nature and resists being active in promoting a conception of what is good for people. The attitude is as follows: "Best to let them pursue the good for themselves and stay out of the way." This is called "holding the center."

Lesson Three: Rule Best by Ruling Least

Taoism is deeply suspicious of active, busy government. Here's the most famous example from the *Daode Jing* of what we mean.

> "The best hierarchy is one that those below simply realize is there.
> Next to that
> Is one that you feel kin to, and extol.
> Next to that
> Is one that you dread.
> Next to that
> Is one you condemn.
> When reliability is inadequate in it,
> There will be unreliability in it.
> Reflectively!
> His ennobling of language:
> Works are completed, affairs proceed
> And the hundred surnames all call this 'our own doing.'"
>
> —*Daode Jing*, chapter 17

The bottom line: The best government is that which makes its presence known least; the best leader is the one who speaks infrequently but effectively. Taoism leaves people to choose and pursue their own way of life, their own conception of the good. Almost all authoritarianism, on the other hand, starts with a self-styled genius (or sage) who professes to know what is good for everyone else. On this subject the Taoist is skeptical … and leaves people alone.

Lesson Four: Follow the "Way of the Female"

Many of us intuitively embrace ideas of advancement, intelligence, expansion, and activity—reflections the male, or yang, side of human nature. To succeed as an effective leader, the *Daode Jing* informs us, we must instead be willing to emphasize retreat, intuition, reduction, and passivity—the "way of the female." This advice has less to do with one's actual gender than with one's outlook on the job of governing.

Rather than being like the demanding father, Taoism asks us to emulate the supportive mother. If our child finds herself with an unconventional orientation or view of her life, we support her in her choices rather than trying to change her. If we would be leaders, the Taoist political suggests, we should similarly nurture and support all ways of life that people spontaneously choose. We remain impartial on the question of the ultimately *right* tao and tolerate all.

So do we tolerate everything? Do we tolerate those ways of life that are intolerant and try to force their own conception of the good on others? Ancient Taoists, unfortunately, did not contemplate these questions or offer any formula for the limits of toleration. They were optimists about nature—human and social nature.

Interestingly, the *Daode Jing* maintains that the "female" approach is the most effective way to *overcome* opposition, political or otherwise.

> "The female constants using stillness.
> She conquers the male,
> Using stillness to act out 'beneath.'
> Hence if great states use 'beneath' on small states,
> Then they take small states."
>
> —*Daode Jing*, chapter 61

The bottom line: Good leaders know that less is often more.

Lesson Five: Change the World by Not-Doing

The Taoist sage/politician accomplishes what the "activist" dreams of doing, but does so by means of a resolutely "passive" leadership style.

Social initiatives, we are warned, often backfire. Authentic simplicity and virtue, on the other hand, when cultivated by the leader and the people, will reliably sustain society over time.

> "Govern your country with integrity,
> And use weapons of war only with great cunning.
> Change the world with not-doing.
> How do I know the way things are?
> By these:
> The more prohibitions you make,
> The poorer people will be.
> The more weapons you possess,
> The greater the chaos in your country.
> The more knowledge that is acquired,
> The stranger the world will become.
> The more laws that you make,
> The greater the number of criminals.

Therefore the Master says:
I do nothing,
And people become good by themselves.
I seek peace,
And people take care of their own problems.
I do not meddle in their personal lives,
And the people become prosperous.
I let go of all my desires,
And the people return to the Uncarved Block."

—*Daode Jing*, chapter 57 (McDonald translation)

The bottom line: Good leaders avoid activism for its own sake; they know political activism often produces results opposite to those intended. They trust society to self-correct, self-enrich, and self-simplify.

Lesson Six: Don't Starve the People

When political troubles arise, when the populace is rebellious, when civil unrest is foreseen, and when there is hardship and poverty, Laozi suspects greed, self-aggrandizement, and heedlessness on the part of the country's leadership.

In other words, if the people are difficult to govern, there's a good chance the government has tried too hard to impose a single way of life on the empire.

"Starvation among the people
Comes from the amount of tax-in-kind
Those above the people 'eat.'

"From this: The people starve.

"The difficulty in governing people
Arises when those above the people
Deem and enact.

"From this: The people are difficult to govern.

"The people take death lightly
Because those above them
Seek life's richness.

"From this: The people take death lightly.

"In general:
Only those who don't deem and enact using 'life'
Are worthy enough to value life."

—*Daode Jing*, chapter 75

The bottom line: Government in general, and leaders in particular, should stay out of the people's business—because failing to do so can, and often does, produce poverty, unrest, and violence. If we are appropriately modest about our confidence in having found the right way to live, we will not be inclined to push, force, beat, or kill people to make them "better" (by our own lights)—or bring about covetous ideas in the populace.

Who Knew?

Those who haven't read the *Daode Jing*, and who are inclined to think of Taoism as a nature-obsessed, ambiguous, and vaguely "airy" school of thought, are usually startled by the detailed elaboration of this liberal (or libertarian) political stance in the *Daode Jing*. The *Zhuangzi* generally prefers to simply avoid the subject of politics. The positions we've just outlined, though, are all consistent with Zhuangzi's skepticism about relying too heavily (or at all) on essentially limited and/or incomplete human knowledge.

It's certainly hard to imagine Laozi or Zhuangzi, with their emphasis on individuality and their embrace of skepticism, endorsing a centralized, activist government that imposes a conception of the correct way to live!

Is It Conservatism?

All the *Daode Jing*'s talk about lowering taxes and shrinking government seems familiar, of course, and to some, the Taoist political ideal may sound familiar.

Actually, though, it isn't like Western conservativism at all since it is inspired mainly by equality and impartiality toward different ways of life. Classically, conservatives, as their name implies, are interested in maintaining or perpetuating the existing social order: supporting old traditions and institutions, largely *because* they're traditional. The Taoists, though, wouldn't have any inherent love of (or trust for) established social institutions; their perfect world is one in which individuals and groups creatively and authentically *self*-correct, *self*-enrich, and *self*-simplify, with the least possible intrusion or manipulation from the government. If that means existing institutions are undermined or abolished in the process, like so many straw dogs, so be it!

> **Tao Then, Tao Now**
>
> "There have, in the past, been instances in which humankind has been successfully left to its own devices; never, however, has there been an instance in which humankind has been successfully governed."
>
> —*Zhuangzi,* chapter 11

The Importance of Asking Questions

To approach the center of Taoism's current political legacy, we have to be willing to look at the two modern political movements that are its intellectual heirs: *libertarianism* and *anarchism.* Neither has gotten much in the way of glowing reviews from contemporary political commentators. Fortunately, though, we live in an open society in which political debate is regarded as worthy of pursuit for its own sake.

That means we can—and should—examine unfamiliar political ideas and evaluate them on their own merits. The mere act of learning about political philosophies doesn't, of course, imply support for those philosophies … only a healthy willingness to ask questions.

What Is Libertarianism?

In fact, Western liberalism derives from an emphasis on individual freedom. Its resonance with the doctrines of Laozi and Zhuangzi does not come from a focus on the individual, though, but from its fondness for variety, plurality, different points of view and a modest assessment of one's own ability to transcend a given point of view. Many similar ideas fill out the Western individualist conception and emerge in people like Thomas Jefferson (who wrote, "That government is best which governs least"). However, Taoist liberalism may be more like the liberalism of communitarian pragmatists like John Dewey than like the absolute individualism of John Locke.

In essence, libertarians believe that the government has no right to push you around—unless it's doing so to keep you from unfairly pushing others around (for instance, by physically harming them or depriving them of property they've attained honestly). Libertarians define "freedom" as the absence of compulsion.

Libertarians argue in favor of an understanding of the term a "free society" that grants the individual *freedom from being placed under any unjustified compulsion.* Libertarians view government as justified only insofar as it is effective in preventing people or groups from initiating unjustified force against *other* people or groups.

Taoist Tip-Off

Don't try to convince a libertarian that the "role" of government is to maintain a healthy society. In the libertarian view, all government is coercion—and government can only be justified when it keeps other unjustified coercions from taking place.

Libertarianism accepts a system of government that performs this limited preventative role (by, for instance, prosecuting and imprisoning rapists and murderers). It views with disapproval a system of government that appropriates personal property, drafts people into the armed services, establishes "correct" moral codes, regulates the possession of firearms, or otherwise attempts to promulgate formally accepted standards of behavior.

In short, libertarianism agrees with Laozi that government should stay out of the social and moral arena … and "practice not-doing" in most cases. (Exceptions to this include protection of the individual's right to life, speech, and property.) To the libertarian, the notion of wu-wei—as a model for governmental restraint—has a powerful appeal.

On Leaving Things Alone

"The Taoist notion of wu-wei matches up well with the libertarian opposition to physical and political force. The libertarian view is that individuals are the sovereign rulers of their own destinies under the triune rights of life, speech, and property. Such rights are protected by the appropriate obligations: prohibition against physical force, prohibition against censorship, and prohibition against theft. Libertarians believe that if people are essentially left alone, they can truly prosper. Taoists believe that prosperity is, by definition, what happens when something is 'left alone.'"

—"Taoism and Libertarianism," by Wolf Logan (www.ramsjb.com/talamasca/freedom/taoliberty.html)

To Learn More About Libertarianism ...

... visit www.libertarian.org, a well-written website that offers an introduction to the movement designed for both "the long-time libertarian" and "the curious newcomer." The site emphasizes that libertarians "share a defining belief: that everyone should be free to do as they choose, so long as they don't infringe upon the equal freedom of others."

What Is Anarchism?

If you wanted, you could trace anarchism back to Laozi and also to people like Henry David Thoreau (who wrote "that government is best which governs not at all").

Anarchism is the political theory that holds that dominance, authority, and hierarchy are not necessary to a harmonious society. Anarchism advocates a cooperative approach to social organization that excludes government altogether.

A much-maligned and deeply misunderstood system of thought, anarchism is usually considered to be a fairly recent movement, one attached mostly to Western societies. The bad taste is created by recent versions of Marxist or Maoist anarchism which glorified violence to take down society. This, of course, is far from the Taoist approach—which would be more likely to promote simple disengagement. The difference may stem from the non-individualist basis: Many Western anarchists, starting with extreme moralistic claims about individual rights, have justified taking up arms to defend those extreme rights. Taoists can justify only getting away.

In truth, it has a pedigree that extends back thousands of years to the Taoists of ancient China. Many modern anarchist organizations appeal proudly to their Taoist heritage.

The English word *anarchy* derives from a Greek expression meaning "without a ruler" or "without authority." Anarchy can be understood to reflect a desire for *all* social groupings to proceed along a cooperative, yin-based, receptive model, rather than along an authoritarian, yang-based, hierarchical model.

Taoists were anarchists in the Chinese context because they denied the necessity of a "final authority" on matters of the way of life. The absence of such an authority is the best recipe for progress in ways of life. Historically, however, Western anarchists have focused most of their energies on the task of convincing people that government, organization, or the rule of law *violates people's natural individual rights to absolute liberty.*

Although the ancient Taoists did not have a clear theory of rule of law, Taoism's effect of reducing punishment and giving people clear guidelines within which to pursue their own conceptions of the good life is one that would probably make constitutional democracy appealing. This approach is quite consistent with "moral authority anarchism" of the Taoist type.

Beyond the Stereotypes

People tend to react emotionally, and negatively, to the word *anarchy* because it has become strongly attached, for whatever reasons, to the notions of chaos and violence. The stereotype of the scheming, black-suited, bomb-throwing anarchist goes back to the silent film era—but anarchy's lineage as a subtle, intellectually rigorous political theory deeply distrustful of government goes back to ancient China.

Anarchism is a fascinating intellectual tradition worth considering on its own merits, rather than on the basis of the stereotypes that have been linked to it. Specifically, the stereotypes miss the fundamentally egalitarian, spontaneous, and mutually supportive impulses of anarchism.

The Most Misrepresented Ideas in Political Theory

"[A]narchism and anarchy are undoubtedly the most misrepresented ideas in political theory. Generally, the words are used to mean 'chaos' or 'without order,' and so, by implication, anarchists [are seen as desiring] chaos and a return to the 'laws of the jungle.' This process of misrepresentation is not without historical parallel. For example, in countries which have considered government by one person [monarchy] necessary, the words 'republic' or 'democracy' have been used precisely like 'anarchy,' to imply disorder and confusion."

—"What Is Anarchism?" (www.anarchyfaq.org)

Anarchy, as we have said, was a politically powerful and deeply influential tradition in ancient China. Modern anarchist movements take many forms and include both nuanced intellectual arguments and hormone-driven exchanges that flirt unconvincingly with both reason and insanity.

When viewed in the proper historical context, with Taoism as its founding philosophy, the idealistic, mutually supportive approach of anarchism becomes both clear and intriguing.

To Learn More About Anarchism ...

... visit www.anarchyfaq.org, a cogent series of essays about anarchism built around frequently asked questions like "What does 'anarchy' mean?" It bills itself as "the creation of many anarchists across the globe and ... a classic example of the power of freedom, equality, and mutual aid."

Tao Then, Tao Now

"[Anarchism means] not the bomb-in-the-pocket stuff, which is terrorism, whatever name it tries to dignify itself with, not the social-Darwinist economic 'libertarianism' of the far right, but anarchism as prefigured in early Taoist thought ... its principal moral-practical theme is cooperation (solidarity, mutual aid). It is the most idealistic, and to me the most interesting, of all political theories."
—Ursula K. Le Guin

The Least You Need to Know

- The Taoist political viewpoint holds that political society should avoid imposing its views about the right way to live.

- We can distinguish two versions of libertarianism: one based on skepticism that any conception can be good for all society (Laozi), and one that starts from the notion of an individual "right" to liberty (John Locke and Thomas Jefferson).

- Modern Libertarianism agrees with Laozi that government should stay out of the social and moral arena and "practice not-doing" in most cases.

- We can distinguish two versions of anarchism: one to Laozi (who had a naturalistic skepticism of moral authority), and one to people like Henry David Thoreau (who emphasized the inherent natural rights of individual freedom).

- When viewed in a libertarian light, Taoism could be rendered compatible with a conception of constitutional democracy—with the rule of law conceived mainly as a way of freeing people from official interference in their private lives (and their own conceptions of the correct tao of living).

Chapter 20

The Tao and Ecology

In This Chapter

- ◆ The lost sword
- ◆ Learn about the Center for Ecoliteracy
- ◆ What is the Alliance of Religion and Conservation?
- ◆ Discover Earthgreen

In this chapter, you learn about three ecological movements in the modern world whose spirit or guiding philosophy (or both) appears to owe something important to Taoism. There are many more we could have profiled, but these three will give you an idea of the way Taoist thought has influenced the environmental movement in the West and around the world.

But before we can tell you that story, we want to tell you this story …

The Lost Sword

Once a traveler on a boat carelessly dropped a precious sword into the depths of a river. The sword was irreplaceable and had been in his family for generations, but the traveler hesitated to take action. Asking the boatman to stop and actually jumping in the cold water seemed like such an inconvenience, especially considering the fine clothes that the traveler was wearing. And who was to say that the search might not take hours? The traveler had a party to go to, and it certainly would not wait for a swimming expedition on the river.

So it was that the traveler kneeled down and scratched an X into the bow of the boat where he stood. This mark, he reasoned, would remind him where he dropped the sword. On his return journey, he would have the boatman use the mark to stop at the same spot. Then he would have time to swim to the bottom of the river and retrieve his sword.

The sword was, of course, lost forever.

Lost Opportunities?

Some opportunities, as this ancient Taoist story suggests, must be acted upon immediately; if they are postponed, irretrievable losses may occur. In the Taoist worldview, protecting the earth is such an opportunity.

In the following profiles, you'll learn about people and organizations trying, in various ways, to jump into the river *now* to retrieve a precious family heirloom: the health of our environment. Their efforts reflect, in our view, core Taoist principles of reverence for nature.

The Center for Ecoliteracy

Chaired by physicist, systems theorist, and author Fritjof Capra (*The Tao of Physics*), the San Francisco Bay area–based Center for Ecoliteracy is dedicated to "fostering the experience of understanding the natural world." Capra, a founding director of the organization, describes the Center's ideals as follows:

> "Being ecologically literate means understanding the basic patterns and processes by which nature sustains life and using these core concepts of ecology to create sustainable human communities, in particular, learning communities. Applying this ecological knowledge requires systems thinking, or thinking in terms of relationships, connectedness, and contest. Ecological literacy means seeing the world as an interconnected whole. Using systems theory, we see that all living systems share a set of common properties and principles of organization. Thus we discover similarities between phenomena at different levels of scale—the individual child, the classroom, the school, the district, and the surrounding human communities and ecosystems. With its intellectual grounding in systems thinking, ecoliteracy offers a powerful framework for a systemic approach to school reform."

Capra argues that the transmission of ecological knowledge will be the most important task of the educational system in the twenty-first century, and he identifies five critical principles essential to an understanding of *ecology*. Familiarizing educators with the principles and offering a learning setting in which educators can share them with children are major goals of the center.

Here's a brief summary of the five principles. All five, it is worth noting, resonate with Taoist thought. (Note: The connections with various passages in the *Daode Jing* are ours, and not the Center for Ecoliteracy's. But one suspects that they probably wouldn't come as a surprise to Fritjof Capra.)

> **Spoken and Unspoken**
>
> **Ecology** is, literally, the study of animals and plants in their natural surroundings. The word comes from the Greek *oikos*, or "house." On a larger scale, ecology is the branch of science that seeks to answer the question, "How does nature work?"

Networks

Every entity within a given ecological group is linked to all the other elements in the group through a "vast and intricate" network of connections. The members of each group owe their distinctive identity—and their being—to these networks, which extend much further, and have deeper ramifications, than may at first be apparent to the casual observer.

In this context, consider the words of Laozi:

> "Subtle, beyond all understanding—
> Approach it and you will not see a beginning;
> Follow it and there will be no end."
>
> —*Daode Jing*, chapter 14 (McDonald translation)

Nested Systems

There is a powerful internal order to the systems of the earth. Specifically, systems operate within systems. Smaller systems have distinct properties and characteristics of their own ... and also operate within the framework of larger processes.

Of the Tao (and, seemingly, of the nested system), Laozi writes in chapter 21 (McDonald translation):

> "There is vitality within it;
> Its vitality is very genuine.
> Within it, we can find order."

Cycles

Ongoing cycles of change, energy exchange, and resource distribution take place within ecological groups. These cycles overlap with larger cycles in larger systems.

Laozi writes in chapter 40: "All movement returns to the Tao."

Flows

Every living organism requires a constant flow of energy and resources. (Ultimately, of course, everything on Earth is dependent on the sun's energy.)

With regard to energy, consider chapter 34 of the *Laozi*, which informs us that (McDonald translation) …

> "The Great Tao flows unobstructed in every direction;
> All things rely on it to conceive and be born."

Development

Life develops on the individual level (as learning and growth) and at the species level (as evolution). This development involves a perpetual "interplay of creativity and mutual adaptation" that strongly recalls chapter 4 of the *Daode Jing* (McDonald translation):

> "The Tao is like an empty container:
> It can never be emptied and can never be filled.
> Infinitely deep, it is the source of all things."

Tao Then, Tao Now

"According to ancient Taoist teachings, our natural state is one of few desires. When our desires are unnaturally increased, psychic and physical imbalance and all kinds of problems result …. Our economy [however,] basically runs on the fuel of 'more is better,' a strategy of purposely and systematically trying to push our desires out of their natural tendencies and strengthen them out of all natural proportion …. The only thing in nature I can think of that grows nonstop are cancer cells. Should we then ask the question: Do we have a cancerous economic system?"

—Ronald Epstein, *Pollution and the Environment: Some Radically New Ancient Views*

Ecoliteracy's Learning Communities

Ecoliteracy has developed relationships with a number of Bay area schools to help "develop awareness, build knowledge, translate knowledge into practice, and reflect on their practice." These "learning communities" allow Ecoliteracy to support educators likely to inspire meaningful change in local educational institutions.

Projects include the following:

- Creek restoration
- Recycling campaigns
- Gardening efforts
- Nutritional workshops
- "Outdoor classroom" development
- Ocean habitat study

... and many more.

Getting the Word Out to Educators and Young People

The Center for Ecoliteracy is a remarkable organization, one that has clearly set as its goal the direct exposure of educators and students on important ideas about ecology, conservation, and respect for the environment. As long-term environmental responses go, this is among the soundest we've seen.

Note again that the Center's geographical scope is quite narrow: the San Francisco Bay area. There's a reason for this. To quote the organization's website: "The practice of acquiring ecological literacy requires a place—whether a garden, a nearby creek, or a local watershed. The terrestrial, marine, and freshwater ecosystems of the San Francisco Bay–Delta provide a vibrant context for fostering ecological literacy."

Tao Then, Tao Now

"Everything is connected to everything else."

—Barry Commoner

Translation: One organization, focusing on one vast watershed. It's a nice idea.

Here's another nice idea: There really ought to be a program like this in or near *every* urban community. Until there is, the Center for Ecoliteracy serves as a superb model for ecologists, philanthropists, educators ... and everyone else in favor of educational goals that support a sustainable relationship with the planet.

For more information about the Center for Ecoliteracy, or to make a donation, visit www.ecoliteracy.org or write …

Center for Ecoliteracy
2522 San Pablo Avenue
Berkeley, CA 94702

Alliance of Religions and Conservation (ARC)

Anyone who has ever questioned the practical value of interfaith movements would do well to consider the good work of the Alliance of Religions and Conservation (ARC).

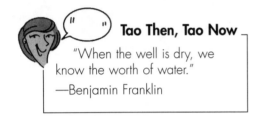

Tao Then, Tao Now

"When the well is dry, we know the worth of water."

—Benjamin Franklin

The ARC is an international charitable organization that "works with religious communities and environmental groups around the world to create and expand efforts to care for the environment." The organization's goal is to help local groups take on conservation plans that embrace the local group's faith tradition and that make the most of local customs and resources.

The organization is based in England. In 1986 Prince Philip, who serves as International President of the World Wildlife Fund, invited religious leaders from five major faiths to consider an intriguing question: What could the world's religious faiths, working together, do to protect the earth's environment? From this question arose a new organization, the World Wildlife Fund Network on Conservation and Religion. Eventually, the grouping of five religious traditions expanded to include nine:

- Taoism
- Sikhism
- Islam
- Judaism
- Jainism
- Hinduism
- Christianity
- Buddhism
- The Baha'i faith

The formal launching of the ARC as an independent charitable entity occurred in England in 1995. The ARC cites many contemporary statements of support for its efforts from religious leaders within each of these traditions. The Taoist excerpt reads …

"People should take into full consideration the limits of nature's sustaining power, so that when they pursue their own development, they have a correct standard of success .... Insatiable human desire will lead to the over-exploitation of natural resources."

Specifically, the ARC's work in support of the earth falls into three categories: Sacred Gifts, Climate Change, and Sacred Land.

Sacred Gifts

Sacred Gifts projects "honor what is already happening" and "indicate significant new commitments" in a given region. According to the ARC, a Sacred Gift project has six distinguishing characteristics. Such a project ...

- ◆ Addresses a recognized environmental need in ways that support good environmental practice.
- ◆ Uses the resources of a faith community to reach, affect, and encourage response in as many people as possible.
- ◆ Has the potential to grow and spread in effectiveness beyond its initial introduction.
- ◆ Shows a cohesiveness and continuity across diverse aspects of a faith's work.
- ◆ Is seen by participants as part of a wider process across the faith community.
- ◆ Addresses one of six key areas in which the faiths have considerable environmental significance, and in which most, if not all, faiths are active: land and assets, education, media, health, lifestyle, and advocacy.

A recent Sacred Gift initiative supported by ARC has been the China Taoist Association's call for members to stop using endangered animals in preparations associated with traditional medicine.

> **Tao Then, Tao Now**
>
> "There is something fundamentally wrong in treating the earth as if it was a business in liquidation."
>
> —Herman Daly

Climate Change

ARC recently established the Climate Change Partnership in collaboration with representatives of many major faith traditions. Under the partnership, those agreeing to the Partnership agree to "voluntary cuts in their energy use and CO_2 emissions, and commit to using—and in some cases even generating—'clean' energy from solar power, waste products, wind power, and other non-carbon fuels."

The ARC then presents these commitments to national governments, urging compliance with international agreements relating to climate change and, in some cases, lobbying for support to help faiths in implementing their commitments. To date, 10 governments, including Russia and Bolivia, have indicated their support for this unprecedented faith/government initiative.

Sacred Land

The ARC's Sacred Land Project celebrates the "environmental and cultural significance of sacred places in Britain" and aims to support local groups of many faiths in identifying and conserving sacred places. To date, the ARC has helped hundreds of groups in Britain and Ireland to build partnerships with religious, environmental, and government agencies in identifying and preserving sacred sites.

A Record of Achievement

Although still quite young, the ARC's record of action and commitment on environmental issues puts to shame that of many governments (notably the United States). Thousands upon thousands of religious communities—churches, mosques, synagogues, and so on—have become involved in conservation through its efforts.

In the years to come, the ARC will continue to take action on the five key goals of its mission:

> **Tao Then, Tao Now**
>
> "The biggest problem in the world can be solved while it is still small."
>
> —Laozi

- To assist and encourage the evolution of practical, educational projects that further the involvement of religions in caring for the natural environment.
- To assist and encourage the evolution of religious and ethical programs within conservation bodies.
- To assist and encourage events that bring together religion and conservation groups to further ties and develop practical conservation projects.
- To raise and grant funds for the above aims.
- To publish and promote materials that explore the links between religion and conservation and that further the aims of the ARC.

To find out more about the ARC, visit www.religionsandconservation.org. To make a donation, mail your check to:

Alliance of Religions and Conservation
3 Wynnstay Grove
Fallowfield
Manchester M14 6XG
United Kingdom

On the Path _____

The World Wildlife Fund International, in collaboration with the ARC and the Central Tibetan Administration (the government-in-exile of Tibet), has undertaken a "systematic project to protect cultural remains and maintain the ecological balance of China's sacred mountains." Many of the mountains in question are regarded as holy sites within traditional Chinese Taoist religious practice. Taoism's sacred mountains have been revered for centuries as places for retreat, meditation, and communion with nature. They are now in danger of being overrun by tourists, logging interests, and the pollution that so often accompanies economic development. To support the World Wildlife Fund International's important efforts on this and other essential projects, visit www.panda.org and click "Support WWF."

Earthgreen

If we had to identify one environmental organization that consciously and effectively mirrors the precepts of Taoism, that organization would be Earthgreen. It's a public, non-profit organization dedicated to spreading the word about important events affecting the earth we all share. Earthgreen is focused on helping people gain a fuller understanding of the intricate relationship between the environment that supports all life on Earth and the machinations of the consumer economy that support what most of us in the West regard as "real life." For a quick reality check on what "real life" is costing the planet, check out the organization's website at www.earthgreen.org.

A Typical Day on Planet Earth

Here is an excerpt from the Earthgreen website (www.earthgreen.org):

"If today is a typical day on planet earth, we will lose 116 square miles of rainforest, or about an acre a second. We will lose another 72 square miles to encroaching desert, the result of human mismanagement and overpopulation. We will lose 40 to 100 species, and no one knows whether the number is 40 or 100. Today the human population will increase by 250,000. And today we will add 2,700 tons of CFCs to the atmosphere and 15 million tons of carbon. Tonight the earth will be a little hotter, its waters more acidic, and the fabric of life more threadbare."

—David W. Orr, Professor of Environmental Sciences, Oberlin College, 1990

"To speak of Limits is natural.
That is why a gusty wind doesn't last the morning;
A downpour doesn't last the day.
If even Heaven and Earth cannot last forever,
How much less can human beings last!"

—Laozi

Earthgreen tells the truth about humanity and the planet, gives you both the "big picture" and the "close-up," and shows you how the two are connected. If Laozi isn't on the contact sheet as the organization's honorary chairman emeritus, he ought to be.

Want to Help?

Do the planet (and yourself) a favor and support this organization's good work. You can do that in one of three ways:

CAUTION

Taoist Tip-Off

The ozone hole above Antarctica is widening ominously. For evidence, visit www. earthgreen.org/destruction.htm. For insights on what Laozi might make of this state of affairs, visit www.earthgreen.org/taoism.htm.

◆ Call 1-800-550-0056 and say, "I want to make a donation."

◆ E-mail martin@delivex.com and with the message "I want to make a donation." (Leave your phone number so they can call you back.)

◆ Send a check to:

Earthgreen
17 Spectrum Pointe Drive, #501
Lake Forest, CA 92360

The Trees of Life

"Taoist protection of the environment has a long and distinguished history … A significant feature of Taoist conservation activity in China is tree planting, especially around sacred temples. In Quihai province, for example, 1.7 million trees have been planted since 1982, turning barren hills into green forests."

—"Taoists and the Environment" (www.panda.org/livingplanet/sacred_gifts/ factsheet_ taoists.html)

The Least You Need to Know

- Don't wait for the return trip; dive in and get the sword now.
- One way to do so is to learn more about, and consider supporting, the Center for Ecoliteracy.
- You should also learn more about, and consider supporting, the Alliance of Religion and Conservation (ARC).
- While you're at it, learn more about, and consider supporting, Earthgreen.

Chapter 21

The Tao and Pop Culture

In This Chapter

- ◆ The Tao of *Star Wars*
- ◆ The Tao of The Beatles
- ◆ Other cool pop culture Taoist connections

In this chapter, you learn about the Tao-inspired mass entertainment that has attracted paying customers in the West in recent years.

Now Playing: The Tao

Popular film, television, and music may seem at first to be unlikely outlets for the expression of Taoist ideas.

All the same, some of these—including a number of works that have now attained iconic status in pop culture—incorporate themes and ideas from the Taoist masters. Some of these references appear to have been perceived only subliminally by the vast audiences they reached … but then, the same can be said of many other Asian expressions of Taoism in the arts through the centuries.

How has American pop culture encountered Taoism? Some answers follow.

Lights, Camera, Wu-Wei: The Tao Goes to Hollywood

The scripts of a number of recent Hollywood blockbusters have been built, with varying degrees of faithfulness, around Taoist concepts. Even more direct examinations of Taoist themes were to be found in a charming, low-budget, independent comedy released in the year 2000. Here's a brief look at these films.

The *Star Wars* Films

Here's the granddaddy of pop Tao: the rip-roaring, light-saber-rattling, galaxy-shaking fantasy-adventure that launched a thousand merchandising spin-offs.

Taoist Tip-Off

The examples that appear here are offered as a representative sampling of Taoist influences on Western popular culture, not as an exhaustive list.

Spoken and Unspoken

The word **samurai** has carried a number of meanings through the centuries, but it is generally understood to refer to a kind of ancient Japanese warrior—either independent (fairly rare) or acting in the service of a lord (much more common). The samurai tradition was deeply influenced by Zen Buddhism.

It surprises some people to learn that George Lucas's epic sci-fi cycle is deeply indebted to the principles of Taoism. Yet one has only to consider the series' tagline—"May the Force be with you"—to encounter the most direct adaptation from the *Daode Jing*. This is the motto of the Jedi, a mysterious fraternity of mystical warriors who bear more than a passing resemblance to the Zen-influenced (and thus Tao-influenced) Japanese *samurai*.

When asked to explain the Force, the aged Jedi knight Obi-Wan Kenobi has this to say: "The Force is what gives the Jedi its power. It is an energy field created by all living things that surround and penetrate us. It binds the galaxy together." Sound familiar? Later, Luke Skywalker hears the dead Kenobi's voice urge him to "use the Force" to empty his mind ... and fulfill his own destiny.

Lucas's "Force" is meant to equate with the Great Tao; the utter clarity of focus of the Jedi recalls the no-mind that Zhuangzi celebrates in his parable of the butcher. It's worth noting, though, that in Taoism the all-pervading Tao would be seen as animating, uniting, *and being identical with* the entire universe—which is not quite the description we receive of the Force. The Jedi's emphasis on *passing along* clarity from person to person—that is, from master to disciple—would certainly have met with some skepticism from Zhuangzi, who regarded this kind of clear focus as essentially impossible to transmit to another.

Consider these additional and striking parallels from the first three films (*Star Wars*, *The Empire Strikes Back*, and *The Return of the Jedi*):

◆ **Doing-without-doing (wu-wei).**
Avoiding conscious intervention in events as they unfold is a constant theme in Taoism—and in the life and adventures of Luke Skywalker. When he first trains in using a light saber, for instance, Skywalker flunks the test and gets zapped by a laser; when Obi-Wan Kenobi forces him to rely on his own instincts by obscuring his vision with a helmet, Skywalker effortlessly turns aside every blast.

Tao Then, Tao Now

The ancient principle of wu-wei, which rejects grasping, effort-oriented action, is reflected intriguingly in Yoda's advice to his pupil Luke Skywalker in *The Empire Strikes Back*: "Try not. Do. Or do not. There is no try."

◆ **Nature over artifice.** Even though their most memorable scenes involve land speeders, light sabers, and massive battle-equipped space stations, a preference for nature over technology is not hard to detect in the *Star Wars* films. Think of the idyllic, pastoral setting of the triumph of the Ewoks (teddy-bear warriors!) in *Return of the Jedi*, or of the training Skywalker receives in the swamp where Yoda lives in *The Empire Strikes Back*. The message: Trees and bayous may well be a source of a kind of power that can overcome even the most magnificent machines.

Tao Then, Tao Now

At the end of the first *Star Wars* film, Luke Skywalker relies on his feelings—rather than a sophisticated targeting device—to deliver the shot that destroys the *Death Star*.

◆ **Things contain their opposites.** Is Darth Vader a "bad guy"? Yes, but … in *The Return of the Jedi*, the evil man-machine reconciles with his estranged son, takes off his ever-present helmet, and (gasp) smiles! Is Luke Skywalker a "good guy"? Yes, but … he is the son of Darth Vader and must overcome his own obstacles and inclinations to "the dark side" to complete his journey. To a certain degree (but only to a certain degree!), Lucas allows Taoist principles of opposition and harmony to guide the development of his heroes and villains.

Taoist Tip-Off

Beware! A Taoist analysis of the *Star Wars* films has its limits. Traditional story structure demands a triumph of good over evil, and in *Star Wars* this demand has, so far, implied a vanquishing of "the dark side" that is not fully supported by the Taoist worldview.

> **Tao Then, Tao Now** _____
>
> The Taoist influence continued in the year 1999, when George Lucas finally unveiled the fourth *Star Wars* film, *The Phantom Menace*. (This movie presents Episode I of the nine-part *Star Wars* saga; the first film released, *Star Wars*, was actually Episode IV in the overall story.)
>
> True to form, Lucas built clear Taoist elements into his plot. For instance, the final image of the film is virtually a cinematic recreation of the yin-yang principle, with the land-inhabiting Naboo reconciled to the water-inhabiting Gungan, and each group representing part of a "symbient circle" in which, we are told, what happens to one group inevitably affects the other.

During *The Phantom Menace*, we also learn that …

- **One's perspective determines one's perceived experience.** Attentive parents accompanying their children to *The Phantom Menace* may have thought twice about the film-critic consensus that *The Phantom Menace* was nothing more than a video-game blown up to full-screen dimensions. Those willing to listen for content got it when they heard Qui-Gon(!) Jinn observe that "Your focus determines your reality." This subtle but profound observation is one of several in the film suggesting that Lucas has read his *Zhuangzi* and that he meant repeated viewings of the film to yield philosophical insights as well as an appreciation for explosions.

> **Tao Then, Tao Now** _____
>
> In *The Phantom Menace*, Qui-Gon Jinn's name suggests the Chinese Taoist term *qigong*, which has been defined as "the practice of using qi for a variety of purposes, including self-healing." *Qi* means "vital energy"; *gong* means "work" or "achievement."

- **Meditative openness to the present should guide our everyday actions.** Qui-Gon Jinn instructs the young Obi-Wan Kenobi that, instead of being distracted by the future, he should keep his concentration "here and now where it belongs." Laozi would have agreed.

- **Change is inevitable.** When he must part from his beloved mother, Annakin Skywalker (the future Darth Vader) hears these words from her: "You can't stop the change, any more than you can stop the suns from setting." Their home planet's sky features two suns; the guiding principle of alteration, however, is apparently the same noticed here on Earth.

- **Spontaneous openness to one's own true nature is the best approach.** This openness transcends rational analysis. "Feel," Qui-Gon Jinn tells Obi-Wan, "don't think." The teaching is so elemental, and so concisely stated, that it almost fades from notice, yet it is the lesson whose pursuit guides the entire drama of *Star Wars* (and a good many other human dramas as well).

The Nature of the Light Saber

"The Jedi hold their light sabers like samurai swords, and their views and discipline sound like nothing so much as Taoism or Zen Buddhism, which have influenced the ideology of the martial arts. The nature of the light saber, which reflects back laser shots to the shooter, is characteristic of the 'Submissive Way' theory of Taoism, by which the attack of an opponent is turned back upon him or her."

—"A Response to Critics" (www.friesian.com/starwars, 1999)

There is much more that could be said about Taoist thought and its relationship to the *Star Wars* movies, particularly with regard to the films' dubious view of the government and its institutions. ("It is clear to me," Queen Amidala observes ominously in *The Phantom Menace*, "that the Republic no longer functions.") Another book will have to take up that topic, however, because it's time to look at another special-effects blockbuster with Taoist overtimes, namely …

The Matrix

This incomparable Keanu Reeves fantasy-thriller puts a postmodern and profoundly paranoid spin on many familiar elements of Taoism, notably Zhuangzi's parable of the butterfly. In that parable, you'll recall, Zhuangzi related the experience of having dreamt convincingly that he was a butterfly, and then, upon awakening, being unable to decide whether he was a butterfly dreaming he was a man or vice versa.

In *The Matrix*, the entire physical world may well be a figment of the imagination, but if it is, it is a delusion brought about, not as a result of the guiding and healing Tao, but by far more sinister forces. To say much more would, perhaps, spoil the plot of one of Hollywood's greatest social protest films (listen closely to Morpheus's remarks about churches and taxation). If you've already seen the movie, take a moment to ponder the fascinating Taoist parallels listed here. If you haven't seen the film, do yourself a favor and rent this on video or DVD tonight.

- **Life is but a dream (or is it a nightmare?).** Neo (Keanu Reeves) asks a friend whether he's ever had that feeling of not being sure if he's awake or still dreaming. Later, Morpheus (Laurence Fishburne) tells Neo that he looks like the kind of man who's prepared to believe anything, because he expects to wake up at any moment. Zhuangzi alert!

Tao Then, Tao Now

In *The Matrix*, Morpheus paraphrases Zhuangzi when he asks, "Have you ever had a dream, Neo, that you were so sure was real? What if you weren't able to wake from that dream? How would you know the difference from the real world and the dream world?"

◆ **The truth must be experienced directly, rather than explained in words.** Morpheus tells Neo that no one, alas, can really be told what the Matrix is; such knowledge is a matter of direct experience. Sounds familiar. Note: In the world of the Matrix, this direct experience is not necessarily a *pleasant* one right off the bat.

◆ **One is everywhere, whether one realizes it or not.** And *emptiness is everywhere.* And *wu-wei.* If the Tao is an emptiness with which one is actually identical, and from which one can make endless withdrawals, then the world of the Matrix offers a similarly paradoxical state of affairs. The Spoon Boy appears to bend a spoon by supernatural means. He explains his skill to Neo: "There is no spoon … it is not the spoon that is bending. It is only yourself."

Crouching Tiger, Hidden Dragon

This martial-arts blockbuster's debt to Taoist traditions was expressed directly by its director, Ang Lee. Lee wrote:

> "We embraced the most mass of art forms [i.e., the Hong Kong martial arts movie] and mixed it with the highest—the secret martial arts as passed down over time in the great Taoist schools of training and thought. What is the Tao, the 'way'? … It's enigmatic, in that it can only manifest itself through contradictions, through the conflicts of the heart rather than through the harmony it seeks …. For example, the martial arts film is very masculine, but in the end, our film finds its center in its women characters. It is the women who, in the end, are walking the path of the way."
>
> —Director's statement (www.magiclanternpr.com/films/crouching.html)

The Taoist celebration of human skill (particularly in fields such as martial arts and calligraphy) is in view for most of *Crouching Tiger, Hidden Dragon.* At one point, the lord Sir Te remarks: "A sword, by itself, rules nothing. It comes alive only through skillful manipulation."

The Tao of Steve

This gentle, charming independent film poses that age-old question: Can a profound understanding of the *Daode Jing* help one score with a whole bunch of chicks? The answer—at least for Dex, the charming if occasionally loathsome sloth who is the film's protagonist—is, yes, but only for a while. Eventually, if you spend enough time reading this Laozi dude, you end up taking a good, long look at yourself in the mirror and wondering what on Earth you're doing with your life.

In the meantime, though, you're free to develop spontaneous skill in the Lothario department. Dex's Tao-derived rules for success with the ladies are as follows:

Eliminate Your Desires

Tao of Steve Rule No. 1: Eliminate your desires. If you're thinking about getting laid, you're finished. A woman can smell an agenda.

Rule No. 2: Do something excellent in her presence to prove your sexual worthiness.

Rule No. 3: After you eliminate desire and prove your excellence, *you must retreat.*

A witty, gentle counterpart to the big-budget *Shallow Hal* (which *doesn't* have a plot that revolves around Taoism), *The Tao of Steve* is a thoughtful, provocative look at the male psyche, the kind of movie that's likely to provoke as many knowing grins as it does belly laughs. It is not sexually explicit or exploitative.

Unlike the other movies we've discussed in this chapter, *The Tao of Steve*'s script deals *directly* with specific questions relating to the Tao. And various wu-wei–related insights on getting laid. And also Steve McQueen's apparent divinity.

Somehow it all hangs together. Perhaps it's better not to try to explain why in mere dualistic words.

Another trait that distinguishes *The Tao of Steve* from the three blockbusters we've discussed in this chapter is financial. It didn't overwhelm multiplexes in quite the same way that, say, *The Phantom Menace* did.

For movie buffs with a weakness for light comedy and heavy Taoist speculation, however, *The Tao of Steve* is a great video rental. If you've made it this far into this book, and you are (or know) a sexually mature male, you'll find something to love in this film. Check it out.

The Tao and The Beatles

Hardcore Beatles fans who read the *Daode Jing* for the first time may well stop short when they get to chapter 47. This chapter is the source for a song lyric that shows up on the B-side of the 1968 single "Lady Madonna." The song—and, in some translations, the *Daode Jing* chapter title—is "The Inner Light."

 **On the Path**

Chapter 47 of the *Daode Jing* inspired The Beatles song "The Inner Light":

"The farther one travels, The less one knows."

This was George's first composition to appear on a Beatles single. Many people assume the song to be of Indian inspiration (thanks to the sitar and other Indian instruments used on the track). Actually, The Beatles are collaborating with Laozi!

Years later, an interview disc with John Lennon would be released under the title *The Tao of John Lennon.*

If there are Tao connections to other inductees to the Rock 'n' Roll Hall of Fame, we haven't been able to track them down. Stay tuned.

The Tao on TV

Finally, let's consider the ultimate television sitcom—the "show about nothing" that kept America glued to its television sets for most of the 1990s. Right about now, you're probably asking yourself—exactly what kind of nothing are we talking about when we talk about *Seinfeld?*

Is it the nothing that heals and sustains and guides the universe, the same nothing that shows up repeatedly in the *Daode Jing?*

Is it radically different than that Taoist nothing? Or is it perhaps identical with that Taoist nothing and yet identical with some other kind of nothing at the same time?

Okay, maybe you *weren't* asking yourself those kinds of questions, but William Irwin, editor of *Seinfeld and Philosophy: A Book About Everything and Nothing* (Open Court, 1999) is. The book analyzes the many popular scripts for parallels with Taoist thought … and with the works of other heavy-duty philosophers like Heidegger, Kant, Sartre, and Aristotle.

The book is a fascinating—and painless—layman's overview of philosophical principles. "I'm not claiming that there's some abstruse philosophy behind the show," Irwin explained in a recent interview, "just that the two can be linked in some way."

As can, one might argue, all manifestations, both visible and invisible, of the Tao.

The Least You Need to Know

◆ The *Star Wars* cycle of films feature some fascinating parallels with Taoist thought. So do *The Matrix; Crouching Tiger, Hidden Dragon;* and the charming, smile-inducing indie comedy *The Tao of Steve.*

◆ The Beatles adapted a chapter of the *Daode Jing* for their song "The Inner Light."

◆ To the extent that *Seinfeld* was in fact about nothing, it was actually about … oh, never mind.

Part 5

Here and Now

Tao now! In this part, you find resources, reviews, and writings to support further exploration and practice.

West Is West

In This Chapter

- ◆ Taoist organizations in the West
- ◆ Help for people with tight schedules
- ◆ Contact information

Many organizations in North America and Europe celebrate and sustain Taoist principles. In this part of the book, you get a representative sampling of these organizations.

The Center of Traditional Taoist Studies

Based in Weston, Massachusetts, the Center of Traditional Taoist Studies (CTTS) is a nonprofit American organization offering classes in Taoist philosophy, religion, qigong, and martial arts. The Boston campus incorporates what is believed to be one of the largest privately maintained Taoist temples in the world.

The Center offers programs designed to "provide the foundation knowledge required to be a student of the Tao."

Tao Then, Tao Now

Master Alex Anatole is the founder and president of the CTTS. An ordained Taoist priest and expert in both qigong and kung fu, Anatole was born in Moscow, where he studied for two decades under Grand Master Lu Tang Tai. In 1966, Grand Master Tai and Master Anatole founded Moscow's first Taoist temple and seminary. In the late 1970s, Anatole set out for the United States to begin a new mission: spreading the teachings of Taoism and its ancient Chinese disciplines to Americans.

Master Anatole's emphasis on traditional Taoist disciplines offers a hands-on example of Taoism in the West. His "modern" approach is simply to appeal directly to Taoism's ancient principles.

Start with Laozi

"Classical Taoism defines a specific path to enlightenment that is clear and unambiguous .... Enlightenment begins by understanding the philosophy of life as taught by Laozi, the founder of Taoism. It is here that '*spirituality*' must be clearly defined, so that the goal of 'enlightenment' is not confused. Without completely understanding the goal of spirituality, the process of enlightenment is akin to driving a car through a dense fog. Once the goal is understood, enlightenment is obtained through applying Taoist principles in everyday life. This is accomplished by training yourself in an array of disciplines designed for mental, physical, and spiritual development."

—From *The Path to Enlightenment*, Center of Traditional Taoist Studies

---

Commitments

The CTTS centers its efforts on a number of areas of study and practice. Instruction and participation in each take place at the Weston facility.

- ◆ **Taoist philosophy.** The CTTS dedicates itself to "the practical application of Taoism" and offers weekly lectures on the teachings of Laozi and Zhuangzi. It is worth noting that the organization views with skepticism the emphasis on the supernatural and the arcane it finds in many contemporary Taoist writings. The CTTS holds "some of the world's leading institutions" accountable for what it identifies as the most serious sin possible within Taoism (namely, confusion), and it emphasizes the right understanding of classical Taoist philosophy as an essential first step within the tradition.

- **Taoist religion.** The CTTS regards its religious practice (or more specifically, its use of images in religious procedures and ceremonies) as a means for establishing a personal link to "the source of qi or the Great Ultimate" in accordance with ancient Taoist rituals. Ceremonies are conducted at the Weston temple.

- **Taoist meditation.** Students receive instruction in ancient Taoist meditation techniques involving relaxation and the opening of the body's energy centers, followed by intense visualizations intended to bring about the "burning" of accumulated stress.

- **Martial arts.** The CTTS conducts training in the ancient practice of kung fu and notes that "throughout history, Taoist religious institutions considered kung fu as an integrated element of their monasteries' practices." The Center regards the mastery of martial arts skills as the effective, proven physical application of its spiritual principles. Think of the discipline as "Tao for those people who must confront enemies"—for instance, the traveling priests of past centuries who were forbidden to carry weapons but who nevertheless had to defend themselves.

- **Taoist healing sciences.** The Center offers instruction in qigong, the practice of traditional Chinese medical arts. It promotes a vision of medicine that sees the Western and Eastern systems of treatment as complementary rather than competitive. The CTTS has established an alliance with Longhua Hospital in Shanghai, which employs both Western and traditional Chinese therapeutic methods to manage a staggering patient load of 850,000 people per year with a staff of approximately 1,200. Compare the figures at one of the most respected American medical facilities, the Washington Hospital Center in Washington, D.C. In the year 2000, the facility treated just 261,000 patients with a larger staff of 1,534.

> **Spoken and Unspoken**
>
> **Spirituality** or **spirit** are defined in many Western dictionaries with terms like "otherwordly" or "incorporeal"—the implication being that spirituality is something far away from one's own body, breath, and experience. Compare the definition of spirituality offered by the CTTS: "The ability to perceive the world as it really exists, understand your limitations, and see life's path with clarity and simplicity."

> **Tao Then, Tao Now**
>
> The CTTS advocates a vision of modern medicine that makes full use of both Western and traditional Chinese approaches to therapeutic practice. It notes that, in contemporary China, a stroke victim is likely to receive, initially, what an American would regard as standard "modern" treatment. The patient's treatment would conclude, however, with traditional Chinese therapies meant to help restore balance and employ the body's own natural healing energies.

To find out more, contact:

Center of Traditional Taoist Studies
Box 134
Weston, MA 02134
www.tao.org
questions@tao.org

A Breath of Fresh Air

Hundreds of book, tape, and workshop organizations are attempting to assimilate Taoist ideas into formats accessible to Westerners with limited time and little or no inclination to attend classes on Chinese philosophy or visit a Taoist temple. Many of these groups, however, offer a soupy, impractical, melange of ideas that have little to do with core Taoist principles. A few actually meet the dual requirement of short-term practicality and consistency with traditional Taoist ideals.

On the Path

Author J. J. Clarke has written a cogent and helpful overview that illuminates the many elements of Taoist influence, practice, and observance in the West. It's called *The Tao of the West: Western Transformation of Taoist Thought* (Routledge, 2000). Chenyang Li has written another valuable book with a similar theme, but with a narrower emphasis on comparative philosophy: *The Tao Encounters the West* (State University of New York Press, 1999).

Tao Then, Tao Now

"In mustering your vitalities, embracing in one, can you fail to distinguish? In specializing in breath and consummating weakness, can you be as a child? In cleansing and voiding your profound mirror, can you be without flaw?"

—*Daode Jing,* chapter 10

We propose, as one representative of Authentic Breathing Resources, a San Francisco–based clearinghouse for information about books, audiotapes, manuals, and workshops developed by author Dennis Lewis. His book *The Tao of Natural Breathing* is probably the best and simplest resource for incorporating traditional Taoist meditative breathing practices.

The Breathing of an Infant

"Unfortunately, few people who experiment with their breath understand the importance of 'natural breathing.' This is the kind of spontaneous, whole-body breathing that one can observe in an infant or young child. Instead of trying to learn to breathe naturally, many people impose complicated breathing techniques on top of their already bad breathing habits. These habits are not in harmony with the psychological and physiological laws of the mind and body. They are not in harmony with the Tao.

"Natural breathing is an integral part of the Tao. For thousands of years, Taoist masters have taught natural breathing to their students through qigong, tai chi, and various other healing arts and sciences. Through natural breathing we are able to support our overall health … and extract and absorb the energy we need for spiritual growth and independence."

—Master Mantak Chia, of The International Healing Tao (Chiang Mai, Thailand), in the foreword to *The Tao of Natural Breathing*

Dennis Lewis, a contemporary Taoist lecturer, argues that the style of breathing that involves the entire body is healthier, likelier to reduce stress, and more supportive of spiritual goals than the shallow breathing most Westerners practice. His advice strongly recalls Zhuangzi's observation that the sages of ancient times "breathed from their heels," and his book has received praise from such diverse journals as *Library Journal*, *Massage Therapy Journal*, *Somatics Magazine-Journal*, the *San Francisco Chronicle*, *Qi Journal*, and *Publishers Weekly*.

Spoken and Unspoken

Natural breathing, according to author Dennis Lewis, is breathing that mirrors that of a healthy infant and, thus, involves the harmonious interplay of the lungs, diaphragm, belly, chest, back, and other parts of the body.

And deservedly so. This is a concise and blessedly easy-to-implement overview for improving everyday *natural breathing*. If you're like many Westerners interested in Taoism—short on time, but looking for a good point of entry to Taoism that will immediately change your life for the better—you may want to consider reading Lewis's book or attending one of his many workshops.

Beyond "Fight or Flight"

Ancient Taoist breathing strategies can help us move beyond the stressful "fight or flight" physical state identified by Western science. As Lewis observes on his website:

"Because of the constant pressure of stress in our inner and outer lives, many of us do not breathe naturally. We have become upper chest breathers. This causes us to breathe faster than we should, often bringing about a chronic state of hyperventilation, a state in which we breathe too fast for the real demands of the situation. Those of us who breathe too fast often find ourselves holding our breath in moments of stress and fear; this is a natural momentary response to the presence of danger that often signals the beginning of the 'fight or flight' reflex we especially needed in our early history on this earth."

The problem, he points out, is that modern life has conditioned us to spend many hours of the day in this fight or flight state with debilitating results to personal health and spirituality. If this sounds familiar to you, and if you'd like to learn more about Taoist breathing principles without committing to weeks or months of study, you owe it to yourself to check out Lewis's work.

To find out more, contact:

Authentic Breathing Resources
PO Box 31376
San Francisco, CA 94131
www.authentic-breathing.com

On the Path

The BTA emphasizes networking and connections among those interested in Taoism in a way that many other groups don't. The group also takes an active role in the support and restoration of Taoism and Taoist sites in China. The BTA has strong connections to the Chinese Taoist Association, the umbrella group that represents Taoist practitioners in China.

The British Taoist Association

Launched by a community of English Taoists, the British Taoist Association (BTA) is "dedicated to the Taoist tradition with the aim of spreading Taoism to the West." The Association is composed of both British Taoist priests (ordained in China) and Chinese Taoist priests.

The BTA's doctrinal emphasis is simultaneously narrow and broad. Although it is identified with a particular school of religious Taoism, it makes no sectarian claims and calls attention to its commitment to support and sustain Taoism in all its forms.

The Many Paths to the Tao

"The Dragon Gate (Longmen) sect is part of the Complete Realization (Quanzhen) school, which is one of the largest Taoist schools in China today …. Although the founder members of the British Taoist Association are priests of the Dragon Gate Tradition, the Association embraces all the different strands of Taoism. We do not regard the Association as a special 'sect' and being a member does not require commitment to a particular master or school of Taoism. We recognize that each person has his or her own path to the Tao, and encourage members to follow whatever teachings and practices are right for them."

—From the BTA website (www.taoists.co.uk)

Reestablishing Traditional Temples

The BTA works closely with the Chinese Taoist Association in support of the restoration of ancient Taoist temples. A recent fund-raising effort helped to bring about the renovation of the Qing Hua Gong temple "located in a village on the outskirts of X'ian."

A current priority is the reclamation of the temple in Zi Yang devoted to the True Immortal Zhen Ren, who lived in a nearby cave during the sixteenth century.

The Dragon's Mouth

A quarterly magazine, *The Dragon's Mouth*, is an ongoing project of the BTA. It offers many articles of interest to Westerners interested in exploring Taoism's various aspects. Recent articles have included the following:

◆ "Lectures on Taoism: Taoist Philosophy"
◆ "The Tao Te Ching: A Taoist Fugue"
◆ "The Way of Qigong"
◆ "The Meaning of Virtue"
◆ "The Wheel of Life"
◆ "Women's Cultivation"
◆ "The Shamanic Roots of Orthodox Taoism"
◆ "The Tao Te Ching in Practice"
◆ "Interview with Min Zhiting, Chairman of the Chinese Taoist Association"
◆ "Mysticism Made Visible"
◆ "Yi-Ching Imagery"
◆ "Tai Chi and Taoist Alchemy"

The Dragon's Mouth is offered free to members of the BTA.

Tao Then, Tao Now

The BTA's mission includes the sponsorship of visits from Taoist priests to the United Kingdom. The aim of these trips is to provide direct exposure to the ancient traditions and insights of Taoist practice.

A Voice of Clarity

The BTA is an invaluable resource for Westerners interested in exploring the many aspects of Taoism. Their website features information on upcoming events, affiliated groups, and information on membership.

To find out more, e-mail taoists@hotmail.org.

Other Groups You May Wish to Contact

Here are some other organizations you may wish to get in touch with.

The Qigong Institute

The group's goals include …

- Promoting medical qigong via education, research, and clinical studies.
- Improving healthcare by integrating qigong and Western medicine.
- Making information about qigong available to medical practitioners.

The Qigong Institute also sponsors lectures, offers online resources, participates in international conferences, and promotes research on qigong.

To learn more, contact:

Qigong Institute
561 Berkeley Avenue
Menlo Park, CA 94025
www.qigonginstitute.com

The Feng Shui Guild

The Guild aims to "promote the use, practice, and teaching of feng shui." Its membership includes teachers, practitioners, and those interested in learning more about feng shui for application in their own work and living spaces. The organization offers an extensive listing of practitioner referrals.

To learn more, contact:

> **The Feng Shui Guild**
> Administrative Director
> 784 East Homestead Drive
> Highlands Ranch, CO 80216
> www.fengshuiguild.com

The Foundation of Tao

The Foundation of Tao describes itself as a "spiritual organization dedicated to providing its members with the knowledge and power to liberate themselves from suffering, dysfunction, afflictions, [and] death." The founder, Stephen Chang, is the author of a number of important books on Taoist practice, including *The Tao of Sexology: The Book of Infinite Wisdom* (The Foundation of Tao, 1996).

The organization conducts a number of lectures and workshops.

To learn more, contact:

> **The Foundation of Tao**
> 2570 Ocean Avenue, Suite 134
> San Francisco, CA 94132
> www.padrak.com/tao

The Least You Need to Know

- The Center of Traditional Taoist Studies offers teaching in traditional Taoist disciplines.
- Authentic Breathing Resources offers easy-to-implement advice on improving breathing techniques.
- The British Taoist Association supports networking efforts that promote direct exposure to ancient Taoists traditions and insights.

Chapter 23

Wired and Wireless

In This Chapter

- ◆ Learn about Taoist links on the World Wide Web
- ◆ Read reviews of our favorite sites
- ◆ Find out what to do next

Are you *really* connected to everything? Well, it sure can seem like it when you're logged on to the Internet. In this chapter, you will learn about some of the best places to look for signs of the Tao on the Internet.

The Tao of the World Wide Web

Following are links, reviews, and brief samplings from our favorite Taoist websites. We're pretty sure you'll like them as much as we do.

If there's such a thing as the virtual Tao, the act of visiting these sites probably has something to do with it.

Taoism Information Page

Address: www.clas.ufl.edu/users/gthursby/taoism/

Category: Resource access

Review: An excellent starting point. The Taoism Information page offers an easy-to-navigate summary of online resources broken down into the following categories: Introduction to Taoism; Chinese Language and Culture; Classical Texts; Acupuncture, Alchemy, and Feng Shui; Buddhism and Confucianism; Taoism and Martial Arts; Taoism and Modernity; Taoist Commercial Sites; and Other Information Sources. The layout is clean and crisp, and the recommended links are easy to access. If you're looking for a simple, direct introduction to the most important strands of Taoist thought and history, this is probably the place to visit first.

On the Path

Looking for a great Taoist spot in cyberspace? We highly recommend the Taoism Information Page. Visit www.clas.ufl.edu/users/gthursby/taoism/.

From the site: "[This site offers] English-language scholarly and philosophical information …. People outside China, including non-Chinese, now seek to engage in practices traditionally associated with Taoism. These may look like opposite concerns, but are not opposed to one another."

Daoism Depot

Address: www.edepot.com/taoism.html

Category: Resource access, articles, and tools for connection with others interested in Taoism

Review: Quite an impressive cafeteria. Offers a well-written introduction to Taoism, numerous resources, and any number of features unavailable elsewhere, including a page on Taoist humor, a Taoist art gallery, *Daoist Magazine*, and a "virtual temple." Not exactly a model of organization and a bit on the sprawling side in some corners, but sometimes that's what you're looking for. A wonderful site to meander through.

From the site: "Welcome to the *Daoist Magazine* … Relax, read the literature and poems, and feel free to submit your own!"

Taoist Mysticism

Address: www.digiserve.com/mystic/Taoist/index.html

Category: Brief overview

Review: An unusually lucid and well-organized summary of key principles within Taoism. The site, created and maintained by Deb Platt, offers a concise overview of the major philosophical and religious points, relevant quotations from Laozi and Zhuangzi, and a helpful glossary. This is the best site we found for a one-stop "refresher" of the Big Ideas connected to the Taoist classics. No filler, no narcissism, no intellectualizing. File it under "must visit."

From the site: "Mysticism is concerned with the nature of reality, the individual's struggle to attain a clear vision of reality, and the transformation of consciousness that accompanies such vision. I've selected quotations from a number of Taoist works which I feel illustrate these issues."

On the Path

Looking for a great Taoist spot in cyberspace? We highly recommend Taoist Mysticism. Visit www.digiserve.com/mystic/ Taoist/index.html.

Databank of *Dao De Jing* Translations

Address: www.edepot.com/taoblank.html

Category: Resource access

Review: This site takes a little getting used to, but once you get the (relatively simple) "splitting" strategy, you'll probably become addicted.

The guiding idea here, apparently, is that no single translation of the *Daode Jing* into English can be considered definitive. This site lets you pick any *two* of the most popular translations and compare each, line by line. For people unlikely to learn classical Chinese anytime soon, it's invaluable. Recommended for those who have already made it through an English-language translation of the classic at least once.

From the site: "Allows you to select and view one of over a dozen different English translations, and to compare the texts to the original Chinese."

On the Path

Looking for another great Taoist spot in cyberspace? We highly recommend the Databank of *Dao De Jing* Translations. Visit www.edepot.com/taoblank. html.

The *Chuang-tzu:* A Translation of Selected Chapters by Lin Yutang

Address: www.clas.ufl.edu/users/gthursby/taoism/cz-text1.htm

Category: Resource access

Review: A responsible and readable translation of important excerpts from this indispensable work. Offered as part of the Taoism Information Page (see the previous section).

From the site: "A word must be added about Chuangtse's attitude toward Confucius. It will be evident to any reader that he was one of the greatest romanticizers of history, and that any of the anecdotes he tells about Confucius, or Laotse, or the Yellow Emperor must be accepted on a par with those anecdotes he tells about the conversation of General

On the Path

Check out The *Chuang-tzu: A Translation of Selected Chapters* by Lin Yutang: www.clas. ufl.edu/users/gthursby/taoism/ cz-text1.htm. We highly recommend it.

Clouds and Great Nebulous, or between the Spirit of the River and the Spirit of the Ocean. It must be also plainly understood that he was a humorist with a wild and rather luxuriant fantasy, with an American love for exaggeration and for the big. One should therefore read him as one would a humorist ... knowing that he is frivolous when he is profound and profound when he is frivolous."

Paths

Address: www.wsu.edu/~paths/

Category: Resource access, tools for connection with others interested in Taoism

Review: This site features some interesting mailing lists, access to the newsgroup alt. philosophy.taoism, and links to various Taoist-related online texts.

The site is not likely to win any awards for graphic design, but it is easy enough to navigate. This is a crossroads providing Taoist cyberwanderers with many useful pathways, as the name suggests.

From the site: "This page is the library for the *paths* mailing list, established to provide a forum for the discussion of the *practice* of Taoism (the Way, the Path)."

Taoist Circle Organization

Address: www.geocities.com/Athens/Aegean/7201/

Category: Tools for connection with others interested in Taoism

Review: Interested in connecting with others on the path? Check out the Taoist Circle Organization, a kind of cyber town hall with a focus on things Taoist.

This is probably the most popular online gathering point. The site offers a philosophy newsletter, chat tools, and various strategies for entering and supporting the online Tao community.

From the site: "I am trying to organize what I have come to call the Taoist Circle. It is a group of people (not necessarily Taoists) interested in learning and expanding their knowledge. In conjunction with this group of people, I put out a free bimonthly newsletter on Taoism. It has news, essays, website reviews, letters from members, articles on Taoist history and practices, book reviews, jokes, quotes, and current listings of many Taoist forms of communication (new sites, newsletters, publications, mailing lists, etc.).

Along with all this also comes a chat room, a message board to post your questions and thoughts to, a mailing list where you can send and receive e-mail from all on this list, a list of members interested in corresponding with other Taoists, and a site where you can submit your articles or thoughts to the newsletter."

Classical Chinese Philosophy

Address: www.geocities.com/tokyo/springs/6339/philosophy.html

Category: Brief overview

Review: Highly recommended for those interested in a ground-level introduction to Taoism, Confucianism, and Legalism—and their many interactions over the centuries.

You don't need any knowledge of Chinese language or customs to find something of value here. Brisk, accessible, and to the point.

From the site: "[This site was created] to clear up some of that strange fog which seems to drift around 'Chinese philosophy.' It's not meant to be a comprehensive guide to all aspects of Chinese philosophy, but it does cover the major schools of thought which have had the greatest impact on Chinese culture: Confucianism, Daoism and Legalism."

Western Reform Taoist Congregation

Address: wrt.org

Category: Articles, tools for connecting with others interested in Taoism

Review: An active Internet-connected group, based in no particular geographic region, that promotes philosophical Taoism as the foundation of spiritual growth. Fascinating and compelling.

From the site: "We do not believe in a god or deity; we believe in an impersonal force called the Tao. We also have no established concept of an 'afterlife.' However, we do believe that the Tao demonstrates to us the proper way to live. Through our beliefs, we learn how to act under any conceivable circumstances; how to handle problems; and how to live life properly, without causing harm to others. The fact that we place our lives and our trust in the Tao is what makes Western Reform Taoism a religion, rather than simply a philosophy."

On the Path

Visit the Western Reform Taoist Congregation to learn more about this distinctive modern expression of Taoism as a religion. Point your browser to wrt.org.

Religious Taoism

Address: www.chebucto.ns.ca/Philosophy/Taichi/religious-tao.html

Category: Brief overview

Review: Christopher Majka's excellent article on the development of Taoism as a religion. Offers a concise yet well-researched overview of the major sects and the history of Taoist practice.

From the site: "Alongside the development of Taoism as a philosophy another more strictly religious interpretation of Taoism was evolving. This 'religious' Taoism had its own temples, priests, rites, and symbolic images."

Alchemical Taoism

Address: www.alchemicaltaoism.com

Category: Articles, resource access

Review: Features essays from students and teachers related to the Healing Tao system of qigong. A fascinating contemporary look at health and sexuality from a Taoist perspective.

From the site: "This website contains a number of essays, diagrams, theory, and practices having to do, largely, with Mantak Chia's 'Healing Tao' (HT) system of qigong. The contents of this website are meant to supplement someone's study of the Healing Tao system; what's presented here is in no way complete on its own."

The Daily Tao

Address: www.nauticom.net/www/asti/asti.htm

Category: Extremely brief articles and excerpts, resource access

Review: Short and sweet. One nugget of wisdom per day, which is probably quite sufficient. There's more than initially meets the eye here, though. Scroll down and you'll find a list of recommended websites.

From the site: "Please don't steal my images. (Be creative—make your own!)"

Yakrider

Address: www.yakrider.com

Category: Articles, resource access, tools for connecting with others interested in Taoism

Review: Insightful discussions on Zen, Buddhism, Taoism, Christianity, religion, poetry, and meditation—and a cute comic strip that illustrates essential principles of Taoism. Offers journeys to both the deep and shallow ends of the pool, as well as that Internet rarity—focused, intelligent conversations.

From the site: "Subscribe to our free newsletter, The Monthly Yak. Each includes our latest comic strip, recipes, poetry, our Yakity Yak on various topics, recommended books or music and a discussion on a Zen or Taoist term."

On the Path

Another excellent Taoist website is the Yakrider site. Visit www. yakrider.com.

Gay Taoism

Address: www.geocities.com/WestHollywood/Village/3200/two.html

Category: Articles

Review: Living with the Tao, from a gay perspective. The essays are subtle and only vaguely focused on the experience of homosexuality. Whatever your sexual preference, you'll find some fascinating material on Taoism here.

From the site: "I wish you the peace that comes from living in harmony with our universe. Here are some good thoughts. I guess they are Taoist. Well, actually, I guess everything is Tao, if not Taoist …."

Su Tzu's Chinese Philosophy Page

Address: uweb.superlink.net/user/fsu/philo.html

Category: Resource access

Review: Comprehensive list of World Wide Web links and resources relating to Chinese philosophy. The page has been the recipient of awards from various reviewers. Well worth checking out, but probably not of deep interest to beginners.

From the site: "This page has been designed for the purpose of organizing the resources on Chinese philosophy that can be found in cyberspace. It is my goal in setting up this page to attract more people, who are interested in searching for the answers of their life, not to limit themselves within the scope of traditional Western philosophies, but to open themselves to some alternatives offered by several schools of Chinese philosophy."

Panlatrevo: Texts and Scriptures

Address: www.panlatrevo.com/texts/

Category: Resource access

Review: A particularly easy to use online library of core Taoist writings

From the site: "Panlatrevo is an Internet resource for scriptures and information on Taoist philosophy."

Internet Encyclopedia of Philosophy

Address: www.utm.edu/research/iep/

Category: Articles

Research: Searchable database of articles on philosophy, some of which relate to Taoism. Helpful for those exploring comparative philosophy.

> **Tao Then, Tao Now**
>
> "Looking at it—it is not visible. Listen to it—it is not audible. Use it—it is not applicable."
>
> —Laozi (on great guiding signs, a topic presumably of interest to philosophers)

From the site: "The Internet Encyclopedia of Philosophy is a nonprofit organization run by the editors. The Encyclopedia receives no funding, and operates through the volunteer work of the editors, authors, and technical advisors. Articles in the Internet Encyclopedia of Philosophy are currently from three sources (1) original contributions by specialized philosophers around the Internet, (2) adaptations of material written by the editors for classroom purposes, and (3) adaptations from public domain sources (typically from two or more sources for per article)."

A Bibliography of Taoism in European Languages

Address: www.clas.ufl.edu/users/gthursby/taoism/bwestern.htm

Category: Resource access

Review: Detailed, but not hotlinked, bibliography of Taoist writings. Helpful for those engaged in scholarly and archival work.

Sacred Texts Timeline

Address: www.sacred-texts.com/time/timeline.htm

Review: It starts at the Big Bang and moves forward to the present day! This impressive timeline places the *Daode Jing* in historical context with Hindu, Christian, Islamic, and other texts. Features links to relevant texts and connects directly to the influential (but hardly cutting-edge) James Legge translation of the *Daode Jing* of 1891.

From the site: "This is a timeline which gives the history of sacred texts, as well as a few other relevant events."

Chinese Language Information Page

Address: www.webcom.com/~bamboo/chinese/chinese.html

Category: Resource access

Review: Welcome help for those struggling with translation issues. The site includes a number of invaluable educational and technical resources.

From the site: "A comprehensive navigational tool pointing you to Chinese language related resources."

Timeline of Chinese History

Address: www-chaos.umd.edu/history/time_line.html

Category: Overview

Review: A (blissfully) concise timeline of Chinese history. Not, perhaps, the most detailed accounting, but a welcome point of entry.

From the site: "If you are interested in what possessed me to do this, please read my motivations. Feel free to make comments or suggestions by leaving me a note."

And Finally ...

There's a lot more to learn about Taoist philosophy in general, and about Zhuangzi in particular. So that means there's one more site we'd like to suggest that you consider visiting. We wouldn't really be standing behind our own work if we didn't recommend at least one Tao-related home page that hits, well, close to home. So check this one out ... and pass along your feedback to the author.

Chad Hansen's Chinese Philosophy Page

Address: www.hku.hk/philodep/ch/

Review: Much of what appears here is a work in progress. But then, isn't everything?

From the site: "This site contains segments of an extended interpretive theory of Classical Chinese philosophy that takes Daoism (Taoism) as the philosophical center. The interpretive theory turns on a new, more philosophical reading of the Daoist philosopher Zhuangzi (Chuang Tzu). My analysis highlights skeptical and relativist themes in his thinking."

What to Do Next

If you find an interesting Taoist link that isn't included here, and that you feel should be included in subsequent editions of this book, please write us, care of the publisher, and we'll take a look at it.

The Least You Need to Know

- There are a bunch of great Taoist-related Internet resources to choose from.
- Our five favorites are the Taoism Information Page, Taoist Mysticism, the Databank of *Dao De Jing* Translations, the *Chuang-tzu* (translation by Lin Yutang), and Yakrider.
- We hope you'll let us know about other great sites that you find.

Chapter 24

Fifty-Two Tao Meditations

In This Chapter

◆ A year of weekly Tao meditations

This final chapter is designed especially for those who have trouble finding time to meditate.

There are 52 weeks in a year, and there are moments of silence and repose to be found during the course of each and every one of those weeks.

For those of us who have difficulty assigning regular meditation practice a clear slot in any given busy week, there are two alternatives. One alternative is to kick ourselves around the block for our continued inability to take time to meditate. Another alternative is to try to find ways to work full attention and balance into the remainder of our days.

In this chapter, you will find 52 very brief Taoist sayings, one for each week of the year. Jot down one of the sayings and leave it someplace where you will see it regularly. This could be on your bathroom mirror, the dashboard of your car, in your cubicle at work, or in the spot near the sink where you do the dishes. The point is to place the saying somewhere you're likely to encounter it and become closer to it over the course of the week. When the new week comes around, change to a new saying.

Of course, if you have time to sit silently in repose and meditate on the meaning of each of the sayings that follow, so much the better. The point is to keep updating the sayings so that they don't become routine for you—and so that you remain open to the effortless path that always reveals itself as fundamentally unified.

A Year of Weekly Tao Meditations

"Tao is beyond words and beyond things."

—Zhuangzi

"To name what can be named is not constant naming."

—Laozi

"Tao is a name that indicates without naming."

—Zhuangzi

"The ten thousand natural kinds work by the Tao and don't make phrases. They sprout, but don't 'exist.'"

—Laozi

Tao Then, Tao Now

"Who am I?"

"Don't know."

—Traditional Zen question-and-answer sequence pondered during meditation

"The massive wisdom sees everything in one. The lesser wisdom breaks things down into numerous parts."

—Zhuangzi

"Guidance pours out, but in using, something is not filled."

—Laozi

"When one is beyond form and appearance, beyond this and that, where is one's comparison to a separate object?"

—Zhuangzi

"The valley's energy never dies."

—Laozi

"Blunt that which is sharp, untie that which is tied, blend that which is bright, gather together the diffused particles."

—Laozi

"When one attempts to exert control over objects, the objects instead gain control."

—Zhuangzi

"Higher worth is like water. Water is good, benefiting the ten thousand natural kinds without wrangling for position."

—Laozi

"One should hear by using one's spirit, one's entire being."

—Zhuangzi

"To hear with the spirit is not assigned to any single faculty, to one's ear or to one's mind, so it requires emptiness in all of one's faculties."

—Zhuangzi

"That which is in excess is reduced; that which is scarce is increased."

—Zhuangzi

"Generate it, nourish it."

—Laozi

"Thirty spokes together make one hub. Where the nothing is lies the cart's use."

—Laozi

"The pivot of Tao passes through a center point at which every affirmation and every negation converges. One who can grasp this pivot occupies a point of stillness at which every movement and every opposition occupies the correct situation."

—Zhuangzi

"Look at it and fail to see its name is 'remote.' Listen to it and fail to hear its name is 'diffuse.'"

—Laozi

"When one's heart is right, one forgets 'pro' and 'con.'"

—Zhuangzi

"What I follow is the Tao, which transcends all technique."

—Zhuangzi

"The non-action of the sage is not inaction."

—Zhuangzi

Tao Then, Tao Now

"Don't waste your life merely sensing; channel thought and feeling to one purpose—and then let it happen. Has this art of turning on one's light been lost?"

—Paul Reps

"To know what is constant is openness. Open—thus equitable. Equitable—thus kingly. Kingly—thus natural. Natural—thus guiding. Guiding—thus enduring—such that it doesn't stop when you bury the body."

—Laozi

"The journey of a thousand leagues begins by putting one's foot on the ground."

—Laozi

"To exercise no thought and find rest in nothing is one's first step to securing repose in the Tao."

—Zhuangzi

"If 'crooked,' then 'intact.' If 'twisted,' then 'straight.' If 'vacuous,' then 'filled.' If 'worn out,' then 'new.' If 'deficient,' then 'endowed.' If 'endowed,' then 'confounded.' Using this: sages embrace one and deem it the social world's model."

—Laozi

"If one can empty one's own boat while crossing the world's river, there will be no opposition and no source of harm."

—Zhuangzi

"Through non-action, there is nothing left undone."

—Zhuangzi

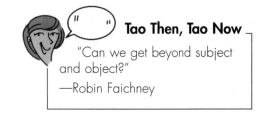

Tao Then, Tao Now

"Can we get beyond subject and object?"

—Robin Faichney

"Because he passes judgment on no one, no one passes judgment on him. Behold a complete man, the man with the empty boat."

—Zhuangzi

"If you hold on too tight, you will lose your grip."

—Laozi

"When one knows the time to stop, knows when one will proceed no further, through one's own efforts, then one has begun properly."

—Zhuangzi

"There is a thing-kind made up of a mix that emerges before the cosmos. Solitary! Inchoate! Self-grounded and unchanging. Permeating all processes without extremity. We deem it the mother of the social world. I don't know its name."

—Laozi

"Take a look at this window. It is only a hole placed in a wall. And yet as a result, the room is flooded with light. Hence, when one's faculties become empty, one's heart fills with light."

—Zhuangzi

"The Tao of Heaven nourishes by not forcing."

—Laozi

"The Tao of the wise person acts by not competing."

—Laozi

"The best warriors do not use violence."

—Laozi

"Those who know they have enough are truly wealthy."

—Laozi

"All things end in the Tao, just as the small streams and the largest rivers flow through valleys to the sea."

—Laozi

"Naming is a necessity for order, but naming cannot order all things."

—Laozi

Tao Then, Tao Now

"If you are everything, or even if you are anything, why say it?"
—Stephen Mitchell

"Perfect Tao cannot be given a name."

—Zhuangzi

"Humanity follows the earth; earth follows Heaven; heaven follows the Tao; the Tao follows only itself."

—Laozi

"A perfect argument does not use words."

—Zhuangzi

"How do I know where creation comes from? I look inside myself and see it."

—Laozi

"Knowledge which stops at what it does not know is the fullest knowledge."

—Zhuangzi

"If you want to become whole, first let yourself become broken."

—Laozi

"Courage that advances itself never gets anything done."

—Zhuangzi

"If you want to become full, first let yourself become empty."

—Laozi

 Tao Then, Tao Now

"Can the Chinese poet from 2500 years ago be heard by me? What will I have to do to listen to him? … Will listening to what I do understand of these poems be enough to ground me so that I can hear what I have not yet understood?"

—Mike Carson

"Death and life have no more supremacy over the perfect man. How little, then, will he be concerned with drawing lines between gaining and losing?"

—Zhuangzi

"If you want to have everything, first give everything up."

—Laozi

"In the days of complete nature long past, men moved quietly and looked about with serenity."

—Zhuangzi

"When you have accomplished your goal, just walk away."

—Laozi

"Do not concern yourself with time, or with right and wrong. Passing into the region that does not end, find rest there."

—Zhuangzi

"Only those who do not cling to their life can save it."

—Laozi

The Least You Need to Know

◆ Even if you don't have time or inclination to commit yourself to a formal meditation plan, you can ponder the sayings in this chapter for a week at a time.

◆ Jot down the saying and place it somewhere you're like to see it every day.

◆ Then change the words … and beware of mistaking them for experience itself!

Appendix A

Recommended Reading

Books

Ames, Roger T., trans. *Huai Nan Tzu*. Albany: State of New York Press, 1994.

Blofeld, John E. C. *The Secret and the Sublime*. New York: E.P. Dutton, 1973.

Briggs, John, and F. David Peat. *Turbulent Mirror*. New York: Harper and Row, 1989.

Capra, Fritjof. *The Tao of Physics: An Exploration of the Parallels Between Modern Physics and Eastern Mysticism, Fourth Edition*. Boston: Shambhala Publications, 1998.

Chan, Luke. *101 Lessons of Tao*. Cincinnati: Benefactor Press, 1995.

Clarke, J. J. *The Tao of the West: Western Transformation of Taoist Thought*. New York: Routledge, 2000.

Dalai Lama, and Glenn H. Mullin, trans. *The Path to Enlightenment*. Ithaca, NY: Snow Lion Publishing, 1994.

Girardot, N. J. *Myth and Meaning in Early Taoism*. Berkeley, CA: University Press, 1983.

Graham, A. C. *Disputes of the Tao: Philosophical Arguments in Ancient China.* La Salle, IL: Open Court, 1989.

———. *Later Mohist Ethics and Science.* London: School of Oriental and African Studies, 1978.

Holy Bible (King James translation). Camden, NJ: Thomas Nelson, Inc., 1970.

Iwrin, William, ed. *Seinfeld and Philosophy: A Book About Everything and Nothing.* Chicago: Open Court, 1999.

Kohn, Livia. *Early Chinese Mysticism.* Princeton, NJ: Princeton University Press, 1992.

Lewis, Dennis. *The Tao of Natural Breathing.* San Francisco: Mountain Wind Publishing, 1997.

Li, Chenyang. *The Tao Encounters the West.* Albany: State University of New York Press, 1999.

Merton, Thomas. *The Way of Chuang Tzu.* New York: New Directions Publishing Corporation, 1965.

Miller, Robert. J., ed. *The Complete Gospels.* San Francisco: Harper, 1994.

Milne, A. A. *The House at Pooh Corner.* New York: E.P. Dutton, 1988.

Mitchell, Stephen, ed. *The Enlightened Mind: An Anthology of Sacred Prose.* New York: HarperPerennial, 1993.

Occhiogrosso, Peter. *The Joy of Sects: A Spirited Guide to the World's Religious Traditions.* New York: Doubleday, 1996.

Pirsig, Robert. *Zen and the Art of Motorcycle Maintenance.* New York: HarperCollins, 1974.

Ram Dass, Lama Foundation, ed. *Be Here Now.* New York: Crown/Hanuman 1971.

Reps, Paul. *Zen Flesh, Zen Bones: A Collection of Zen and Pre-Zen Writings.* Boston: Shambhala Publications, 1994.

Thompson, Mel. *Eastern Philosophy (Teach Yourself)*. Lincolnwood NTC/Contemporary Publishing Company, 1999.

Watts, Alan. *The Book on the Taboo Against Knowing Who You Are*. New York: Vintage Books, 1989.

———. *The Tao of Philosophy*. Boston: Charles E. Tuttle, 1999.

———. *Tao: The Watercourse Way*. New York: Random House, 1977.

Wu, Kuang-Ming. *The Butterfly as Companion*. Albany: State University of New York Press, 1990.

———. *Chuang Tzu: World Philosopher at Play*. New York: Crossroads Publishing, and Chico, CA: Scholar's Press, 1982.

Yamada, Koun. *The Gateless Gate Tucson*. Tucson: University of Arizona Press, 1991.

Zhang, Longxi. *Qian Zhongshu on Philosophical and Mystical Paradoxes in the Laozi*. New York: William Morrow and Company, Inc., 1999.

Zohar, Danah. *The Quantum Self*. New York: William Morrow and Company, Inc., 1990.

Two Online Translations of the *Daode Jing* You Should Check Out

www.hku.hk/philodep/ch/Daoindex.html
Chad Hansen's translation

www.cybernex.net/~jegkirsh/johntao.html
J. H. McDonald's translation

Two Online Translations of the *Zhuangzi* You Should Check Out

www.edepot.com/taochuang.html
Yutang Lin's translation

www.coldbacon.com/chuang/chuang.html
Burton Watson's translation

Tai Chi Resources

Alabama

Taoist Tai Chi Society
Bob Varley, President
PO Box 70215
Montgomery, AL 36107-0215
334-832-1907
alabama@ttcs.org

Alaska

Taoist Tai Chi Society
Mark Johnson, President
PO Box 85331
Fairbanks, AK 99708
907-456-8827
alaska@ttcs.org

Arizona

Taoist Tai Chi Society
PO Box 22331
Flagstaff, AZ 86002
arizona@ttcs.org

California

Jian Mei Association
PO Box 3568
Burbank, CA 91508-3568
818-563-1878

Taoist Tai Chi Society of the
USA—California
Richard Partridge, President
Rob Rothfarb, Webmaster
4111 19th Street
San Francisco, CA 94114
415-241-1537
Voicemail: San Francisco/East Bay:
415-241-1537;
Peninsula/South Bay: 650-562-3802
california@ttcs.org

Tai Chi Academy
PO Box 71016
Sunnyvale, CA 94086
408-836-8500
sifuchuck@taichiacademy.com

Colorado

Arvada Site
6625 Wadsworth Boulevard
Arvada, CO 80003
303-431-6094
ttcsden@earthlink.net

Taoist Tai Chi Society of the USA—
Colorado/Denver
1060 Bannock Street
Denver, CO 80204-4049
303-623-5163
Fax: 303-623-7908

Connecticut

Malee's School of Tai Chi and Kung Fu
Manchester, CT
860-646-6818
Fax: 860-647-1308
www.malees-tai-chi-kung-fu.com
info@malees-tai-chi-kung-fu.com

Florida

Taoist Tai Chi Society
Sean Dennison, Executive Director
Lee Cohee, President
Tallahassee (National/State
Headquarters)
1310 N. Monroe Street
Tallahassee, FL 32303
Phone and fax: 850-224-5438
florida@ttcs.org

Bonita Springs/Naples
brandon.fl@ttcs.org

Clearwater
clearwater.fl@ttcs.org

Jacksonville
jacksonville.fl@ttcs.org

Key Largo
key.largo.fl@ttcs.org

Miami
miami.fl@ttcs.org

Sarasota
sarasota.fl@ttcs.org

St. Petersburg
st.petersburg.fl@ttcs.org

Stuart
stuart.fl@ttcs.org

Georgia

T'ai Chi Ch'uan Atlanta
PO Box 77312
Atlanta, GA 30357
404-881-0030

Taoist Tai Chi Society
Vicki English, President
PO Box 5252
Valdosta, GA 31601
georgia@ttcs.org

Americus
americus.ga@ttcs.org

Illinois

Taoist Tai Chi Society
Margie Butler, President
PO Box 1801
Palatine, IL 60078
847-253-7375
illinois@ttcs.org

Rockford Taichi
Rockford, IL
www.rockfordtaichi.com
jcriscimag@aol.com

Indiana

Taijiquan at Indiana University
www.indiana.edu/~taichi/
cpearce@indiana.edu

Iowa

Taoist Tai Chi Society
Mary Dusterhoft, President
PO Box 294
Iowa City, IA 52244
319-338-6769
iowa@ttcs.org

Kentucky

Taoist Tai Chi Society
Leila Faucette, President
2117 Payne Street, Suite 306
Louisville, KY 40206
502-893-8550
kentucky@ttcs.org

Massachusetts

Harvard Tai Chi Tiger Crane Club
Heather Watchel, President
Cambridge, MA
htctc@fas.harvard.edu

Michigan

The Peaceful Dragon School of Tai
Chi Chuan and Chi Kung
Sally Rich, President
PO Box 7034
Ann Arbor, MI 48107
734-741-0695
www.peacefuldragonschool.com
wasentha@peacefuldragonschool.com
or michigan@ttcs.org

Livonia
38121 Ann Arbor Road
Livonia, MI 48150-3466
Phone and fax: 734-591-3530

New Hampshire

Taoist Tai Chi Society
Maury Beaumont, President
PO Box 203
North Conway, NH 03860-0203
new.hampshire@ttcs.org

Exeter
exeter.nh@ttcs.org

New Jersey

Taoist Tai Chi Society
Tony Bunucci, President
Nutley, NJ
new.jersey@ttcs.org

New York

Taoist Tai Chi Society
Dave Hansen, Administrator
Jane Edwards, President
1021 Kenmore Avenue
Buffalo, NY 14217
Phone and fax: 716-876-7218
new.york@ttcs.org

New York City (Manhattan)
212-946-1476
nyc@ttcs.org

Syracuse
PO Box 8026
Syracuse, NY 13217
syracuse.ny@ttcs.org

The New York School of T'ai Chi
Chuan
306 West 38th Street, Suite 1502
New York, NY 10018
212-502-4112
www.taichichuan.org/

The Center for Traditional Qigong
and Taijiquan
PO Box 249
New York, NY 10012
212-330-8327
adamswallace@yahoo.com

Long Island School of Tai-Chi-Ch'uan
87 Tyler Avenue
Sound Beach, NY 11789
516-744-5999
bobklein@villagenet.com

William C. C. Chen
12 West 23rd Street, 2nd Floor
New York, NY 10010
212-675-2816
WmCCChen@aol.com

Ohio

Taoist Tai Chi Society
Rick Seemann, President
PO Box 1034
Westerville, OH 43086
ohio@ttcs.org

Toledo
PO Box 585
Toledo, OH 43697
toledo.oh@ttcs.org

Oregon

Portland
Allen Pearce, President
239 NW 13th Avenue, Suite 211
Portland, OR 97209
503-220-5970
Fax: 503-220-5034
oregon@ttcs.org

Rhode Island

Way of the Dragon
866 Broadway
PO Box 14561
East Providence, RI 02914-0561
www.waydragon.com

South Carolina

Taoist Tai Chi Society
Myrtle Beach/Grand Strand
south.carolina@ttcs.org

Tennessee

Taoist Tai Chi Center of Oak Ridge
(TTCC)
86 Ogden Lane
Oak Ridge, TN 37830
865-482-7761

Oak Ridge Senior Center (ORSC)
Emory Valley Road
Oak Ridge, TN 37830
865-482-8334

Texas

TaiChi People
1914 B. Guadalupe
Austin, TX 78705
512-236-1503
Fax: 512-236-0336
taichiherb.com
taichiherb@aol.com

Taoist Tai Chi Society
PO Box 490
Round Rock, TX 78680
texas@ttcs.org

Washington, D.C.

Stephan Berwick
703-820-4319
stefanb@erols.com

Wisconsin

Suwandi Rusli
4723 Sheboygan Avenue, #304
Madison, WI 53705
608-236-4628
ruslis@cae.wisc.edu

Feng Shui Resources

Arizona

Jeane T. Haase
Foo Dog Feng Shui
373 W. Windowmaker Road
Tucson, AZ 85737
520-241-3449
foodogfengshui@aol.com

Jane Jung
Eastern Feng Shui
211 W. Roger Road, Unit 8
Tucson, AZ 85705
520-696-3131 or 520-401-0626 (cell)
questions@jjshometeam.com

Diane deSimone
547 East Roger Road
Tucson, AZ 85705
520-293-5290

California

Holly Ziegler
The Open Door Feng Shui
Consulting
PO Box 1036
Arroyo Grande, CA 93421
805-489-8823
FengShui-RealEstate.com
Holly@FengShui-RealEstate.com

Caroline Patrick
Caroline's Arts and Feng Shui
Shoppe
129 First Street, #K
Benicia, CA 94510
707-748-1127
Fax: 707-747-9315
www.fengshuiartistry.com
caroline@fengshuiartistry.com

H. H. Grandmaster Prof. Lin Yun
Yun Lin Temple
2959 Russell Street
Berkeley, CA 94705
510-841-2347
www.yunlintemple.org
info@yunlintemple.org

Janice Sugita
468 S. Camden Drive, #220
Beverly Hills, CA 90210
310-652-1642
jssugita.comsugitart@aol.com

Kathleen Thurston
Divine Order
20 Manor Road
Fairfax, CA 94930
415-453-2588 in California
808-325-6755 in Hawaii
kathleen@divineorder.net

MaryAnn Russell
Complete Feng Shui Solutions
17711 Amberton Lane
Huntington Beach, CA 92649
714-840-2829
mamrussell@mindspring.com

Dr. Carol A. Suter
4199 Campus Drive, Suite 275
Irvine, CA 92612
949-552-3545

Jeremy Belmont
5850 W. 3rd Street, #186
Los Angeles, CA 90036
626-573-9322 or 1-800-592-8339
101fengshui.com
jeremybelmont@hotmail.com

Sharon Jeffers
Living Solutions
PO Box 46215
Los Angeles, CA 90046
323-850-0812
www.livingfengshui.com
livingfengshui@yahoo.com

Feng Shui Consultations by Cathleen
McCandless
PO Box 2664
La Jolla, CA 92038-2664
858-454-7933
www.fengshuiwisdom.com
cathleen@fengshuiwisdom.com

Sidney Nancy Bennett
Feng Shui Perceptions
San Francisco, CA 94101
415-456-7989
members.tripod.com/~Reid_J/FengShui/
fengshui.htm
fengshui2@Juno.com

Dr. Edgar Sung
2578 Noriega Street, #203
San Francisco, CA 94122
415-681-1182
www.edgar03.com
sung@edgar03.com

Colorado

Karen Craig
Paradise Consulting, Inc.
19755 Flint Lane
Morrison, CO 80465
303-697-5215
www.fengshui-paradise.com or
www.sacredspacenvironments.ne
kcraig@ecentral.com

Connecticut

The New England School of Feng Shui
Directors Amy Mims and Susan Pildis
PO Box 1085
Cheshire, CT 06410
203-268-9483
www.neschoolfengshui.com
amymims@aol.com

Susan Pildis
Awareness
PO Box 141
Cheshire, CT 06410
203-272-3765
www.awareness-fengshui.com
susan@awareness-fengshui.com

Miriam Tsao
113 Heritage Hill Road
New Canaan, CT 06840
203-972-3771 or 646-621-3260
TMTsao@aol.com

Lurrae Lupone, M.Ed.
Nova Vita/QI-MAG Feng Shui Consulting
PO Box 9
South Lyme, CT 06376
203-245-7326 in Connecticut
941-454-8639 in Florida
Lurrae@yahoo.com

Micheley Angelina
Feng Shui Transformations
20 Butlertown Road
Waterford, CT 06385-2040
860-443-7330
www.transformational.com/fengshui.htm
micheley@transformational.com

Florida

Carol J. Cannon, BBEI
Environmental Placements, Inc.
#144, 5030 Champion Boulevard, G-6
Boca Raton, FL 33496-2496
561-496-6852
www.cannonfengshui.com
carol@cannonfengshui.com

Juan M. Alvarez
Feng Shui Cultural Centre
73 Merrick Way
Coral Gables, FL 33134
305-448-0859
fengshuicom.net
fengshui@fengshuicom.net

John Huang, Ph.D.
Authentic Feng Shui Design
PO Box 781
Orlando, FL 34760
407-877-6288
yyhuan@hotmail.com

Wendy Victor, FSII
208 Via Tortuga
Palm Beach, FL 33480
561-832-2519
WendyVictor@msn.com

Katrine Karley, BTB
1702 Kestral Park Way South
Sarasota, FL 34231
941-926-8887 or 941-360-8887
www.AbsoluteHarmonyFengShui.com
kkarley8@aol.com

Julie Nevills
Psycholochi
5122 Northridge Road, #201
Sarasota, FL 34238
941-921-1628
www.psycholochi.com
janevills@home.com

Ludy Aniela Goodson
2113 Charter Oak Drive
Tallahassee, FL 32303-4805
850-531-9819
ludyaniela@altavista.com

Trish Allen McCabe
Feng Shui by Design
PO Box 148
Winter Park, FL 32790-0148
407-826-010801
Trish@FengShuiByDesignOnline.com

Georgia

Tracy R. Miller
Gazelle Feng Shui
6595 G Roswell Road, #773
Atlanta, GA 30328
404-320-0302
tracymiller@gazellefengshui.com

Robin Polk
Feng Shui Forward
6595 G Rosewell Road, #773
Atlanta, GA 30328
818-345-4660

Laura Taylor
Laura Taylor Designs
300 Fountain Oaks Lane
Atlanta, GA 30342

Gunda Perry
Feng Shui Consultant
2957 Haverford Lane, SE
Marietta, GA 30067
770-426-270
gperry@life.edu

Pat Santhuff
Healthy, Wealthy, and Wise, American
Feng Shui
6531 Gray Hawk Way
PO Box 871215
Stone Mountain, GA 30087-1215

A. J. Southard, D.D.
Yin Yang and You
PO Box 444
Whigham, GA 31797
229-762-3294
fengshui@surfsouth.com

Hawaii

Sharon Jeffers
Living Solutions
PO Box 66
Waimea, HI 96796
323-850-0812
www.livingfengshui.com
livingfengshui@yahoo.com

Illinois

Patricia Iwan
AAA Feng Shui Ltd.
13211 So. Avenue M
Chicago, IL 60602
773-646-3427
aaafengshui.com
aaafengshui@aol.com

Margo Dumelle
Harmony Feng Shui
411 North Elmwood Avenue
Oak Park, IL 60302

Indiana

Carol Bridges
Nine Harmonies School of Feng Shui
4215 N. Indian Hill Road
Nashville, IN 47448
812-988-0873
www.bloomington.in.us/~9harmonY

Kansas

Valerie Dow
Natural Habitat
PO Box 21
Haysville, KS 67060

Mary Knowles
Essential Feng Shui
2331 N. 51st Street
Westwood, KS 66205

Kentucky

Barbara Hancock
An Eye for It
111 Claremont Avenue
Louisville, KY 40206-2728

Pamela H. Owen
Owen Design and Placement
PO Box 37138
Louisville, KY 40233

Louisiana

Lou Stewart
Space Solutions
76119 Danielson Lane
Covington, LA 70435
985-892-6460
stewart22@aol.com

Maryland

Shelly Moreton Daly
Feng Shui Design Consulting of Maryland
5804 Greenspring Avenue
Baltimore, MD 21209
410-664-4370
fengshuimd@earthlink.net

Carol M. Olmstead, FSIA
Certified Feng Shui Practitioner
5201 Camberley Avenue
Bethesda, MD 20814
301-530-2112
fengshui@powerwords.com

Dr. Cleeretta H. Smiley
Smiley's Holistic Feng Shui Institute
2209 Ross Road
Silver Spring, MD 20910
301-565-9453

Karen Zopf
716 Hickory Lot Road
Towson, MD 21286
443-414-3560
kzopf@hydeinc.com

Massachusetts

Anatoly Tsirelson, M.S.C.E.
A.R.T. Consulting
41 Centre Street
Brookline, MA 02446
617-566-5995
www.fengshuiart.net
anatoly@fengshuiart.net

Rollin Shaw
Intelligent Space
36 Crest Drive
Dover, MA 02030

Linda Varone, R.N., M.A.
Feng Shui Sanctuary
405 Waltham Street
PO Box 166
Lexington, MA 02420
781-643-8697
FengShuiSanctuary.com
lindavarone@mediaone.ne

Michigan

Dennis Fairchild
Aquarius Rising
1025 E. Maple, #105
Birmingham, MI 48009-6435
248-646-3555
WFD6@aol.com

Minnesota

Lorraine Adan
6901 W. 84th Street, #254
Bloomington, MN 55438

Barbara Bobrowitz
Balanced Environment
1520 S. Timber Ridge NE
Fridley, MN 55432

Carole J. Hyder
Balanced Environment
901 W. Minnehaha Parkway
Minneapolis, MN 55419

Judith Kroening
A Charmed Life
701 19th Avenue South
Minneapolis, MN 55454

Dr. Jennifer Glende
The Healing Circle West
14420 Woodruff Circle
Minnetonka, MN 55391

Eric Albrecht
Natural Harmony, Inc.
3925 Zircon Lane W.
Plymouth, MN 55446

Missouri

Nancy McDonald
Fortunatus Feng Shui
3009 SE 2nd Street
Blue Springs, MO 64014
816-224-2232
FortunFS@aol.com

Montana

Shera Gabriel
Created Environments
Box 89
Charlo, MT 59824

Nebraska

Patricia S. Flodman
2150 S. 61st
Lincoln, NE 68506

Nevada

Margie Miles
Innovative Options, Inc.
557 California, Suite #39
Boulder City, NV 89005

New Hampshire

Raven Gregg
Feng Shui Consultant
89 Walnut Hill Road
Derry, NH 03038
603-434-4913

Margaret M. Donahue
Feng Shui Connections
4 Baldwin Street
Windham, NH 03087
603-537-9954
fengshuiconnections.com
pdonahue@bit-net.com or
goodchi@MediaOne.ne

New Jersey

Shelley Solomon
845 Kings Court
Cherry Hill, NJ 08034
856-779-2467
dancingenergy@yahoo.com

Monica Collins
16 Evergreen Street
Clinton, NJ 08809
908-238-1310

Teresa Polanco
100 Grand Cove Way, Suite #4LS
Edgewater, NJ 07020
201-941-7515
virtualight@aol.com

Tracey Taylor
Tracethemark
PO Box 129
New Milford, NJ 07646
201-599-3880
mytaylor@optonline.ne

New York

Martha Rohl
139 Prospect Street
Babylon, NY 11702
631-587-7523
mrohlfengshui@aol.com

Arnold L. Koch
Certified Feng Shui Practitioner
PO Box 983
Vestal, NY 13851-0983
607-722-7719
www.americhi.com
fengshui@americhi.com

Jennifer Frank
Ten Thousand Ounces of Gold
67-35 Yellowstone Boulevard
Forest Hills, NY 11375
718-261-4348
www.TenThousandOuncesOfGold.com
jennifer@TenThousandOuncesOfGold.
com

Linda Williams, FSIA
119 E. Hartsdale Avenue, 3L
Hartsdale, NY 10530
914-686-0670
www.FengShuiNY.com
Linda@FengShuiNY.com

Hannah Scott
PO Box 1008
Millbrook, NY 12545
Phone and fax: 845-677-6475
hannah_fengshui@yahoo.com

Anthea Appel
Chi of Earth
636 7th Avenue
New Hyde Park, NY 11040
917-648-8721
www.chiofearth.com
jade3dragon@aol.com

Ann Billow
Billowing Design
140 West 79th Street
New York, NY 10024
212-873-4881
Billowingdesfengshui.com
BillowingD@mindspring.com

Janet Hicks, Ph.D.
JOH Enterprises
161 Varick Street, Suite 1017
New York, NY 10013
212-946-1102
www.joh9.com/fengshui.htm
jhicks@joh9.com or sjbridges@rcn.com

Benjamin Huntington
Mountain Institute of Tribeca
23 Leonard Street, 4th Floor
New York, NY 10013
212-334-7762
www.mountaininstituteoftribeca.com
info@faceyourself.com

Pamela Laurence
23 Leonard Street, 4th Floor
New York, NY 10013
212-334-7762
www.faceyourself.com
info@faceyourself.com

Evelyn Seed
Feng Shui Consultations by Evelyn
Seed
162 W. 56th Street
New York, NY 10019
212-246-1639

Vincent Smith
434 E. 52nd Street, #9G
New York, NY 10022
212-751-7161 or 413-738-5520
vmsdesign@aol.com

Judith Wendell
Sacred Currents
11 East 88th Street
New York, NY 10128
212-410-1832
www.sacredcurrents.com
judith@sacredcurrents.com

Barbara DeStefano
DeStefano and Associates
53 Rondout Harbor
Port Ewen, NY 12466
845-339-4601

Ohio

Diane Knepper
The Feng Shui Connection
9581 Lansford Drive
Cincinnati, OH 45242

Dawn Schwartzman
Interior Services, Inc.
1360 Kemper Meadow Road
Cincinnati, OH 45240

Penny Crabtree
2105 Jennifer Lane
Findlay, OH 45840

Oklahoma

Taye K. VanMerlin
Contemporary Feng Shui Solutions
4618 N. Classen Boulevard
Oklahoma City, OK 73118

Nina O'Brien
617 Old Bugle Road
Edmond, OK 73003

Karen K. Hench
1309 Ravenwood Court
Bartlesville, OK 74006

Rick Phillips
Designs with Intention
123 East 21st Street
Tulsa, OK 74114
918-584-7425 or 1-800-379-6752
www.designswithintention.com
dezinguru@aol.com

Oregon

Barbara C. West
Sacred Design
PO Box 5327
Eugene, OR 97405

Diane Baker
Feng Shui Design and Consulting
2324 N.W. Marshall Street
Portland, OR 97210
503-228-0379

Katy Nielsen
7125 SW 3rd Avenue
Portland, OR 97219

Patricia Ann Warren
Faces Unlimited, Inc.
1598 SW Upper Hall Street
Portland, OR 97201

Pennsylvania

Janice Girgenti
Feng Shui Studios
1107 Westbury Road
Jenkintown, PA 19046
215-572-1650
FengShui123@aol.com

Helen Berliner
107 Brook Circle
Lansdale, PA 19446
215-362-0758
www.HelenBerliner.com
sambhok@aol.com

South Carolina

Libba Beerman
2007 Deer Island Road
Hilton Head Island, SC 29928
843-363-2329
libba-t@webtv.net

Texas

Kimla Dodds
Design with Feng Shui Today
107 Ranch Road 620S, #30-B
Austin, TX 78734
1-800-925-8196
KimlaMarie@aol.com

Nancy Wesson
Balanced Living Through Design
9206 Knoll Crest Loop
Austin, TX 78759
512-343-1204
www.life-synergy.com
n_wesson@hotmail.com

Donna Collins
The Everyday Feng Shui Company
PO Box 670274
Dallas, TX 75367-0274
214-880-0851
Fax: 214-352-8805
everydayfengshui@yahoo.com

Naoise Nickolay
Creative Feng Shui
16318 Mahogany Crest Drive
Cypress, TX 77429
281-684-6819 or 281-225-6285
naoise@earthlink.net

Christy DeWolfe
DeWolfe Feng Shui
5114 J. I. Bruce Drive
Temple, TX 76502
254-770-0581

Utah

Claudia Batey
104 K Street, #3
Salt Lake City, UT 84103

Vermont

Peter J. DeLuca
PJD Designs
970 Route 100
Weston, VT 05161-5414
802-824-6615 or 802-824-4695
deluca@vermontel.net

Virginia

Jeannie Marie Tower, BBEI
EcoAlchemy Design
Alexandria, VA 22305
703-684-6502 in the United States
+44(0)20-7385-0020 in London
www.fengshuimagic.com
fsmagic88@aol.com

Cecile Wendover Clover
PO Box 6701
Charlottesville, VA 22906
804-973-7223
clover@luckycat.com

Mary Branch Grove
3727 Prosperity Avenue
Fairfax, VA 22031
703-442-7735
www.fengshuidirectory.com/grove
dragon@patriot.net

Robyn Bentley
PO Box 6952
Richmond, VA 23230
804-358-7075
www.fengshuidiva.com
robynbentley@aol.com

Ellen Whitehurst
Sacred Spaces, Sacred Places
Virginia Beach, VA 23451
757-412-2600 or 1-800-627-1092

Leigh Saint Germain-Borthwick
Interior Balance
2805 Hidden Lake Drive
Williamsburg, VA 23185
757-564-1974
hilinas@email.msn.com

Washington

Kevin Fong
321 High School Road, NE #182
Bainbridge Island, WA 98110

Cynthia Chomos
Sacred Interiors, Feng Shui and Color
Services
PO Box 17285
Seattle, WA 98107
206-919-0107
www.CynthiaChomos.com
cchomos@nwlink.com

Denise Linn
Denise Linn Seminam, Inc.
PO Box 75657
Seattle, WA 98125

Libby Sturman
EAS Design Co.
5808 E. Greenlake Way, N
Seattle, WA 98103

Charlene P. Weaver
Feng Shui Creations
2648 15th Avenue W, #1101
Seattle, WA 98119

Angie Leonard
Albertine's Attic
14522 SE 27th Circle
Vancouver, WA 98683

K. Connor Momno
211 North 24th Avenue
Yakima, WA 98902

Wisconsin

Kate Trnka
Harmony Consultations
PO Box 2341
Appleton, WI 54912

Pamela Tollefson
Feng Shui Design
129 W. Brown Deer Road
Bayside, WI 53217

Krasna Svoboda
Clear Space
2210 Westlawn Avenue
Madison, WI 53711

Taoist Temples

California

Yi Guan Tao Temple
11645 Lower Azusa Road
El Monte, CA 91732

Taoist Temple
12 China Alley
Handford, CA 93230-4613
559-582-4508

Temple of Kwan Tia, Inc.
PO Box 630
Mendocino, CA 95460
www.taorestore.org/Mendocino.html

Oroville Chinese Temple and Garden
1500 Broderick Street
Oroville, CA 95965
916-538-2496

Taoist Sanctuary of San Diego
4229 Park Boulevard
San Diego, CA 92103
619-692-1155
www.taoistsanctuary.org

Chi Sin Buddhist and Taoist
Association
1051 Powell Street
San Francisco, CA 94108

Foundation of Tao
Dr. Stephen Chang, Founder
Dr. Nancy Worthington, President
2570 Ocean Avenue, Suite 134
San Francisco, CA 94132

Mountain Wind
PO Box 31376
San Francisco, CA 92103
415-282-4896 or 415-641-7716
www.breath.org

Universal Society for the Integral Way
(Hua Ching Ni)
PO Box 1530
Santa Monica, CA 90406-1530
310-576-1902
www.usiw.org

Colorado

Fung Loy Kok Taoist Temple
1060 Bannock Street
Denver, CO 80204
bking@du.edu

Florida

Tao Institute
1000 Sawgrass Village Drive
Ponte Verda Beach, FL 32082
904-273-4919

Idaho

Genessee Valley Taoist Hermitage
PO Box 9224
Moscow, ID 83843-1724
208-285-0123

Massachusetts

Center for Traditional Taoist Studies
Box 134
Weston, MA 02493
Tao.org

Michigan

Shannon Roxborough
PO Box 43556
Detroit, MI 48243
chinesetao@aol.com

New Hampshire

Red Lotus Healing Tao
PO Box 89
West Nottingham, NH 03291
603-942-7634
lotus108@aol.com

The College of Tao
PO Box 1222
El Prado, NH 87529

New York

American Taoist Healing Center
396 Broadway, Suite 502
New York, NY 10013
212-274-0999

Taoist Arts Center
342 E. 9th Street
New York, NY 10003
212-477-7055

Oregon

Quigong Friends Network
HC 71125 Radar Base Road
Burns, OR 97720
541-573-4203

The Abode of the Eternal Tao
4852 W. Amazon
Eugene, OR 97405
1-800-574-5118

Texas

Teen How Taoist Temple
1501 Delano
Houston, TX 77003
713-236-1015

Virginia

Singing Wind Healing Tao Center
1011 N Edgewood Street
Arlington, VA 22201
703-528-2044

Washington, D.C.

Center for Dao-Confucianism
1318 Randolph Street NE
Washington, DC 20017
202-526-6818
tkang@wam.umd.edu

Taoist-Related Health Resources

Alabama

Mary Johnson, L.Ac., Dipl.Ac.
Holistic Health Horizons
305 E. 16th Street
Anniston, AL 36207
256-235-0388
holistichealth@peoplepc.com

Alaska

Taoism Center for Wellness
615 E. 82nd Street, Suite B11
Anchorage, AK 99518
907-344-5533
www.alaska.net/~pilkin

Arizona

Southwest Institute of Healing Arts
609 N. Scottsdale Road
Scottsdale, AZ 85257
602-947-5161

Arkansas

Andrew Wilson, D.O.M.
6301 Mulberry
Pine Bluff, AR 71603
501-993-7255

California

Eric Lai, L.Ac.
8530 Whilshire Boulevard,
Suite 500
Beverly Hills, CA 90211
310-358-9566

Colorado

Julianne Despain, Dipl.Ac.,
Dipl.C.H, P.T.
Calm Spirit Acupuncture and
Chinese Herbs
11890 W. 64th Avenue
Arvada, CO 80004
303-467-5337 or 303-467-1131

Connecticut

Marc Harlan Gerstein, L.Ac., Dipl.Ac.
Acupuncture Association of Hartford
112 Cottage Grove Road
Bloomfield, CT 06002
860-243-3903 or 413-256-6756
marcg@javanet.com

Delaware

Xiaoyan Gong, O.M.D., Dipl.Ac.
Gong's Oriental Care
161 S. DuPont Highway
New Castle, DE 19720
302-328-6288 or 302-324-8275
xiaoyangong@hotmail.com

Georgia

Warren Cargal, Dipl.Ac.
455 Paces Ferry Road, Suite 201
Atlanta, GA 30305
404-233-5080
wcargal9@bellsouth.net

Hawaii

Tai Hsuan Foundation
College of Acupuncture and Herbal
Medicine
PO Box 11130
Honolulu, HI 96828
808-947-4788
Fax: 808-947-1152
home1.gte.net/escompu/thf.home.htm

Idaho

Gwen Millar, L.Ac.
171 W. River Street, Unit 102
Ketchum, ID 83340
208-725-5517 or 208-726-5499
calmshen@primenet.com

Illinois

Claudette Baker, Dipl.Ac., L.Ac.
1757 Glenview Road
Glenview, IL 60025
847-998-8860
Fax: 847-998-8863

Indiana

Lei Xiao, Dipl.Ac., Dipl. Herb
Essence of China Acupuncture and
Herb Clinic
9790 E. 96th Street
Fishers, IN 46038
317-585-0758 or 1-888-815-4159
www.essenceofchina.com
mail@essenceofchina.com

Iowa

Irene Dougherty, R.Ac.
9 E. State Street
Marshalltown, IA 50158
515-752-6255
sstar39@hotmail.com

Kansas

Richard Morantz, L.Ac. (CA)
1103 Massachusetts Street
Lawrence, KS 66044
785-841-1587

Kentucky

Elizabeth Whittemore, Dipl.Ac., R.N.,
B.S.N., M.Ac.
PO Box 331
Pewee Valley, KY 40056
502-243-2187

Louisiana

Lisa S. Lee-Alevizon, M.D., L.Ac.
Holistic Health
1031 W. Tunnel Boulevard
Houma, LA 70360
504-223-3811

Maine

Alice Meattey, L.Ac., Dipl.Ac.
74 State Road
Kittery, ME 03904

Maryland

David Blaiwas, L.Ac.
6935 Laurel Avenue, #203
Takoma Park, MD 20412
301-270-2117 or 301-854-9950

Massachusetts

John Varner, L.Ac.
A Common Practice
54 Jeffrey Lane
Amherst, MA 01002
413-256-1904

Michigan

Beverly Yee, L.Ac., MTOM
Cumberland Center for Natural
Health
21823 Boulder
East Pointe, MI 48021
810-778-1135
byee002@aol.com

Minnesota

Edith Davis, L.Ac.
393 N. Dunlap Street, Suite 850
St. Paul, MN 55104
612-647-1277 or 651-999-0114
edithrdavis@juno.com

Missouri

Afua Bromley, L.Ac., Dipl.Ac.
5219 Delmar Boulevard
St. Louis, MO 63108
314-308-1605 or 314-773-6064
www.universalhealth.net
afuabromley@hotmail.com

Montana

Jerrie Nelson, C.A.
1001 S. 24th Street W., Creekside 2
Billings, MT 59108
406-656-7416 or 406-656-5682

Nevada

Huiwen Zhang, O.M.D.
Legacy Oriental Medical Center
3300 E. Flimingo Road, #18
Las Vegas, NV 89121
702-898-7899 or 702-898-7898

New Hampshire

Sean Doherty, Dipl.C.H, Dipl.Ac.,
M.Sc., M.S., DNBAO
Nashua Natural Medicine
76 Northeastern Boulevard, Unit 36A
Nashua, NH 03062
603-579-0956 or 603-579-0957
sean@nashuanaturalmedicine.com

New Mexico

Barbara Maddoux, DOM
801 Encino Place NE, Suite B-3
Albuquerque, NM 87102
505-243-5848 or 505-292-0668

New York

American Taoist Healing Center
396 Broadway, Suite 502
New York, NY 10013
212-274-0999

Oregon

Patricia Rupert, L.Ac.
1000 SW Vista, Suite 1112
Portland, OR 97205
503-274-8880

Pennsylvania

David Mortell, R.Ac., Dipl.Ac
5655 Bryant Street
Pittsburgh, PA 15206
412-363-0886

Rhode Island

Cate Chason, D.Ac.
469 Angell Street
Providence, RI 02806
401-247-1058

South Carolina

Zeyi Chen, M.D.
5 Daniel Street
Charleston, SC 29047
843-571-6913 or 843-571-1440

Tennessee

Daniel Lee, D.A., A.P.
Holistic Acupuncture and Herbs
2805 Foster Avenue, #204
Nashville, TN 37210
615-332-8351
www.acupuncture-net.com
acupuncture@dreamwiz.com

Texas

Healing Tao Institute
Dr. Jampa Mackenzie Stewart
PO Box 9312
Austin, TX 78766
512-447-9507 or 1-800-432-5826
(1-800-HEAL-TAO)

Utah

Kris Justesen, O.M.D.
Ahshi Acupuncture and Chinese Herbs
545 E. 4500th S., #E230
Salt Lake City, UT 84107
801-263-9380 or 801-263-9925
www.alpinewellnesscenter.com
kjustesen@alpinewellnesscenter.com

Vermont

Robert Davis, L.Ac.
38 Wright Avenue
South Burlington, VT 05403
802-862-8880 or 802-862-8887
acupunctureVt@earthlink.net

Virginia

Singing Wind Healing Tao Center
1011 N. Edgewood Street
Arlington, VA 22201
703-528-2044

U.S. Virgin Islands

May Trieu M.S., M.D., O.M.D.
TCM Healing Center
42 Kronprindsens Gade
St. Thomas, USVI 00802
340-774-1420 or 340-715-1420
drmaytrieu@hotmail.com

Washington

Monica J. Legatt, L.Ac., Dipl. NCCAOM
Heart of Seattle Acupuncture
509 Olive Way, Suite 404
Seattle, WA 98101
206-623-7213
Fax: 206-467-2777
www.seattleacupuncture.com
Legatt@workmail.com

Washington, D.C.

Susan McConnell, Acupuncturist
3006 Arizona Avenue, NW
Washington, DC 20016
202-966-3061

West Virginia

Qingquo Shang, L.Ac.
Center for Alternative Health
50 River Walk Mall
South Charleston, WV 25303
304-744-1318 or 304-744-1328

Wisconsin

Curry Chaudoir, L.Ac., Dipl.Ac.
Acupuncture and Holistic Health
Associates
5150 N. Port Washington Road, #102
Milwaukee, WI 53012
414-332-8888

Wyoming

Rebecca Hawkins, L.Ac., PT, Dipl.Ac.,
ATC
East Meets West Health Care
430 S. Jackson Street
PO Box 3086
Jackson, WY 83001
307-690-9395
acupuncture@jhinct.com

Index

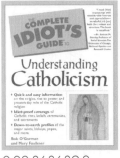

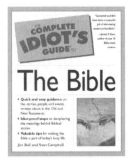

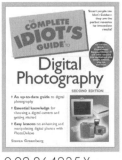
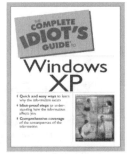